TradCLIMBING+
The positive approach to improving your climbing

Adrian Berry
John Arran

Uncredited photos by Adrian Berry
Other photos as credited
Illustrations by Ray Eckermann and Alan James
Edited by Alan James
Printed in Europe on behalf of Latitude Press Limited
(ISO 14001 and EMAS certified printers)
Distributed by Cordee (cordee.co.uk)

First published by ROCKFAX in December 2007
This edition published by ROCKFAX in June 2017
© ROCKFAX 2007, 2017

All rights reserved. No part of this publication may be reproduced, stored in a retrieval system, or transmitted in any form or by any means, electronic, mechanical, photocopying or otherwise without prior written permission of the copyright owner.
A CIP catalogue record is available from the British Library.

This book is printed on FSC certified paper made from 100% virgin fibre sourced from sustainable forestry

ISBN   978 1 873341 91 9
rockfax.com

Cover: Martin Kocsis on Keelhaul (E2) at Bosherston Head, Pembroke, Wales. Photo by Mike Hutton
This page: Steve Ramsden on Fay (E4), Lower Sharpnose, Cornwall, England.

Alex Barrows on the crux of *Quietus* (E2) Stanage Edge, The Peak District, England.

Contents

Introduction 4

Starting Out.........................8

A guide for newcomers showing the various ways to get into trad climbing, the important differences between climbing indoors and outside, plus an introduction to the key safety skills and terminology.

Gear 28

A comprehensive look at the myriad of gear available, with advice on what to buy to build up your climbing rack.

Protection 58

A thorough analysis of how to place protection, with tips on how to make the very best of every feature found on the rock.

Ropework......................... 96

Starting with all the knots you will need for any situation, this chapter looks at how advanced ropework skills will keep you safe, and allow you to focus your energy on the important business of getting to the top.

Technique........................ 160

There's no use in having the best gear placement and ropework skills if you can't do the moves - this chapter takes a trad-specific approach to moving efficiently and securely.

Tactics 190

Tactics is about how to best use the skills you already have to get those routes in the bag and is a major part of the climbing game.

The Mind......................... 206

For many climbers, the mind is the weakest link. By taking a more positive approach your mind can be turned from being a weakness to being your best asset.

Multi-pitching..................... 238

Getting high off the ground adds a dimension to climbing, one that can leave life-long memories. Here's how to do it safely and efficiently.

Training.......................... 254

Improving your performance through training is the quick way to progress, this chapter looks at physical, technical and mental training using a practical approach.

Destinations 274

So you're climbing like a pro, here's where to go! There's trad climbing to be found all over the world, so quit your job, pack your bags and check out these destinations!

Introduction

About this book

This book is for climbers who want to try their hand at trad climbing - that mystic art where every climb can seem like two climbs: one consisting of moves that lead up the climb, the other, a hunt for protection that safeguards the moves.

While climbing continues to diversify into safer, more athletic pursuits, and the number of climbers continues to grow, participation in trad climbing is still strong. Perhaps it is the rewards from testing both mind and body and finding an inner strength that is ordinarily unused. Perhaps it is the thrill of taking-on nature at its most raw and pushing your own limits. Whatever it is, there's no doubt it's a compulsive experience.

Trad climbing rewards the ability to move decisively and confidently. It requires an intuitive understanding of the limits of equipment and, of course, the ability to keep a cool head when things aren't going your way. It also rewards the ability to work closely with a partner as well as the ability to sort things out when you're on your own.

Because it involves so many skills, trad climbing is a sport that takes a long time to master. This book should help to speed things up a bit.

Whether you are yet to rack-up for your first trad lead, or have a burning desire to push yourself to the very limit, if you want to become a better climber - and not just a safer climber, then this book is for you.

At the very least, we hope that this book will save you some time by learning from the authors' mistakes, rather than your own!

Patrick McBride and Rob Greenwood taking a belay on *South Face Direct* (VS), Chair Ladder, Cornwall. Photo by Duncan Skelton.

Introduction

What's Trad Climbing+ all about?

All motivation can be classed as either positive or negative. Positive motivation is present when you have a goal that you wish to reach. Getting to the top of a climb, breaking into a new level of difficulty, or even having a go at a new style of climbing for the first time are all positive goals. Negative motivation is what keeps us from doing something harmful - nobody wants to fall and get hurt, or fail on a climb that we're not physically ready for. Negative motivation keeps us safe and sane, and it is just as important as positive motivation.

Most instructional books focus heavily on teaching how to satisfy our negative motivations: how to build solid belays, place reliable runners and so on. In other words - they show how to be a safer climber. At the other end of the bookshelf are 'performance climbing' books that concentrate on the physical training aspects of climbing - the focus on these books is very much to make us stronger climbers. The intention behind this book is to bridge these different approaches with the focus solely on trad climbing.

In other words, this book has been written to present a balance of the negative 'safety' aspects of trad climbing, with the equally useful positive skills, such as technique, strategy and mental preparation, that will lead you to the top.

We hope this book will help you in your journey, and that the ideas contained will make a real difference to your enjoyment of climbing, wherever it takes you.

Happy climbing!

Sarah Clough on *Parachute* (VS) Stoney Middleton, The Peak District, England. Photo by Nick Smith.

About the Authors

Adrian Berry learned to climb on the sea-cliffs of South Wales where he dreamt of one day climbing on rock that didn't break off, and protection that wasn't behind the bits of rock that broke. After many years, he discovered Peak gritstone where the rock was solid, but occasionally had no protection. Outside of the UK, Adrian has travelled extensively, though has yet to find climbing as interesting and varied as in the UK. After a spell representing Great Britain at competition climbing, Adrian returned fully to rock and added numerous hard new routes to the sea-cliffs and inland gritstone crags. When the 'last great problems' became, at last, too great, Adrian played a key role in developing the provision of climbing coaching in the UK. Currently, Adrian works as a writer, photographer, and climbing coach.

positiveclimbing.com

Above: Adrian on *Blind Vision* (E10) Froggatt, The Peak District, England. Photo by Tim Glasby. Below: John making the first free ascent of the 500m E6/7 *Bloody Mary* in the Karakorum mountains of Pakistan. Photo by Anne Arran.

John Arran spent his teenage years struggling up easy trad routes in most areas of England and Wales. Eventually he learned how to climb well and first became known for soloing hard climbs in Colorado. Returning to the UK he has since made a name for himself in competition climbing, in sport climbing, by onsighting trad new routes up to E7 and by headpointing trad new routes up to E10. He loves climbing on all rock, even if it is loose and there's not much protection. In recent years he and his wife Anne have taken to establishing hard big-wall free-climbs in remote locations, such as the 1000m wall behind Venezuela's Angel Falls. When not travelling the world as an international election consultant, he devotes much of his time to climbing photo-journalism and coaching.

thefreeclimber.com

About trad climbing

Trad climbing is great. We all know it is, but explaining why isn't so easy. It demands a unique and ever-changing blend of the physical, the technical and the emotional. It's a healthy sport; a natural challenge. It takes us to amazing and beautiful places. It helps build trusting relationships. It's fun, memorable, absorbing, scary and fulfilling. All of these are true, but the whole is greater than the sum of the parts. To really know why trad climbing is great you have to try it and find out for yourself.

For some people, a perfect day out is venturing into the hills, climbing well within their grade on fine rock, with good friends and a healthy safety margin. Others are more interested in pushing their physical and psychological limits, striving for ever harder or bolder challenges. Others again will be adventurers, preferring the lure of an unexplored valley or unclimbed line to the more conventional guidebook favourites. Maybe the climbers who've really got it sussed are those who enjoy all of these, and plenty more besides.

Trad climbing is any rock climbing that doesn't rely on a route having been equipped in advance with permanent bolts or similar for protection. It remains very much the same activity as it was for the 19th century pioneers, who would daringly seek new ways up intimidating cliffs. The technology has improved; we now enjoy a level of security that would have been unthinkable even a few decades ago. The number of climbers, and the number of catalogued climbs, has also grown enormously; but the enduring ethos is perfectly suited to our modern and environmentally aware world. We climb using only what nature has provided and we strive to leave each climb exactly as we found it.

A common misconception about trad climbing is that it's scary. The reality is that, as long as you know what you are doing, you have almost complete control over the level of risk you are prepared to accept. You choose the routes, and there are so many well-protected trad routes at every grade you could spend your whole life climbing safe ones. You choose what protection to place and where to place it, which usually gives ample scope for backing up any gear you're not completely happy with. At any time you can also choose to come down. Such abundance of choice and personal responsibility isn't common in other sports but it certainly adds to the satisfaction you feel when you get to the top of a climb. Not only will you have risen to the physical and technical challenge, but you'll have done so having made sound and perhaps critical decisions at every stage.

Trad climbing is not just about climbing hard nor about climbing in control. It's not just about staying safe nor about taking risks. It's not just about being ambitious nor about being content. It's about all of these things, and plenty more besides. Perhaps that's why we enjoy it so much.

Sophie Leaker seconding *Plumb Line* (Diff), Three Cliffs, Gower, Wales.

Starting Out

This chapter looks at the basic methods involved in trad climbing and the emphasis will be firmly on safety. We will look at the various aspects of all types of climbing that are good preparation for getting into trad.

The latter part introduces the principles behind how the safety systems work, the basic skills of putting on a harness, how to communicate at the crag and how grades are used to indicate the difficulty of a climb.

Getting into trad climbing

You don't need to have done any other sports to climb and many good climbers come from a background of not being particularly 'sporty'. However, a reasonable level of strength and fitness will make your early experiences more enjoyable and will allow you a more rapid progress through the grades.

Traditionally, climbers have been introduced to trad climbing as the one and only form of climbing, but with the rapid rise of indoor climbing, bouldering, and sport climbing, there is now a number of introductions to trad climbing that make it a lot more accessible.

Even if you are introduced directly into trad climbing, it is most likely that your first experiences will be top-roping or seconding easy, single pitch routes where your safety is assured by an experienced partner and you can relax and enjoy the feeling of climbing rock.

Sarah Clough leading *Hamlet's Climb* (HVD), Wharncliffe, South Yorkshire, England.
Photo by Nick Smith.

Starting Out

Moving from indoors to trad climbing

Indoor bouldering

Indoor bouldering is a popular way to try climbing without learning anything about rope-work and is a great first step. Bouldering on climbing walls is a great way to learn the basic movement skills involved in rock climbing and also to build up specific upper body strength. An often overlooked benefit of bouldering is its ability to teach perseverance and the tenacity to deal with repeated failure before success is won. Indoor bouldering is also a great way to meet other climbers who may be very willing to introduce you to other forms of climbing.

Photo by Alex Messenger

Indoor top-roping

At its most basic, indoor top-roping involves no more technical skills than indoor bouldering - plus an experienced partner can take care of all the rope-work. It will, however, soon be worth learning the basic skills of putting on a harness, tying on using a solid knot, and belaying for yourself. Acquiring these skills is not difficult and you should be able to learn from an instructor or experienced climber on your first session. Knowing these basic, but essential, skills will allow you to visit a climbing wall without needing someone more experienced to climb with.

Apart from the basic rope skills, indoor top-roping teaches us to trust the equipment, knots and our partners. This trust is crucial for advancement onto greater things; without it climbing is always going to be a very stressful business!

Lastly, top-roping indoor routes teaches us to conserve our strength and to move efficiently, or else suffer the dreaded forearm pump! Naturally, this exercise will also start training your body to deal with fatigue and will lay the foundations for the stamina that may be needed soon.

Photo by Nick Smith

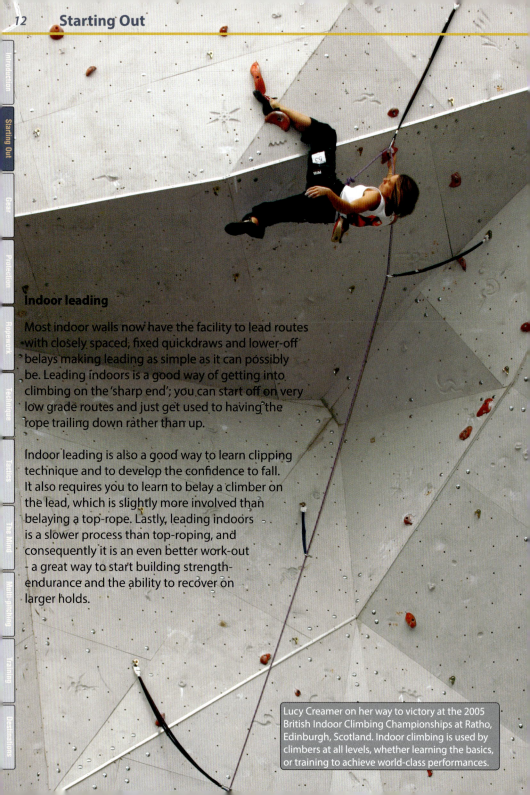

Starting Out

Indoor leading

Most indoor walls now have the facility to lead routes with closely spaced, fixed quickdraws and lower-off belays making leading as simple as it can possibly be. Leading indoors is a good way of getting into climbing on the 'sharp end'; you can start off on very low grade routes and just get used to having the rope trailing down rather than up.

Indoor leading is also a good way to learn clipping technique and to develop the confidence to fall. It also requires you to learn to belay a climber on the lead, which is slightly more involved than belaying a top-rope. Lastly, leading indoors is a slower process than top-roping, and consequently it is an even better work-out – a great way to start building strength-endurance and the ability to recover on larger holds.

Lucy Creamer on her way to victory at the 2005 British Indoor Climbing Championships at Ratho, Edinburgh, Scotland. Indoor climbing is used by climbers at all levels, whether learning the basics, or training to achieve world-class performances.

Starting Out

Moving from outdoor bouldering to trad climbing

Moving outside for the first time introduces some important differences from climbing indoors. Outdoor rock climbing is always going to take place in a less controlled environment than indoors and the need for you to take responsibility for your own safety is more apparent and often more critical than it is indoors.

The main difference with bouldering on rock is that you shouldn't expect to have matting underneath you at all times - it is your responsibility to ensure that there is adequate matting. This is a good introduction to the skill of assessing risk and being responsible for your own personal safety. In addition to matting, the art of spotting (helping to protect a falling climber from injury by directing them away from hazards) needs to be learnt, and this emphasises the advantage of trust between climbing partners.

Outdoor bouldering is a great way of getting used to climbing on real rock. The holds are often much smaller and the moves less obvious than indoors, plus you need to learn to 'top-out' when you get to the top, rather than reversing a few moves and jumping down. Bouldering on rock is one of the best ways of developing the sort of strength and technique needed for when you get on rock routes. Bouldering at any time in your climbing career is a good way of making quick progress through the grades.

Boulderers attempting the *Lung Dyno* (V4) at Quantum Field, Castle Hill, New Zealand.

Climbing outside

If you have never climbed outside, then there are some things worth thinking about before you head to the crags.

Hazards

Rock climbing has more *objective* dangers than indoor climbing. These are the dangers that cannot be reduced simply by becoming a technically more competent climber. Objective dangers include being hit by falling rocks (often dislodged by other climbers), being caught by incoming tides on sea-cliffs and getting stuck in bad weather in remote locations.

Being aware of the natural hazards found at climbing locations is mostly common sense born from experience. The more time you spend climbing outside, the more you will be able to tune into the environment. Clues like broken rocks littering the base of the crag will tell that rock-fall is common, high tide lines will indicate how far the tide comes in and whether your escape will be possible.

Climbing in high mountain environments requires a whole host of skills, such as navigation, clothing choice and how to deal with emergencies. These skills are beyond the scope of this book, but are necessary for those venturing further from the path.

Self-reliance

Unlike in urban environments, there is no state-funded rescue service waiting to get you out of trouble (in the UK). The charity-funded volunteer mountain rescue teams provide a superb rescue service, but are not there simply to make life easier for us when we get lost trying to find the crag, or suffer a minor injury. Always try to get yourselves out of trouble and only call upon Mountain Rescue (call 112 and ask for 'Mountain Rescue') when you know you, or another, is in peril, and you have exhausted your solutions.

Elsewhere in the World, the rescue services vary from excellent to nonexistent and you should always familiarise yourself with local rescue services when on a trip.

Self-responsibility

At the core of self-responsibility is the fact that it is our choice to climb and venture into wild places and in doing so we choose a higher level of risk than we face in everyday life. When things do occasionally go wrong, it is important that we take responsibility for our own actions that put us in the situation, rather than look to others to blame.

Walking into the fabulous granite walls in Val di Mello, Italy. A long way from the climbing wall.

Starting Out

Access and behaviour

Some climbing areas are on private land and permission to climb must be given by the landowner before you may even approach the crag. Landowners have very little incentive to allow climbers to use their land and so such permission should always be appreciated. Guidebooks detail the access situation to the areas they cover and will include any conditions, such as keeping to established paths, or periods when you aren't allowed to climb because of temporary restrictions - for example, when birds may be nesting.

Bad behaviour at the crag is often cited as the reason why landowners have closed the crags. Making noise and leaving a mess is just asking for often hard-won access to be denied. Bad behaviour at a climbing wall may end up with you being excluded from the wall, bad behaviour at the crag may end up with everyone being excluded.

Many landowners are concerned with issues of legal liability. If you are injured at the crag, remember, it was your choice to be there. Suing the landowner is not only likely to remove permission to that crag, but could lead to many other crags being closed as word gets around.

It's worth noting that actions such as lighting fires and stripping vegetation from routes may well be illegal.

National parks have by-laws that often prohibit acts that alter or pose the risk of altering the protected environment. Wild camping is often not permitted, and even where it is, you should always leave a campsite in as good as, or better condition than, it was when you found it. Taking away others' rubbish is a small price to pay to maintain a beautiful place, and our access to it.

Ethics and styles

Ethics are often viewed as being more complicated than they actually are. There really are three main ethics:

1) Don't damage the rock
2) Be considerate to others
3) Be honest about what you do

More complicated issues arise when it comes to placing and replacing fixed *in situ* protection like pegs and bolts, when local ethics should be followed by consulting local climbers for their opinions.

Much 'ethical' debate is actually concerned with the style of an ascent. Being able to define the various styles in which it is possible to climb a route makes it easier to communicate clearly what we have done, and reduces the likelihood of misunderstandings. So long as we are honest about what we do, there is rarely an ethical dimension to how we climb a route.

Starting Out

Sport climbing

Sport climbing is leading rock routes that are protected by *in situ* (fixed in place) bolts. Sport routes require just a rack of quickdraws to connect your rope to the bolts. Although very similar in style to leading indoors, sport climbs generally have more widely spaced bolts and you need to learn to place your own quickdraws. While many belays on outdoor sport routes can simply be clipped and lowered from as you can indoors, many will require you to thread a belay, which requires a greater awareness of ropework. Another difference between climbing sport routes and indoor routes is that you need to be able to judge the quality of *in situ* bolts, as there is no regular inspection system in place.

Sport climbing is a great way getting fit, learning the skills of route-reading and energy conservation and developing a 'go for it' attitude. Falling is commonplace in sport climbing, and is a great way of getting used to the sensation of falling and the need for trust.

For newcomers in climbing, sport climbing is a good way of learning about 'crag awareness'. Hazards like falling rock and poorly placed bolts increase our ability to manage risk and reinforce the fact that we are responsible for our own, and frequently others', safety.

SportCLIMBING+

The first book in the Plus Series covers all aspects of sport climbing. Taking a practical approach, the book focuses on improvements that climbers can make immediately.
rockfax.com

A young climber sport climbing in Val Masino, Italy. Sport climbing is a great way of building the confidence needed to lead trad routes and it is a good idea to sport climb regularly alongside your trad climbing if you want to reach your potential.

Starting Out

Seconding

Seconding routes is the term used to describe climbing a route after somone else has led it first and fixed a belay at the top. It is a good way of learning some of the skills necessary to go on to leading trad routes yourself. Seconding teaches crag-awareness, rope-work, communication skills and a general familiarity with trad climbing. Seconding trad routes will require you to learn to belay and climb using double ropes.

Seconding is a good way of learning how gear is placed and extended, and it is a good idea to second a number of routes before attempting to lead one in order to see how the various pieces of protection can be utilised.

Even when you are regularly leading trad routes, seconding is a good way to push yourself on harder routes and build up your confidence so that you can have a go at leading them.

Many climbers are happy to only, or mostly, second routes without feeling they need to tie into the 'sharp end'. Seconding routes is an enjoyable way of getting to climb routes you might otherwise never get to experience. As a second, you naturally play a valuable role in ensuring your partner is being belayed safely. Additionally, as a second you can make a positive difference to your partner's confidence: by ensuring they know they are being belayed safely, and are psychologically well supported from down below, you can strongly influence the outcome of the day.

Ben Harding seconding *The Loosener* (HVS) St. Govan's Head, Pembroke, Wales. Photo by Nick Smith.

Chris Moor leading *Double Diamond* (HVS), Lundy, England. Photo by Nick Smith.

Starting Out

Leading trad

Finally, we get to leading trad! Your first trad leads should feel pretty tame affairs, especially if you have already experienced other styles of climbing such as bouldering and sport climbing. Your first leads should not be technically taxing and the protection should be obvious and plentiful. Get an experienced climber to recommend some routes to try, look for routes a full three grades below what you can second.

Slabby single pitch routes with cracks that provide good protection are good choices for first leads as you can stand around as long as you like without worrying about getting tired. Choose friendly venues where you can see what you are going to climb clearly from the base of the route.

While it takes a wide range of skills to be safe to venture onto the lead on trad routes, the learning process only really starts here and there's no getting away from the fact that your first season leading trad is possibly going to be your most hazardous. Take things slowly and only move on when you're comfortable with what you're doing.

If you want to improve your ability to lead trad routes - whether you want to push yourself onto higher grades or want to be able to climb at your present level with greater skill and control - you need to get out leading routes as much as possible.

Not only is it important to do as many leads as you can, but it is also important to vary the style of routes you try, from slabby to steep, from one rock type to another. When you feel ready, your natural progression will be to attempt multi-pitch routes, again lowering your grade significantly to start off with, then increasing it as you become more comfortable with the style.

The skills, techniques, tactics and even clever tricks of trad climbing are the subjects of the remainder of this book.

Starting Out

Before you can set off on your first trad climbing experience, we need to cover a couple of useful pieces of equipment - the harness and chalk-bag. *There is much more on gear in chapter 2.*

Putting on a harness

There are two important things you need to get right when putting on a harness. Firstly, you need to make sure that the waist belt is sufficiently tight and secondly, you need to ensure that the buckles are secure.

The waist belt needs to be adjusted so that there is plenty of room for you to breathe comfortably, but is tight enough to make it impossible to slide down over your hips. If your waist belt is too slack, there is a risk that if you fell off and inverted upside-down, you could fall out of your harness. Before setting off, take a second to grab the sides of your harness and try to slide it down over your hips, needless to say, if it can be slid over your hips, it needs to be re-fastened a little tighter and tested again.

Buckles come in two distinct designs, and it is important to be able to tell the difference between the two.

Ziplock buckles

These are the most recent innovation in buckles, and have the advantage on being the simplest to secure.
A Ziplock buckle is automatically secure, you just pull the free end to tighten, and it will be secure.

Thread-back buckles

The original buckle design requires a two step process to make it secure. Firstly, the buckle needs to be tightened by pushing and pulling the waist belt through the buckle. When it is sufficiently tight, the end of the waist belt must be threaded back through the buckle. Before the buckle is threaded back, all sides of the buckle are visible, making it look like a slightly square letter 'O'. After it has been threaded back, one side of the buckle is obscured, making it look like a letter 'C'.
Remember: 'O' is for Open, 'C' is for Closed.

Above: a thread-back buckle in its 'Open' position. Below: the same buckle after it has been correctly threaded-back into the 'Closed' position.

Starting Out

Chalk-bags

Many people's first piece of equipment is a chalk-bag but, even with such a simple piece of equipment, it is important to get it right at the outset.

Attach your chalk-bag to your waist separately from your harness using a piece of cord or tape. While it is more convenient to use a specifically made belt with a plastic buckle, using a piece of standard accessory cord (between 4 and 6mm) means you have something stronger that may very well help get you out of trouble one day. Tie your chalk-bag cord with a simple reef-knot. Avoid attaching a chalk-bag directly to your harness, even if your harness is designed to have a chalk-bag clipped to it - the bag will hang too low and you won't be able to move it into a more convenient position.

At all costs, avoid clipping your chalk-bag to your harness with a karabiner; this will likely orientate your chalk-bag to one side, making it hard to chalk-up the hand on the 'wrong' side.

While fine for indoor climbing, chalk-balls are not well-suited for climbing outside. Loose chalk gives a thicker covering, giving greater protection against the rock, and allowing the backs of the hands to be chalked-up - which is important for crack climbing.

Lastly, chalk-bags can be fun too...

See page 32 for more on chalk-bags.

Alex Barrows on pitch one of *Diocese* (VS), Chair Ladder, Cornwall, England.
Chalking up is a useful way of taking a mini-breather before a hard section of a climb - the last thing you want is to have to fight to find your chalk-bag!

Starting Out

How it all works

The standard method for climbing a route involves **leading** and **seconding**. Leading is, as the name suggests, going first up a climb with the rope trailing below. When seconding you follow the climb, with the rope held from above you by the leader.

While both leader and second are protected by the rope while they climb, the second has a much higher level of protection and should not go far should they fall. The leader is only as safe as the protection they can arrange while climbing and so leading a route has a higher level of risk than seconding. Because of this, it is usual for a novice climber to second a number of climbs before attempting a lead.

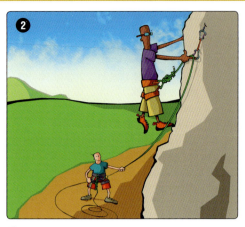

❷ Now that the leader is on belay, he can start to climb. The second feeds the rope out through the belay device so as not to impede the leader's movement. As the leader gains height, they must find **protection** (also known as **running belays** or **runners**) to ensure their safety. The protection is clipped to the rope with a **quickdraw** (also called an **extender**) so that the rope may pass freely as the leader moves past.

❶ After choosing a **route** to climb, the leader has tied into one end of the rope and the second has tied into the other (it is a good idea to use the **buddy system** where you check each other's knots and harnesses). The second then puts the leader **on belay** by passing the rope through their **belay device**. The device allows the second to control the rope and **arrest** (hold) any falls should they occur.

❸ The leader has taken a fall from the climb! His well-placed protection has held and his partner has **locked-off** the belay device to prevent any more rope from passing through it. Phew!

Starting Out

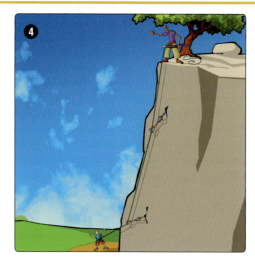

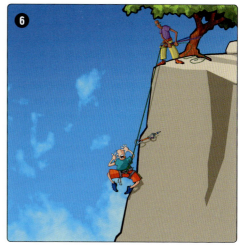

4 The leader has reached the top of the route and has secured himself to a **belay**. A belay is a solidly fixed anchor (one or several pieces of equipment) that the leader can attach to. The leader then informs the second that they are safe and can take the leader **off belay** by removing the belay device from the rope. The leader will then pull up any slack rope and put the second on belay so they can start to climb.

6 Now it's the second's turn to fall! But no need for drama - the leader has locked-off the belay device and the second has fallen only a very short distance.

7 The second has arrived at the top of the route. Now that both leader and second are safely on top, the leader may take the second off-belay, dismantle the belay and both leader and second can untie from the rope, sort out the **gear**, descend to the base of the cliff and move on to their next climb.

5 As the second climbs, the leader takes in the slack rope. When the second arrives at a piece of protection, it is their job to remove it and carry it with them by attaching it to their harness.

Communication

Good communication between climbing partners is essential to avoid confusion and mishaps. In order to avoid miscommunication, climbers have developed a system of calls designed to inform one another unambiguously of what is going on. These calls do vary a little especially in other countries. The most important thing is to get your point across and be sure that you have.

Climbing calls

"(You're) on belay!"
Your partner has put you on belay.

"That's me!"
Called when the rope is taken in to the point where the only thing stopping it is the climber tied into it. This tells your partner at the top of the pitch that the thing on the end of the rope is you and not something the rope has snagged on.

"Climb when ready!"
The leader at the top shouts this when it is safe for the seconder to start climbing.

"Climbing!"
The seconder shouts this to inform the leader that they have set off.

"Slack!" or "rope!"
Used by the person climbing (leader or seconder) when they need some rope paying out.

"Take in!"
Used by the person climbing when they need some slack rope taken in. Avoid the call "*Take in* the *slack*" in case only the last word is heard!)

"Watch me!"
Used by the person climbing when they are in trouble and may fall.

"Take!"
The person climbing yells this when their weight is about to come onto the rope.

"Below!" or "rock!"
Informs anyone below you that you've dropped something or pulled off some loose rock.

"(I'm) safe"
Shouted by the leader when they make them self safe at the top of a climb and do not need to be on belay anymore.

"You're off" or "off belay"
Used to inform the leader that they have been taken off belay.

"Rope (below)"
Warns those below that you are lowering or throwing a rope down.

"(I'm) off / (rope) free"
Used to inform the person waiting at the top of an abseil that you are off the abseil rope and they can come down.

"OK"
A very commonly used call - but worth avoiding as it can mean anything!

Non-verbal calls

There are often situations where, due to the length of a pitch, the noise from a roaring sea, or a howling wind, it's impossible to hear each other. In such situations it is wise to agree a non-verbal sign for 'climb when ready' before the leader sets off - three significant tugs on the rope for example. Be very careful that your signal can't be given by mistake, such as by tugging at the rope in an attempt to free it and being taken off belay in mid-climb!

Climber on *Wen* (HVS) Wen Zawn, Gogarth, Wales. When communication is difficult, a pre-agreed code of rope tugs can be very useful.

Grades

In the UK, we use an **adjective grade** to give an overall indication of the difficulty of a climb. This takes everything into account, including the protection, the strenuousness, the difficulty of the moves and the general level of exposure and commitment. Adjective grades start at 'Easy' and progress through increasingly elaborate word combinations until they arrive at 'Extremely Severe' at which point the thesaurus was ditched and we split the grade into E1, E2, E3 and so on.

UK adjective grades were first used long ago when climbing equipment was nothing like as good as it is now. If your first climb was Hard Severe, it may be tempting to reflect that it wasn't actually very *hard* or *severe*, but go back on it with leather boots, no protection and yet-to-be-cleaned loose rock and you will probably develop a greater appreciation for why adjective grades all sound a little melodramatic.

UK trad grades are given for the difficulty of onsighting (*see page 192*) a route, so even if the route has never been climbed onsight (true for many of the harder routes) an estimate of the onsight difficulty is made.

The limitation with having just one grade for overall difficulty is that it doesn't tell you much about *why* the route is difficult. A climb graded E1 may have very easy climbing but no protection, another may have a single hard move (called a **crux move**) but excellent protection. To make things clearer, we use a **technical grade** for each pitch of a route. This indicates the difficulty of the hardest move, taken in isolation. So our dangerously unprotected E1 could be graded E1 5a, and our hard-but-safe E1 could be graded E1 5c. An average E1 would be E1 5b.

It is not just danger that can inflate an adjective grade relative to a technical grade. A very strenuous route with good protection could be graded E1 5a, as could a poorly protected but physically mild route. The only way to tell whether the 'E1 5a' you're about to try is strenuous and safe or non-strenuous and bold is to read the description in your guidebook and look out for words like 'pumpy' or 'runout'. Or, of course, you could look up at it and see for yourself!

Using a guidebook in Arapiles, Australia. The Australian grading system quite sensibly starts at '1' and has no +'s, -'s, a's, b's, c's, d's, X's or V's. The only problem is you never know if the route you're getting on is going to be scary or just plain hard...

Starting Out

Sport Grade	British Trad Grade (For bold routes)	UIAA	USA	Norway	Australian	South Africa
1	Mod (Moderate)	I	5.1		4	6
2	Diff (Difficult)	II	5.2		6	8
2+		III	5.3	3	8	9
3-	VDiff (Very Difficult)	III+	5.3	3	8	10
3	HVD (Hard Very Difficult)	IV-	5.4	4	10	11
3+	Sev (Severe)	IV	5.5	4+	10	12
4a	HS 3c BOLD / 4b SAFE (Hard Severe)	IV+	5.6	5-	12	13
4b		V-	5.6	5-	14	13
4c	VS 4a BOLD / 5a SAFE (Very Severe)	V	5.7	5	14	14/15
5a		V+	5.8	5	15	16
5b	HVS 4b BOLD / 5b SAFE (Hard Very Severe)	VI-	5.9	5+	17	17
5c		VI	5.10a	6-	18	18
6a	E1 5a BOLD / 5c SAFE	VI+	5.10b	6	19	19
6a+	E2 5a BOLD / 6a SAFE	VII-	5.10c	6+	20	20
6b	E3 5b BOLD / 6a SAFE	VII	5.10d		21	21
6b+			5.11a	7-	22	22
6c	E4 5c BOLD / 6b SAFE	VII+	5.11b		22	23
6c+		VIII-	5.11c	7	23	24
7a	E5 6a BOLD / 6c SAFE	VIII	5.11d	7+	24	25
7a+		VIII+	5.12a		25	26
7b	E6 6b BOLD / 6c SAFE	IX-	5.12b	8-	26	27
7b+	E7 6c BOLD / 7a SAFE		5.12c		27	28
7c		IX	5.12d	8	28	29
7c+	E8 6c BOLD / 7a SAFE	IX+	5.13a	8+	29	30
8a		X-	5.13b		30	31
8a+	E9 7a BOLD / 7a SAFE	X	5.13c	9-	31	32
8b		X+	5.13d	9	32	33
8b+	E10 7a BOLD / 7b SAFE	XI-	5.14a		33	34
8c			5.14b	9+	34	35
8c+		XI	5.14c		35	36
9a		XI+	5.14d		36	37
9a+			5.15a		37	

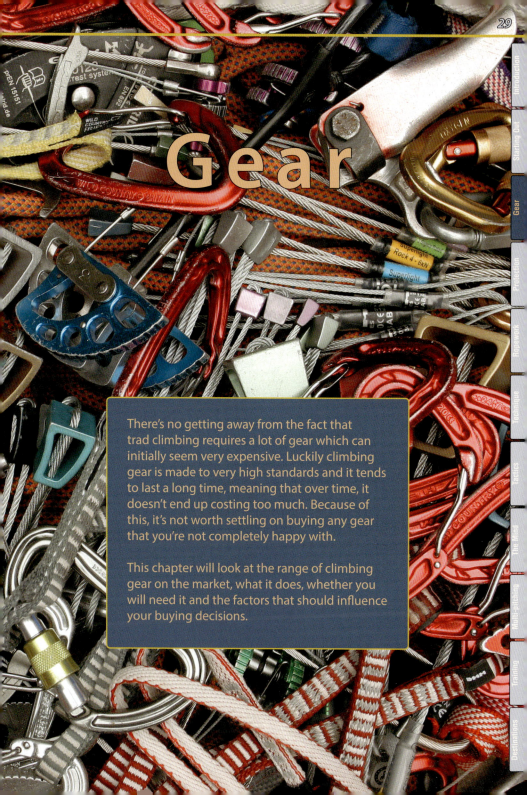

Gear

There's no getting away from the fact that trad climbing requires a lot of gear which can initially seem very expensive. Luckily climbing gear is made to very high standards and it tends to last a long time, meaning that over time, it doesn't end up costing too much. Because of this, it's not worth settling on buying any gear that you're not completely happy with.

This chapter will look at the range of climbing gear on the market, what it does, whether you will need it and the factors that should influence your buying decisions.

Climbing shoes

Climbing shoes are the most important piece of climbing equipment you will ever buy. To best understand climbing shoes, think of them as equipment rather than clothing, in a similar way to how a skier would think of their skis.

For a complete beginner, tight fitting climbing shoes are a painful distraction, and it is preferable to have shoes that allow your toes to flatten. **Board lasted** shoes - where the shoe 'last' is stretched over a stiff 'board' sole - are more forgiving in this respect. If you go on to engage in hard technical climbing, the ability to stand precisely on smaller holds will begin to outweigh the desire for comfort.

A snug fitting **slip lasted** technical climbing shoe, where the shoe is softer and more flexible, opens up a world of climbing that is just not possible in anything else simply because they are much more sensitive. However, you will need to fit them with your toes bent, and here's why: take off your shoes and socks at home and stand next to the skirting board that runs around the bottom of the wall. Now, *keeping your toes straight*, try to stand on the skirting board. You will find it completely impossible. Now try it again, but this time bend your toes tightly into a 'fist' - much easier!

This demonstrates that to be able to stand on small edges with sensitive slip-lasted shoes you need to bend your toes into a fist. Also, naturally, you need your toes to be tight against the rand of the shoe as any dead space will cause the shoe to flex and slip off the hold. This all adds up to the fact that, for climbing shoes to deliver the best performance, you need to have your toes bent and touching the inside of the rand. Initially this will seem quite radical and uncomfortable, but in no time at all you will get used to the position and it will eventually feel quite comfortable. You can tell if your toes are in the right position in the shoes because they will form an

Above and below: a well fitted climbing shoe for technical climbing. Note how the knuckles of the toes have formed a distinct ridge along the top of the shoe. The side view shows how the toes are in the position where they can transfer the maximum force through to the footholds.

obvious ridge in the upper of the shoe. If you can wear normal socks under your climbing shoes, your shoes are probably too big for you. If you do wish to wear socks, consider buying some ultra-thin liner socks. If you get ankle-high liner socks, maybe no-one will even notice?

Gear

All-day comfort?

Comfy shoes are good for long multi-pitch climbs where you will be climbing well within your grade. Be aware though that, if you intend to climb *hard* all day, you are still going to need to wear your best shoes and put up with a bit of discomfort.

Stiff or soft?

Stiff shoes take the strain off your feet when standing on small holds for long periods. However, the cost is in the ability to adapt the shape of your shoe to closely match the contours of rounded footholds, also known as **smearing**. Smearing is much easier with soft shoes such as unlined slippers - which can only be used for edging if you've strong feet and a tight fit. Stiff shoes are generally better for climbing cracks where lateral stiffness makes foot jams less painful, and enables you to make maximum use of small toe-end holds in the cracks.

Laces, slip-ons, or velcro?

For getting the tightest fit, it's hard to beat lace-up shoes. Velcro fastenings have the advantage of being easy to take on and off - great for bouldering and multi-pitch routes where you may wish to take your shoes off at the belays. If you buy shoes with velcro fastenings, you may want to cut off any spare strap as they can easily catch, undoing the shoe.

Slippers are usually the softest shoes and the close fit is achieved through using elastic, though when the elastic wears out, the fit will suffer.

Top: a medium performance lace-up shoe balancing comfort with performance.

Middle: a high performance lace-up shoe designed for maximum performance rather than comfort.

Bottom: a velcro-fastened high performance slipper.

Gear

Harnesses

A good trad climbing harness is characterised by the facility to rack plenty of gear. Look for a harness with five or more gear-loops, this will allow you four gear-loops for protection and quickdraws, and one at the back for less urgent items like your belay device. Curved gear loops generally take more gear than square-cut ones as you can rack gear along the entire length of the gear-loop, right up to the waist-belt.

You shouldn't be expecting to spend too much time actually hanging in your harness, so comfort isn't the prime concern. The comfort of your harness is primarily the result of having the right size for your body. Women need a harness with different proportions from those required by men and there are a wide range of female-specific models. The other factor in comfort is the amount of padding: a well padded harness with wide leg-loops and waist-belt will offer increased comfort, but will be slightly heavier, will restrict movement, and the increased padding can make things a bit sweaty when it gets hot.

A Ziplock buckle - this type of buckle does not require you to 're-thread', though it is slightly more prone to work loose over a long period.

Five gear loops provide enough space for all your gear. 'Square' gear loops provide less space for gear than curved ones.

Front belay loop. This is only used for attaching your belay device, or securing yourself to a belay on a climb. You do not tie your rope into the front belay loop. Some harnesses also have a rear belay loop, though in practice this is of limited use.

Adjustable/elasticated leg-loops - wide enough to provide an acceptable amount of comfort, but slim enough to allow freedom of movement. Harnesses designed for use in winter climbing often have adjustable leg-loops, which can also be handy if your thighs are larger or smaller than average. For most people though, fixed size leg loops are preferable.

Chalk-bags

Look for a bag with furry lining, big enough to take a whole hand. Most allow a toothbrush to be connected - for cleaning chalky holds. As with most things, the more expensive ones last longer than cheap ones. If you attach your chalk-bag with 1.5m of accessory cord (around 5mm), you will always have a spare prusik loop. *More on Chalk-bags on page 21.*

Gear

Belay devices

This is usually the first piece of hardware that you purchase. A belay device is used for both belaying and abseiling and there should be no need to take a separate abseil device such as a figure-of-eight. A belay device is used in combination with a pear-shaped screw-gate karabiner - also known as an HMS karabiner - and a safe pair of hands.

For trad climbing, you need to be able to control a wide range of rope sizes, from skinny 8mm lead ropes to 10.5mm or thicker abseil ropes, and you may need more than one device.

There are a number of devices on the market that are specifically made for half-ropes, with noticeably narrower slots. There is no doubt that these are much more suitable for handling skinny half-ropes, but if you need to make an abseil approach on a fatter single rope, you will need to either use a friction hitch (*see page 103*) or take a second device. Be wary of devices that have very wide slots (such as the original *ATC*) - they are not designed for skinny half ropes. More recent devices have incorporated 'teeth' to allow them to operate with a wider range of rope sizes.

Devices range in the amount of **grab** they apply. A device with a good deal of grab will lock-up easily, but will be more difficult to feed rope through smoothly. A beginner may choose to have the assurance of a more grabbing device, whereas a more experienced user will be able to give a more fluid belay with a less grabbing device without compromising safety.

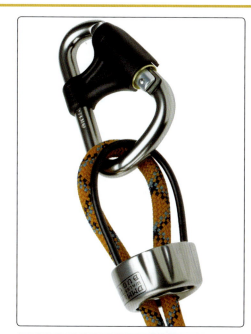

DMM Bug and Belay Master. The Belay Master karabiner has a clasp that prevents the karabiner rotating into an undesirable position.

Lastly, auto-locking belay devices are not recommended to be used for lead belaying on traditional gear, as they transmit more force onto the protection. They are fine for belaying a top-rope.

Nut keys

One of the great banes of trad climbing is getting the protection back out of the rock! Nut keys are designed to help remove stuck wires, though they are also handy in threading slings through the rock and cleaning out soil from cracks in the pursuit of a gear placement.

Nut keys are best attached using a standard karabiner. While there are 'accessory' karabiners available that are small and neat, it is better to have a full-strength karabiner - you will probably find yourself belayed off it one day!

Helmets

Helmets are more commonly used now than ever before. Helmets were traditionally designed to protect your head from impacts by falling rocks from above, but increasingly models have been designed to protect against impacts to the side, such as you may experience in a fall.

Head injuries are often very serious but helmets can obstruct your freedom of movement and become uncomfortable in high temperatures. Whether or not you choose to wear a helmet is very much a personal decision based on the risks posed. It is common for climbers to wear helmets on some routes, such as loose sea-cliffs, and not on others where the risk of head injury is reduced such as on very steep routes with good protection.

Helmets and risk compensation

While there can be no room for doubt that wearing a helmet will reduce the severity of a head injury in the event of an impact, helmets only offer limited protection and, as with all things, prevention is better than cure.

There is a danger that wearing a helmet makes you feel safer, and because of this you will be likely to take bigger risks, negating much of the increased safety afforded by the helmet and maybe even putting you in increased danger.

Wearing a helmet should not affect your sense of vulnerability and self-preservation - the 'grey matter' inside your helmet is of more value in avoiding head injury than the helmet itself.

To be safer, wear a helmet - but don't rely on it.

Prusik loops

Prusiks are used to attach the climber to the rope by means of a secure but moveable knot and generally carried on multi-pitch routes, when leading or seconding routes where a fall could leave you hanging in space, or when you approach a route by abseil. Some climbers carry them at all times.

Prusik loops are simply lengths of accessory cord with the ends tied together with a double fisherman's knot to form a loop (climbing shops won't tie them for you, so buy the cord and tie them yourself - *see page 101*). Each prusik loop is made from around 1.5m of accessory cord. The narrower the cord, the more readily it will bite the rope, but naturally, at the cost of strength. 4mm - 6mm is the range most commonly used with thinner ropes requiring thinner prusiks. A prusik loop can also be used as a chalk-bag string which gives a convenient way of carrying one.

A single small screw-gate karabiner is generally used to make use of your prusiks, and used to store them out of the way at the back of your harness.

See pages 102 and 152 for more on prusiks.

Katherine Schirrmacher on *The Mau Mau* (E4) Dinorwic Slate, North Wales. Wearing a helmet is very much a matter of personal choice.

Meilee Rafe starting up *The Arrow* (E1), St. Govan's Head, Pembroke, Wales.

Karabiners

Also known as *krabs* or *'biners*, karabiners are the means of connecting one thing to another, and a full rack may contain thirty or more of these simple but effective clipping devices. Karabiner strength is rated in three ways: the strength along the length of the karabiner with the gate closed; the strength along the length of the karabiner with the gate open; and the strength across the width of the karabiner. The first rating is always significantly higher than the other two.

Snap-link karabiners

The vast majority of karabiners you use will be snap-links which are available with wire-gates or solid-gates. Both offer similar strengths but the very lightest karabiners these days tend to be wire-gates although solid-gates will still light enough for most. Be wary of cheap karabiners of both types which can be unreliable after only a short period of use.
If you are building up a lead rack you will save money if you buy karabiners in sets of five or more.

Screw-gate karabiners

These are used in critical positions where it is crucial that the gate isn't opened accidentally, radically reducing the strength of the karabiner.

A notched wire-gate snap-link

Nose

Gate

Most screw-gate karabiners have a simple collar on the gate that is turned to lock the gate and are by their nature always solid-gate. There are a number of variations on the screw-gate theme producing models that are either more secure but difficult to operate, or less secure but impossible to forget to lock - such as twist-lock models.

Specialist shapes

Most karabiners are shaped in what is known as the off-set 'D', which is the strongest shape. Other shapes have more specialist uses, the pear-shaped 'HMS' karabiner is ideal for use with a belay device (*see page 33 for a special HMS belay krab*). Oval karabiners are popular with aid climbers and are an excellent choice for racking a collection of wires.

A notchless screw-gate

Notched or notchless?

There is a trend in karabiner design to get rid of the notch in the nose of the karabiner. Removing the notch makes it a little easier to unclip thin items such as wires and bolts, especially where the karabiner is under a little load. Wire-gate karabiners without notches generally have larger noses than those with.

Ropes

There are three different types of ropes used in trad climbing: *dynamic half ropes*, *dynamic single ropes* and *static ropes*. Ropes are sold in various lengths, the minimum you will find is 50m. The longer the rope you use, the fewer belays you need to take, which *usually* saves time, however you will end up taking in more slack on routes with shorter pitches. Ropes longer than 50m can also have a longer life as worn ends can be cut, leaving a rope that is still long enough to use.

Dynamic ropes

Dynamic ropes have an elastic nature that allows them to stretch when loaded. Only dynamic ropes should be used for lead climbing as the stretch significantly reduces the force on the gear and the climber. The degree of dynamism of a rope is referred to as its **impact force** (and is measured in daN). The lower the impact force, the softer the rope will be to fall on, which reduces the chance of equipment failure. On the down side, ropes with more stretch are harder to take in tight and you tend to fall a bit further.

Half ropes

Half ropes are the most popular choice for trad climbing and come in a range of diameters (usually around 8.5mm) and are used in pairs (**double ropes**). Half ropes allow protection to be used when it is distributed over a wide area, without causing rope-drag. They also always the weight of a fall to be distributed over two or more pieces of protection if used intelligently which can be crucial if the protection is a marginal placement. Half ropes are not to be confused with **twin ropes** which are two ropes treated as a single rope and are never clipped into a piece of protection on their own. Twin ropes have little use for most trad climbing.

Single ropes

Single ropes are used on their own when leading pitches where the protection is in a straight line, such as bolt-protected sport climbs or crack climbs. Single ropes come in a range of diameters from around 9mm to 11mm. The thinnest single ropes can be used as half ropes without an excessive weight penalty and make a good first purchase if you intend to use your rope for trad and sport climbing.

Static ropes

Static ropes are ropes with little or no stretch and they are never used for leading. The most likely use of a static rope in trad climbing is as an abseil rope. When abseiling on a dynamic rope, the constant stretching can cause the rope to wear against the rock with hazardous consequences. Static ropes are a great investment if you regularly climb in areas such as sea cliffs where an abseil approach is necessary. Static ropes really prove their worth should you need to ascend them (*see page 152*) either to escape or for other reasons such as taking photos.

Miles Gibson on the classic crack climb *London Wall* (E5) Millstone Edge, The Peak District, England.
Even on a fairly straight crack climb like this double ropes are a good idea so that you can divide the load between two runners in the event of a fall, or so that you can pull one rope through to clip a high runner without exposing yourself to a big fall.

Gear

Leading gear

The gear detailed so far is enough for any climber getting into trad climbing who is prepared to second routes. The gear from here on will form the basis of a leading rack.

Wired nuts (wires)

Also known as 'nuts', 'rocks' and 'stoppers', wires provide good protection in almost all rock types. Wires come in sets that are numbered and colour-coded for ease of selection (*left*). Fortunately, different manufacturers have largely numbered sizes in line with each other so it is possible to build up a collection of wires from different manufacturers without having different numbering systems to think about.

Microwires

Microwires (*right*) come into play on harder, less well-protected climbs where tiny cracks are all there is to work with.

In the very smallest sizes it is not possible to thread the wire through the nut without making the wire so thin that it is useless. To get around this problem, the smallest wires bond the wire directly into the nut. The original brass 'RP' microwires remain a favourite amongst many climbers. In some sizes, wires where the nut is bonded directly to the wire are significantly stronger than those where the wire is looped through and 'swaged'.

Offset wires

Off-set wires are so called because one side of the nut is narrower than the other, allowing for the wire to be placed where a normal-shaped wire would not fit, such as in flared cracks - they are particularly good in peg-scars. Some microwires are available in an off-set shape.

Superlight rocks

These 'single-wire' wires are yet another variation on a theme. Lighter than the standard wire due to the reduced nut size and single wire, they fit into slender placements where a normal wire wouldn't go. Because they use only one wire strand, they are less strong in the larger sizes than an equivalent normal wire. They are great as a backup set that won't add noticeably to the weight of your rack.

Sliders

This is a general term for wired nuts where the nut has an additional moving part that allows it to jam into thin, parallel cracks. Often, a sliding nut will be the only full-strength protection that can be placed in a thin slot. Sliding nuts are not often used, and can be hard to come by.

Meilee Rafe on *German Schoolgirl* (E2 5c), Dinorwic Slate, Wales. A couple of sets of wires is an essential part of a lead rack on just about any trad climb.

Other passive protection

Hexes

Hexes are the most satisfying pieces of climbing gear to place: they are big and you just know you're safe when you've buried one into the cliff.

Hexes are mostly used in irregular cracks where the placements are too big for wires. They have the advantage over wires in that they have slings permanently attached, meaning they often don't require the use of a quickdraw (*see page 46 for more on quickdraws*).

The use of hexes is most popular on lower grade routes where wide cracks are more commonly encountered and where speed of placement is less of an issue.

See page 74 for more on placing hexes.

Tricams

Tricams are clever little pieces of gear that provide true camming action without any moving parts. Lighter (and cheaper) than spring loaded camming devices, they boost the range of your rack without weighing you down. While they are no longer a 'must-have', their narrow profile means they sometimes offer protection in features such as small pockets where absolutely nothing else will do.

See page 75 for more on placing Tricams.

Classic hex territory: *Crack of Doom* (VS), Almscliff, Yorkshire, England.

Camming devices (cams)

Also known by the trade-name 'Friends', cams were originally developed for parallel cracks that wires could not protect. Since then they have developed into a crucial and versatile part of every trad climbers gear collection, mainly due to the range of sizes they can cope with and the speed at which they can be placed.

Cams work by transferring a 'pull' force directly out to the sides of a crack: the more the pull, the more the outward force and the greater the grip on the sides of the crack. The spring-loaded cams are moved into position by a trigger, which also serves to remove the device when it is no longer needed.

A set of cams is the most expensive purchase in building up a trad rack, but a full set is essential if you want every advantage modern gear offers.

When building up a set of cams, you will probably want to combine the different products from several manufacturers, as the different designs have advantages and disadvantages in different sizes.

In the smallest sizes, it is useful to have the cams grouped closely together in order to allow placements in small pockets as well as cracks. Double-stem cams, such as Metolius's *TCUs* and DMM's *4CUs* are designed to present the cams closer together than single stem cams. *Aliens* achieve a similar result by integrating the springs into the cams. Some cams also have the advantage of extendable slings, allowing them to be extended without using a quickdraw.

In the larger sizes stability is more of an issue, so it is more of an advantage to have the cams spaced out - making a single stem device such as a *Wild Country Friend* a more attractive option.

Camming range is also a key selling point, with double axle devices, produced by Black Diamond, DMM and Wild Country proving popular. The increased range means that you need fewer units to cover the whole spread of crack sizes. Various designs are also now available that offer increased camming range but often at the expense of cost and/or complexity.

Maintenance

After you've bought your cams, buy some lubricant and remember to lubricate the moving parts regularly - their holding power is reduced if they are not properly lubricated. This is particularly important if you use them on sea cliffs.

More on using cams on page 76.

Lee Meadows before the crux rockover on *Tody's Wall* (HVS), Froggatt Edge, The Peak District, England. Photo by Nick Smith.

Slings and quickdraws

Slings

Slings are used in a wide variety of trad climbing situations, from arranging protection on rock spikes to attaching to belays, and can even serve as make-do harnesses.

Slings typically come in looped lengths of 30cm, 60cm and 120cm, and widths from 8mm to 12mm. Slings are made from either nylon or Dyneema - with the latter allowing much thinner slings of similar strength. The most commonly used slings are 60cm, which are typically worn over the shoulder, and 120cm, which are usually doubled-up and worn over the same shoulder. Much longer slings, up to 400cm, are available; known as cordelettes, these are specifically designed for arranging belays.

There is often a temptation to marry up a sling with a screw-gate. While this is strangely satisfying there is no real point unless you intend to use the sling in a belay: a snap-link karabiner is usually fine.

Quickdraws

A quickdraw is simply a sling with a karabiner at each end. They are used for extending protection to reduce rope-drag and help prevent unseating protection (*see ropework on page 136*). They are also known as **extenders**.

While it is quite possible to use for trad climbing the same quickdraws you use for sport climbing, the optimum design addresses quite different needs, so it is wise to acquire a separate set.

A good trad climbing quickdraw is light, easy to clip, adaptable to different situations, and ideally, able to be adjusted to different lengths (*see sling-draws on page 48*). Typically a lead rack will contain between six and twelve quickdraws, depending on the length of pitches being attempted. Quickdraws should be arranged so that both karabiners are facing the same direction so that it can be placed with both gates facing away from the rock.

One karabiner should be dedicated to clipping the rope and identified by a rubber retainer holding it in place.

Screamers

In situations where very marginal protection has to be relied upon, there exist quickdraws that are designed to absorb much of the force of a fall by ripping stitching apart. The main strength of the quickdraw remains intact, and hopefully, by reducing the impact force, the protection it is clipped to will also remain in place. They are only effective on short falls though.

Retainers

When you go to clip a quickdraw, the last thing you need is to find that the clipping karabiner has turned upside-down. Retainers hold the karabiner in the right position and designate it as the rope end - this is important since the non-rope end gets scratched over time and these scratches can damage your rope. Many quickdraws come with retainers built-in but if yours do not, these can be purchased separately in packs, or alternatively, elastic bands or finger-tape can be used to perform the same function.

Petzl 'Strings' - good for wider tapes.

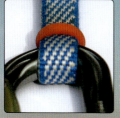

Sheep castration rings - available from all good farming suppliers - and some outdoor shops.

1.5 inch plumbing washers.

> Caution should be exercised when using retainers with open slings, especially long slings as there is a possibility of arranging things so that the only thing connecting the karabiner to the sling is the retainer - which will of course fail under body weight.

Cecile Rittweger on the lip of *Flying Buttress Direct* (HVS) Stanage Edge, Peak District, England. Using a long sling to extend protection placed under a roof is vital to avoid rope-drag problems higher up.

Slingdraws

A slingdraw consists of a thin 60cm sling with a pair of karabiners, one of which is held in position with a retainer.

❶ In its extended position it provides a far greater extension than that provided by any other quickdraw.

❷ By simply passing the captive karabiner through the other ...

❸ ... and clipping the remaining bight (loop) of sling, it is magically transformed into ...

❹ ... a short quickdraw that can be easily racked and used like any other quickdraw.

With only the captive karabiner in place, the slingdraw can be used as a normal sling, removing the need to carry additional 60cm slings.

Every trad climber would benefit from having slingdraws for at least half of their quickdraws.

Undoing a slingdraw can produce a knot if it's not done right. The trick is to undo it the opposite to the way you clipped it up - with a bit of practice you can consistently 'shrink' them and extend them the same way.

The sewn section of the sling can cause problems when looping the slingdraw. This can be alleviated by attaching the retainer krab close to the sewn section.

Max Adamson on the traverse of *Manzoku* (E1 5b), Stennis Head, Pembroke, Wales.
Extending gear prior to making a traverse will significantly reduce rope drag, slingdraws are a quick and easy way of doing this.

Gear 49

Other bits and bobs

Rope ascenders

We've already looked at prusik loops, which are a simple, non-mechanical means of ascending ropes (*see page 152 for more*). There are several mechanical tools available for ascending ropes. These devices make lighter work of ascending a *single* rope than prusiks. Single is stressed because most dedicated rope ascenders, unlike prusiks, cannot be used to ascend a pair of ropes, which is a serious flaw when you find you've just made a long double-rope abseil to the wrong place and want to go back up!

Single rope ascenders

There is a clear trade-off in rope ascenders between weight and ease of use. At one end of the scale are items such as the Petzl *Tibloc* which are amazingly light, but take a large degree of care in use. At the other end is a full-handled device like the Petzl *Ascender*, which are very easy to use, but bulky, heavy, and not the sort of gear you'd take 'just in case'. In the middle are devices such as the Wild Country *Ropeman MK2*, which are a bit more to carry than the Tiblocs, but easier to use and kinder on your rope.

The big advantage of mechanical ascenders is that, unlike a prusik, they only work in one direction. This makes life a bit easier when used in a rescue situation, such as a hoist. Unless you are expecting to be ascending ropes, a pair of prusik loops (and the ability to use them) is as much as you are likely to need to get out of trouble.

Shunts

It would be logical to entitle this paragraph 'double rope ascenders', but to date, the Petzl *Shunt* is still the only player in the field. The Shunt was designed for protecting a double rope abseil, and this they do very well. They are also capable of ascending double ropes. They work equally well with single ropes and their only disadvantage is the weight and bulk.

Far Left : A Petzl Tibloc
Above: A Wild Country Ropeman MK 2
Left: A Petzl *Shunt*, still the only double-rope ascender on the market.

Gear

Guide Plates as ascenders

There are many belay devices now that offer us the ability to use the device as an auto-locker. This allows the device to be used as part of a rope ascending setup and has the advantage of being able to handle two ropes. When combined with a shunt, you have everything you need to ascend a pair of ropes.

Pulleys

These make life much easier should you find yourself having to rescue someone by hoisting. Other than that, they are only of use in hauling a heavy bag. if you're expecting to do this fairly regularly, you would be well-advised to invest in a device such as a Petzl *Mini Traxion*, which integrates a pulley with a cam and can also be used to ascend ropes and even to self-belay.

Rope-cutters

Lastly, if you have ever got your rope caught in a crack while abseiling you may find you need to cut it free. We're told that it is possible to chew through a rope, but it takes a lot longer and will undoubtedly leave you with a sore jaw - but a good tale to tell.

You don't need a great big knife - even a pair of miniature folding scissors will cut through a 10.5mm rope in under a minute, especially if the rope is under tension. Mini-scissors will also serve you well if you suffer the less traumatic but significantly more frequent occurrence of a broken finger nail.

Lastly, while we're on the subject of dealing with epics, a small **head-torch** is a 'must-have', even if it just lives in the lid of your pack. Small LED head-torches are light and good for getting out of trouble.

Top left : A DMM Pivot - one of a number of belay devices which can be used with a prusik or shunt to ascend a pair of ropes.
Below left: A Petzl Mini Traxion
Top right: Petzl Spatha knife
Middle right: Folding scissors
Right: A compact head-torch.

Building a rack

A 'rack' is just a term for a collection of climbing equipment that makes climbing possible with some degree of safety. The items that make up a rack, and quantities needed, are very much determined by the style of climbs being attempted. Long, well-protected face climbs may need three sets of wires, lots of quickdraws and a few cams, whereas short gritstone routes can be protected by a few cams and a handful of wires. The aim is to have enough gear to never have to climb past a useful placement, but not so much that the weight of it is excessive.

It is usual in trad climbing to use a pair of half ropes, and for each partner to supply one rope, though for routes under 25m, a single 50m half rope can simply be doubled-up.

To give an idea of how racks vary, here are some examples:

Seconding only

Harness
Helmet
Shoes
Chalk
Belay device
Pear-shaped screw-gate
Nut key and karabiner
Prusik loops with screw-gate karabiner

Leading short pitches (20m or less)

All the above, plus:
4 x Quickdraws
4 x Slingdraws
2 x 120cm sling
6 x Cams (1 - 3.5 Friend or equivalents)
2 x Sets of wires (1 - 10)
4 x Hexes or very large wires (10+)
2 x Screw-gate karabiners
12 x Extra karabiners

Leading long pitches (20 - 60m)

All the above, but:
6 x Slingdraws
8 x Quickdraws
3 x Sets of wires

For high grade routes (E1ish and above)

As above, but add:
2 x Micro-cams (0 and 0.5 or equivalents)
1 x Set of microwires

Note, on some rock types, such as slate, you will need these at all grades.

Multi-pitch routes

As above, but add:
2 x Screw-gate karabiners
4 x Cams (covering a wide range)

Sarah Kekus on *Calisto* (E1) St. Govan's East, Pembroke, Wales.
Routes in Pembroke are usually long single pitches with plenty of gear possibilities making a heavy demand on the size of rack needed.

Gear

Carrying it all the crag

A backpack is essential for getting your gear to the crag, though it doesn't have to be a fancy 'climbing pack' with attachments for ice tools and ski-poles - unless you're intending taking it up into the mountains.

When choosing a pack, make sure you have plenty of room for your gear, plus water, food, guide books, the clothes you thought you'd be wearing but it's too hot for, and anything else you might want to take - like cameras, first aid kits and head-torches. Naturally, you'll want it to comfortably fit your back.

Rope-bags

Although mostly used in sport climbing, rope-bags are a good way of keeping your rope tangle free without having to coil it. Rope bags have small ground-sheets built-in which keeps your rope out of the dirt. Most rope-bags are able to handle two fifty metre half ropes with ease.

Rope buckets

Rope buckets are like rope bags, but more useful in trad climbing situations where you need to feed the rope out from a hanging container. Examples of where a rope bucket is handy include abseiling on a windy day where you don't want to let the ends of your rope swing around, and hanging belays above the sea where your ropes can be neatly stashed without getting wet or tangled up.

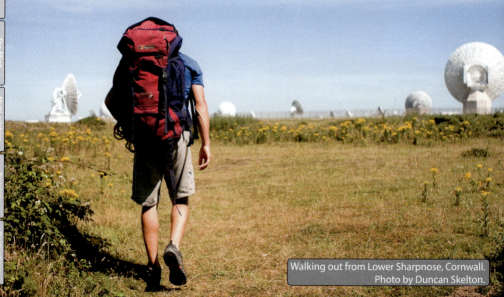

Walking out from Lower Sharpnose, Cornwall. Photo by Duncan Skelton.

John Arran carrying a haul bag (*see page 249*) up to the base of what was to be a new route *Welcome to Crackistan* in Pakistan's Nangma Valley. Photo by Anne Arran.

Gear

Caring for your gear

Climbing gear is incredibly robust and doesn't require a great deal of care, but that's not to say you can ignore the subject completely. The following are the most common causes of damage to your gear and, as with all things, prevention where possible is better than cure.

Acid

The surest way of damaging ropes and similar 'software' is to bring them into contact with an acid. A typical scenario would be to store your gear in the back of your car where battery acid has leaked. If you suspect acid has been in contact with your gear (touch it to your tongue and you will be able to taste it) discard it.

Dirt

Getting grit into gear will cause wear. Gear with moving parts should be regularly cleaned with warm, soapy water, rinsed, dried and lubricated. Ropes can pick up dirt like magnets and eventually the handling will start to noticeably suffer, simply rinse under a shower and leave to dry naturally.

Fraying

Wired nuts should be retired if you find any wire starting to fray. Runners which have been stuck and removed with some violent tugs often bend or fray near the nut end. Damage to wires can be avoided by taking care not to bend them when they're stuffed down the bottom of your pack. The trigger wires on cams are also prone to fraying - these can usually be replaced, although it is quite expensive.

Worn metal

Gear with moving parts will wear to the point of retirement. The most commonly encountered example of hazardous wear are cams. If you have a camming device where the cams have a noticeable sideways movement, then it should be permanently retired. Any sideways movement, especially on larger cams, will be a weak spot.

Other items susceptible to wear include karabiners and belay devices, though considerable wear is needed to reduce their strength. Karabiners with sharp grooves worn into them should not be used to clip the rope into since the grooves will abrade the rope - this is the reason quickdraws have a 'rope end' and a 'gear end'.

A 4CU that's seen better days.
Photo by Duncan Skelton

Gear

Worn nylon

A rope, cut half through from one careless two foot swing across a granite edge ten pitches up El Capitan in Yosemite, California. Photo by Ian Parnell.

When rubbed against rock, nylon will quickly show signs of wear. A light 'fur' where the nylon threads have been pulled *intact* is nothing to worry about, and will actually protect the nylon against further damage, though broken fibres and cuts are reasons to replace the item. Ropes are protected by their outer sheaths and so light damage to the sheath is not a reason to retire it. If at any point the white core of the rope becomes visible underneath the sheath, the rope should be retired. If this occurs close to the end of the rope it is possible to cut it completely at that point and continue using the shorter rope.

Sunlight

The affect of sunlight on your rack is not something to worry about unduly, though it is a good idea to store your gear away from direct sunlight wherever possible. Slings (not being protected by an outer sheath) are more susceptible to damage than rope and it is worth replacing your quickdraws when the colour noticeably fades.

Salt

Climbing on sea-cliffs is likely to deposit salt on your gear. Aluminium, the metal that most of your hardware is made from, corrodes quickly when in contact with salt, causing karabiners to get stiff and cams to lock up. Rinsing and lubricating regularly will prevent this damage. If you find yourself on a climb and the cam you need to place has seized-up, holding it close to your mouth and blowing spit into the seized parts may loosen it up enough to get you out of trouble.

Traumatic damage

If you suspect gear may have been damaged by a fall, or other high impact, closely inspect the item. Look for any bends or cracks (perhaps using another identical item to compare). If you find damage, retire the gear. If you cannot find any damage but nevertheless have lost confidence in it then retire it. If you don't trust it, it's no good to you, even if it's perfectly fine.

Keeping your own gear

Marking your gear is the surest way to make sure your treasured kit doesn't find its way into someone else's backpack never to come back. Various methods have been used over the years including the tried and tested insulation tape, paint and marker-pen. You can even order packs of customised stickers that include your phone number and email address (look online).

Sarah Clough leading *Gabriel* (VS), Stoney Middleton, The Peak District, England. Photo by Nick Smith.

Protection

It is easy to see the moves of a climb as a positive aspect, and the placing of protection as a negative aspect, of the sport. While the moves lead you to the top, protection is there to stop you getting hurt when you fall. It is easy to slip into the mind-set where you spend much of your time on the route concentrating on the next piece of protection rather than on the next move.

In practice, having confidence in your protection is essential to being able to focus entirely on successfully completing the moves, and being able to do the moves efficiently and quickly will save more energy for placing protection.

When both aspects are approached in a positive way you have more chance of reaching your the ultimate goal - the top of the route!

Placing protection

Placing protection is a fundamental part of trad climbing. Protection comes in all shapes and sizes but what distinguishes trad climbing from sport climbing - where protection is fixed in place in the form of permanent bolts - is that the leader has to place the majority of the protection themselves while climbing.

Advances in the technology of climbing protection has made a huge difference to the safety of trad climbing and, consequently, have opened up well-protected routes that were previously considered to be highly dangerous or even unclimbable. As technology has moved on, protection has got stronger and more reliable. While falling off trad routes is never going to be risk-free, long gone are the days when the maxim was 'the leader never falls'. Falling off today is an inevitable consequence of progressing through the sport and knowing how to place protection correctly may be the difference between getting frustrated and falling off the crux (again) or getting airlifted off the crag.

With improved technology, protecting climbs is also less damaging to the environment. No longer do we have to hammer in pegs that damage the rock and eventually get stuck - rusting away slowly. Protection should be placed, used, then removed without trace and only where absolutely necessary should protection be fixed *in situ* (in place).

In this section we are going to look at the art of placing protection in the rock and how to get it back out. How the protection works in relation to ropes will be dealt with in the ropework section (*page 96*). The question of where we place protection, how much of it, and how to place it without getting too pumped, will also be dealt with later - under tactics (*page 190*).

Vic Barrett climbing *Sunset Crack* (HS), Froggatt, The Peak District, England. Photo by Alex Messenger.

Luke Roberts slotting a wire into *Lucky Strike* (E2) Rusty Walls, Pembroke, Wales.

Protection

Placing wires

Placing wires securely and quickly is a skill that takes a lot of practice. The objective is to be able to look at a feature in the rock, decide which part of it will provide the best wire placement, estimate the right size and place it quickly without having to experiment. It takes a lot of practice placing wires to be able to do this and if you've limited experience, or are a bit rusty, then you can expect to have to fiddle around for a while with different-sized wires, and different placements, before you get something you're happy to climb above.

Choosing the right placement

Wires require features in the rock where a natural tapering (a reduction in width) is present. The more the tapering of the rock matches the tapering of the nut on the wire you're attempting to place, the more suitable it will be.

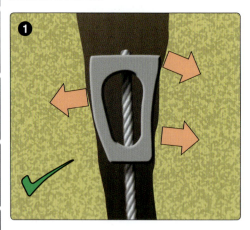

❶ A typical 'bomb-proof' wire placement. The nut is connected to solid rock in three places and as the crack continues to taper, even if the rock crumbles a little, the nut will simply slide down into an ever better position.

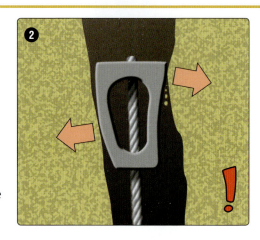

❷ With only two points of contact, this is a very poor placement. The crack here has very little taper and the nut has only just caught on the rock. Although this might well satisfy a good tug-test, a fall could easily pull the nut through.

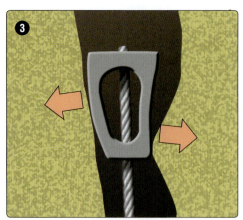

❸ It is tempting to assume that the number of points of contact is the deciding factor in determining the quality of a placement, but where the points of contact are, is as important. While there are still only two points of contact, this is a much stronger placement than the one above, the only weakness is the fact that it is not very stable - a smaller size would be better here.

Protection

Now let's view things from a different angle, after all real cracks come in 3-D...

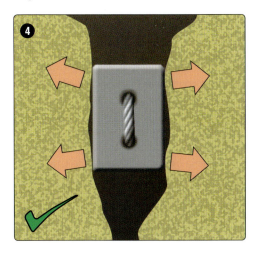

4 Viewed from above, there are no problems with this placement, with four points of contact this is going to be a very stable placement.

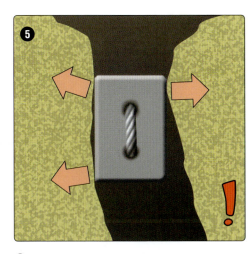

5 While this placement may have looked fine from the side, it is far from ideal as all the force is being applied through the limited points of contact. Even if it is strong enough to hold a fall, it could easily be unseated and fall out.

Judging the rock

A crucial thing to look at in evaluating a wire placement is the rock: a placement is only ever as good as the rock it's in, so when choosing whether to place a wire check that the rock is thick enough on each side of the placement.

The most perfectly placed wire is of no help if it's behind a thin flake (or loose block!) that will simply break off when loaded. Generally, the deeper you can place a wire the better, since there is more rock to hold it in place.

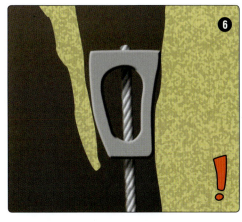

6 While this placement has three points of contact, the crack is only formed by a thin flake and so the strength of the rock is the weak link here and a fall would be very likely to snap the rock.

Sometimes within a crack you will find the surface of the rock is less solid than the weathered rock on the outside. Granite often has loose crystals, especially within cracks. If there is some loose material in a crack, it is a good idea to give it a quick rub with your fingers - or nut key even - to make sure that the surfaces you are placing a nut next to are as solid as possible.

Protection

Selecting the right wire

Wires covering a full range of sizes should be stored in a cluster on two karabiners - one for small wires, one for larger wires. Some use three karabiners - small, medium and large.

A key skill when placing a wire is being able to identify the correct wire when you grab this cluster off your harness. It is an easy skill to practise: simply walk along the base of a crag with a set of wires and place as many as you can - aiming to get the right size first time. With practice you'll soon be able to tell the size from a quick glance at the rock.

Placing a wire can be satisfying and confidence inspiring. Mick Ryan on *Lavaredo* (VS), Carreg Alltrem, North Wales. Photo by Alan James

Often, you will find there is more than one size that will fit. To decide which size to use, consider these aims:

1) Bigger nuts have a larger taper than smaller nuts, meaning there's more rock holding them in - so less chance of being pulled through.

2) However, smaller nuts can be jammed more securely into placements where a large nut may be prone to falling out.

3) Be wary of very small nuts, where the thinner wire significantly reduces their strength - if you can place a nut larger than a size 1 then do so.

One wire, two sizes

All wires cover two sizes because the width of the wire is larger than the depth (often one size exactly). This is handy if you are running low on wires. This feature can be very useful, particularly in using pockets and slots: a good trick is to place the nut into a pocket and get it to catch by turning it a half-turn inside the pocket. This 'half-turn' technique also works well in cracks and breaks where the fissure widens inside the rock.

It is worth noting that the reduced taper on sideways placements does mean that the nut is more likely to pull through than if a larger size had been selected and placed 'normally'.

Above: an off-set wire in a flaring crack. The side inside the crack is narrower than the side showing, which fits this crack better than a standard nut.

Opposite: Charlie Woodburn takes to the air on *Orange Robe Burning* (E6), Trevallen, Pembroke.

Setting the wire in the right position

Wires work in a limited range of directions: a wire placed to withstand a downward force will often be easily unseated by an upwards, or even a sideways, pull. Because of this, it is important to *seat* a wire in the direction that you anticipate it is most likely to be loaded.

Common sense tells us that this direction is straight down, but in reality a fall will often initially load a wire with a significant outward pull. The exact angle will depend on how you fall off and how far above the placement you fall. Take a look at the photo on the left, this is a fairly typical fall from a vertical route. Note the angle of the red rope - this means that the wire is being subjected to a significant outward pull.

Because of this, it's worth making sure that the wire you place will be able to withstand this outward force. The exact angle you seat the wire at will vary with the angle of the rock. Steeper climbs will produce a greater outward pull on the protection, slabs producing only a little (but nearly always some).

A major factor is the length of your fall, with very short falls resulting in a mostly outwards trajectory at the moment the protection is loaded. Anyone who has taken a short fall onto a hand-placed peg can testify to this!

As a rule-of-thumb, on a vertical climb, aim to seat your wires at an angle of around *twenty degrees* relative to the rock, on a steeper climb this angle should be greater, on slabby climbs, less. The same principle holds true for all leader-placed protection, it is just more crucial for wires.

Protection

Wire placement tricks

Stacking wires

If you find yourself with a crack that's too wide for any of the gear you're carrying, and you really can't find anything else, try stacking two wires together - ❶. Jam them together as hard as you can, then clip the downward pointing one with the longest quickdraw you have (any movement will easily unseat it) - ❷. Now gingerly continue, vowing to buy a few more cams or not use them all it so quickly next time.

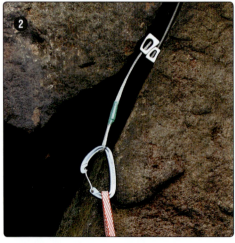

James Rowe leading *Groove Route* (HVS) Rivelin Edge, The Peak District, England. Photo by Nick Smith.

Protection

Interlinking wires for reach

One of the benefits of wires over nuts on cord is that you have a bit more reach, but sometimes that just isn't enough. If you find yourself just out of reach of a good wire placement, simply link two wires together by pulling the nut down on a 'booster' wire, passing the wire loop through the base of the wire you're attempting to place, and then looping it over the nut to form a perfect reef knot. The result is surprisingly rigid and enough to hold it in place and can give you a good 15cm extra reach. You can clip the booster wire, but it is stronger if you clip the wire you've placed. Don't forget to check the placement as you climb past it since the wire often doesn't seat itself properly in the crack when placed in this way.

Alex Hughes on *Long Tall Sally* (E1) Burbage North, The Peak District, England.
For most climbers, the bomber wire on this route is just out of reach until you've done the crux. Using this technique you can place the wire high above you before you make a hard move.

Evaluating your placement

Having placed a wire, you need to give it a visual check. You should look to make sure there is plenty of contact between good solid rock and the nut. If you're not happy with your placement, remove the wire and try something else. When you're happy with your placement, it's time to jam it in.

Jamming

A good wire placement can be jammed in place by making increasingly violent tugs on it. Your first tug should be gentle - if you give it a big initial tug and it pops out, there's a chance you'll topple over backwards and may take a big fall. So go gently to begin with until you're pretty sure it's a solid placement, then really jam it in. Your second may curse you when it comes to taking them out, but it's the only opportunity you have to test the placement and is greatly preferable to watching your wires pop out and slide down the rope.

Extending and clipping

Up to this point, the wire you are placing will still be attached to a racking karabiner with a cluster of other wires on it. It may be tempting to place a quickdraw on the wire and get it clipped before you remove the racking karabiner, but this usually causes unnecessary complexity. By leaving the racking karabiner attached, it will probably get sandwiched between the rock and your quickdraw with the weight of the rope on it, making it hard to remove. When you've jammed your wire in, just unclip your racking karabiner, return it to your harness, take a quickdraw and clip it up.

Will it hold?

The following tables show the strength rating of two different types of small wires available. Wild Country's *Mini Rocks* utilise looped wire, whereas Black Diamond has the wire pressed to the nut. Comparing the similarly sized Mini Rock 0.75 and the Mini Stopper 5, it is clear that the Stopper is the stronger option by 2kn. However, as the sizes increase the advantage reverses, with the Wild Country Rock 2 being a full 4kn stronger than the slightly larger Stopper 6. Both types, of course, are sufficiently strong for most situations that you will use them in.

Wild Country Mini Rocks and Rocks

Size	Strength
0 (4.4mm)	2kn
0.25 (4.9mm)	4kn
0.5 (5.6mm)	4kn
0.75 (6.9mm)	4kn
1 (7mm)	7kn
2 (8.2mm)	12kn

Black Diamond Micro Stoppers

Size	Strength
1 (3.7mm)	2kn
2 (4.6mm)	3kn
3 (5.1mm)	5kn
4 (5.9mm)	6kn
5 (7.4mm)	6kn
6 (8.8mm)	8kn

Another point that comes out from this is the clear jump in strength from the Rock 2 upwards - showing that if you can place anything larger than a Rock 1 - you should.

Protection

Esoteric wire placements

Wires can be used for more than just placing in cracks and pockets. Thin wires with moveable nuts can be used to great effect in the following situations:

Clipping hangerless-bolts

If you come across a bolt without a hanger, such as an old aid bolt - ❶, or a new expansion bolt where someone has stolen the hanger, you can use a wire to make the best of it.

You need to select a smallish wire so that the size of the nut doesn't get in the way, but not so small that the wire isn't very strong (avoid using a size 1). Obviously, this trick can't be done with wires where the nut is bonded to the wires.

Now slide the nut down the wire - ❷, this can be tricky if you only have one hand free, so if you're expecting to have to do this on a route, it's a good idea to do it before you leave the ground.

All you need to do now is pop the loop of wire over the bolt and push the nut up as far as it will go to secure it - ❸. It can now be clipped with a quickdraw.

Making use of micro-threads

Where there is a hole through the rock which is too narrow to thread a sling (*see page 87 for more on using slings*), there's a good chance that you can get a wire through it. If you can't clip both ends of the wire in a loop, you may be able to simply put a karabiner through the wire loop to hold it in position. The fact that the wire is bent will reduce its strength, but it's much better than nothing. This also works with flattened bolt hangers by threading the 'eye'.

Protection

Opposing wires

As we've already mentioned, it is important to anticipate the direction of load and place a wire so that it pulls the right way. Frequently, however, the direction of load and what the rock will allow you are at odds. A common instance of this is when placing wires in a horizontal break, where the wire needs a sideways pull in order to hold but the most likely direction of loads is straight down.

What is needed in this instance is another wire (or any other piece of gear) that wants to be pulled in roughly the opposite direction - this is referred to as *in opposition*. One way of doing this is to join the two wires using a sling and a couple of clove hitches to get just the right configuration (*see photo*). This can be a bit fiddly if you only have one free hand and it can be easier to just use a couple of quickdraws, though be wary of creating a three-way pull (*see page 107*) on a karabiner.

A quicker but less adjustable way to oppose a couple of wires is to clip a 60cm sling to one wire, then pass it through the karabiner clipped to the other, before passing it through the loop formed between the two karabiners - ❶. Now pass it through the second karabiner again and pull it tight - ❷. Though less adjustable, this has the advantage of being able to be arranged with one hand.

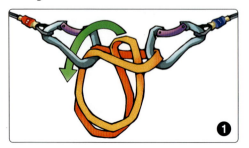

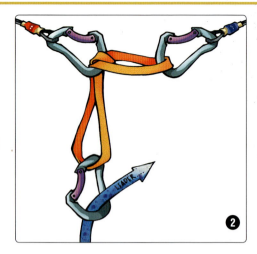

It may be tempting to simply take a sling and clip one end of it to each wire, then simply clip the middle. The danger with this is that should either one of the wires fail, the protection point will most likely fail completely.

A compromise method that will shock-load but not necessarily fail if one wire fails, involves clipping each wire with the opposite ends of a sling, then clipping the two sides of the sling, but critically clipping a loop in one of the sides - ❸. This method has the advantage of being automatically adjusting.

See page 122 for more ways to equalise protection points.

Luke Roberts uses opposing wires to protect the notorious initial section of *The Arrow* (E1) St. Govan's Head, Pembroke, Wales.

Protection

Removing wires

Before we look at some of the tricks for removing wires, it is important to stress that 'what goes in, should come out'.

The first thing to do when you start struggling to remove a wire is talk to your leader: they may tell you how they placed it from an odd angle, or that they didn't even place it and it was already stuck!

Gently does it

Sometimes a well-placed wire gets stuck because the second uses too much force initially trying to remove it. When you come across a wire to be removed, first unclip it from the rope and give it a tap with the quickdraw - this is nearly always enough to unseat it. If that doesn't work, use a nut key and give it a harder knock. Avoid grabbing the wire and tugging it unless you're completely out of options - tugging the wire is a good way of jamming it in for good and can also damage it.

If a wire is really stuck, then you are going to need both hands free to get it out. If you want to second the pitch clean, leave it and abseil for it later. If you're not bothered about sitting on the rope, climb a few moves past the wire and ask for a tight rope - the stretch in the rope will deliver you at the right place.

Using both hands and a nut key you should be able to get the wire moving inside the crack. If it is really stuck, consider clipping a couple of quickdraws together and attaching them to the wire and to your belay loop. Climb past the wire until the quickdraws come tight, then jerk the wire upwards.

Another technique is to clip together a chain of three or four quick draws, attached one end to the stuck wire, then whip the quickdraw chain upwards to give a big tug on the wire.

A final trick is to find a rock and use it as a hammer on your nut key. Be careful you don't drop it if there are people below.

If you've managed to get the wire loose, but still can't retrieve it, be patient, eventually it will come.

Stuck wires

Sometimes you may be forced to leave a wire in place but please be aware of the problems this can cause for climbers in the future. It may be nice sometimes to find a stuck wire on a hard move - it is easier and quicker for you to clip, and should be solid - however, eventually the wire will rust and ultimately snap, the nut will corrode in the rock, probably never to be retrieved. This leaves the route with one less gear placement, often in a crucial position.

If you do come across a wire that someone has abandoned, and you manage to get it out, it's yours! And if it's still fresh, you can add it to your rack with the knowledge that you've done your bit to clean up the crag environment.

Removing a well-placed wire from *Door Post* (HS), Bosigran, Cornwall, England.

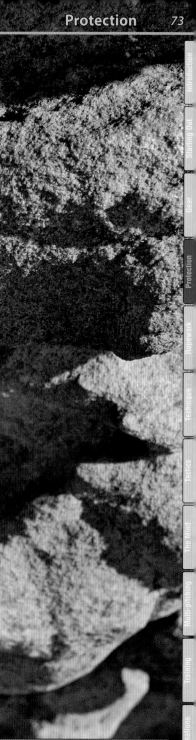

In a perfect world, all wires would be as good as this! The Grampians, Australia.

Protection

Placing hexes

The same advice given in placing wires applies to hexes but the complex shape of hexes means that they can offer a number of different placement possibilities.

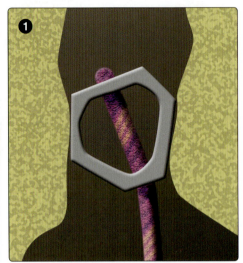

1 This is a 'standard' hex placement using the two sides that present the narrowest shape.

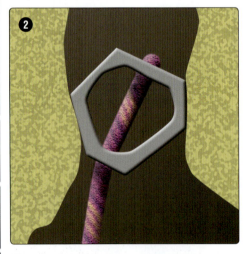

2 Using the other sides of the hex, a slightly wider placement can be made.

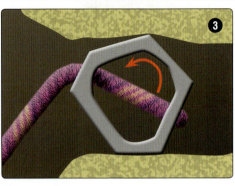

3 Hexes can also be used as basic cams. To cam with a hex, place the hex so the cord/tape/wire exits from the top, a good tug will lock it into place.

4 Here, the widest placement is possible by using the width of the hex.

Other uses for hexes

Apart from providing some very solid protection, hexes are handy when you've run out of quickdraws. Simply pull the cord (or whatever) that loops over the top of the hex out - sliding the hex down the cord - add a karabiner to the top and you have yourself a quickdraw.

Sliding the hex down the cord is also a handy way of racking them so that they don't swing around and get in the way.

Placing Tricams

A Tricam is basically a single cam with no moving parts. Rather than pivoting on an axle like a spring loaded camming device, Tricams pivot on a single point that is in contact with the rock.

The best Tricam placements are where there is a small depression in one side of the crack, or pocket where the Tricam's spike can be seated. On the other side of the device is a pair of rails; the device should be placed so that the tape sling runs between these rails. This can be achieved by placing it with the spike pointing upwards, or downwards. Tricams can even be placed sideways so that the tape runs only partly over one of the rails.

Once you have placed your Tricam - a fiddly process especially if you are trying to do it one-handed - it needs to be firmly seated by giving it a sharp tug.

While Tricams can't 'walk' like sprung cams, it is always worth adding enough extension so that they are not dislodged by the movement of the rope.

When it comes to removing a Tricam, you will need to return it to its 'un-set position' with a nut key. If the Tricam has been heavily loaded, you may well need to exert considerable force with both hands to get it back. Take care not to damage the sling if you have to resort to hammering it out.

A good Tricam placement in a shot-hole on Llanberis slate. Taking a set of Tricams on slate can often offer placements you might otherwise struggle to make use of. A good tip for making use of shot-holes if you don't have Tricams is to insert a large nut narrow end first, with the cord or wire doubled back. Loading the piece will cam the nut into place.

More on Tricams on page 42.

Protection

Placing cams

Cams are the most complex pieces of protection and cam placements are the most difficult to judge. Cams can be placed in cracks, breaks (horizontal cracks) and pockets and each cam can vary in size. The big advantages that cams have over passive protection like wires and hexes is that they can be placed in parallel cracks where there is no natural constriction, and also that one piece of protection covers a wide range of crack widths.

A classic pocket placement for a cam - in this instance a three-cam unit (*TCU*) fitted perfectly (a four-cam unit would not fit such a narrow placement).

Checking the rock

The first thing to look at - as with all protection - is the rock. As with wires, the deeper the placement, the more rock there is to hold the cam. Placing a cam behind a thin flake of rock is very likely to snap the flake off. Cam placements on popular routes on soft rock, like gritstone, are getting gradually worn - ❶. Initially this is resulting in improved placements in the shape of cam-shaped recesses in the rock, but in time these placements will deteriorate - and there is a strong chance that shallow placements will start to fail as the edge of the crack breaks off.

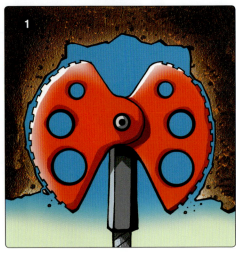

Choosing the right size

Having identified a likely place for a cam, and checked that there is no problem with the rock, the next stage is to select the right size of cam. Before reaching for your rack, take a really good look in the crack and get an idea of how wide it is, and where a cam is going to provide the best placement. While cams fully function throughout a wide range of sizes, the best size is one that fits with the cams half closed - midway in its camming range - ❷.

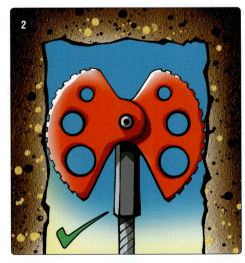

When a cam is fully open (- ❸), there is a risk that should it bite into soft rock, it would open fully and fail. In addition, when a cam is at the widest part of its range, the springs that hold the cams in place are at their weakest, resulting in a placement that may be prone to 'walking'.

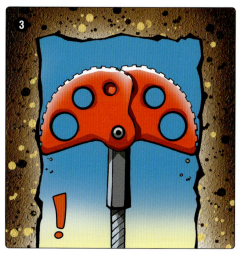

At the other end of the range, 'bunching up' the cams as tightly as possible (- ❹) may give a very secure placement, but comes at the risk of your partner not being able to get it out. This is the number one reason that cams get stuck for good.

Sarah Kekus on *Stingray* (E2) Carreg-y-Barcud, Pembroke, Wales.

Protection

How cams work

First a bit of technical stuff: if you don't like maths then skip this bit and just read the *real world* section opposite.

If you've ever bridged up a chimney, you know how cams work. When climbing a chimney, your weight is transmitted to the sides of the chimney via your legs. The wider a chimney is, the wider your legs are, the greater the outward force you exert, and the more stable you will be - up until you find yourself in the splits - when it doesn't work any more.

When climbing with sticky rubber shoes on rock with plenty of friction (like granite) you can get away with a narrower bridging angle than you can on low friction rock (like slate) where the lack of friction needs to be compensated for with a greater outward force, and a much wider bridging angle. A cam works in an identical way: force applied through the stem of the cam is transferred outwards through the cams.

Bridging angle

Here, the rock has less friction, meaning the force must be transmitted outwards far more than downwards. The same would be true if the rock had a high friction, but the climber's shoes had less: if the climber had aluminium soled climbing shoes (for some bizarre reason), he would be able to stay in place on most rock types if his bridging angle was 152.5° - that's a camming angle of 13.75°.

Bridging up a chimney with sticky rubber and rough rock means you can have a reduced bridging angle, allowing the force to transmit downwards, as well as outwards. Here, the bridging angle is 90°, which produces a camming angle of 45°.

Camming angle

Same physics, different object. Substitute the climber for a cam and exactly the same rules apply. The only real difference is that the force comes from 'below' rather than 'above'.

When we were discussing the angle of the climber's legs while bridging, we referred to the bridging angle. In the world of cams, we refer to the camming angle. To work out a camming angle, just take the bridging angle away from 180° and divide by two.

The main difference between a bridging climber and a cam is that a cam contacts the rock with aluminium alloy rather than sticky rubber. Because aluminium alloy isn't nearly as sticky as rubber, the camming angle needs to be much lower for a cam, than for a person.

The original prototype cam was designed for granite and had a camming angle of 15°. Later models were given a reduced camming angle to ensure more reliable placements in lower-friction rock. Many camming devices have settled on a camming angle of 13.75°, as used in Friends, though some are lower (smaller range, better grip) and some are bigger.

What this all means in the real world

Understanding camming angles immediately helps in gauging the holding strength of a cam placement. In particular it tells us to be wary of smooth rock: the rougher the rock, the better the placement. Parallel-sided cracks in most rock types give surprisingly good cam placements, but we should take care with very low friction rock such as slate and sea-washed limestone, where parallel placements are not as reliable. Conversely, very rough rock will provide better than average placements, meaning that good placements can be found even in quite flared cracks.

It is helpful to look at a cam placement as a sum of the placements of each of its individual cams - usually there are four, sometimes just three. When you have placed a cam, survey the individual cams and look for any that are engaged in an unusual way. For example, you may find that in an irregular crack, the cams are all at different degrees of rotation - if any cam is close to fully open, it is worth trying to replace it.

Using features within the crack

Most cracks have features inside that can be taken advantage of to improve the quality of a cam placement. Concave dishes are obvious places to situate individual cams. Edges within a crack are also well worth hunting out - by pacing a cam against even a slender edge, less reliance is placed on friction.

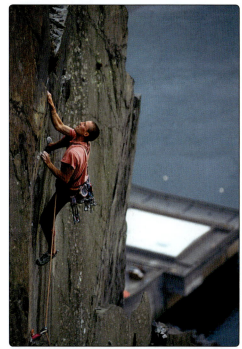

Steve McClure on *Manatese* (E4) Rainbow Walls, Snowdonia, Wales. Placing cams in smooth rock such as slate should always be done with more care than on rough rock like granite. Photo by Alex Messenger.

Protection

Keeping all cams in contact

It doesn't take a genius to work out that an optimal placement is one with all cams in good contact with the rock. Having said that, there are time when the only placement you can get will have one or even two cams not engaged, in such situations all you can do is clip it and tell yourself it's better than nothing - which it is.

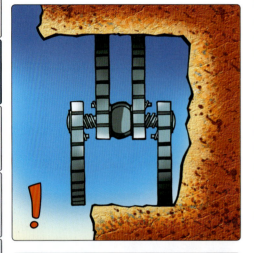

Above: the orientation of this cam only allows three of the cams to make contact with the rock - clearly not what you want.
Below: by simply turning the device around, all four cams make contact producing a good placement.

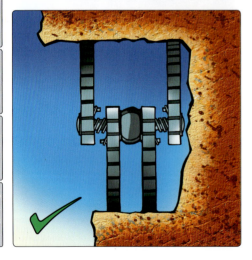

Which way around?

Cams with four individual cams nearly always have the cams closer together on one side than the other, this produces a quite different footprint on each side. In most placements this makes very little difference, though in some placements such as shallow corner cracks, getting all four cams in contact with the rock can only be achieved by placing the cam one way round. If you can't get a good placement it's often worth taking the cam out and turning it around before trying again.

In horizontal placements (such as shown on the facing page), placing cams with the wider cams at the bottom is the method approved by the manufacturers. In practice for all but the most marginal of placements it makes little difference, and if you can get a better fit with the narrow cams facing down it would be better to place it that way around.

Offset cams

One of the most difficult features to make use of with a conventional camming device is a flaring crack where the width of the crack varies so much that there is insufficient range in the cams to fit both the wide side and the narrow side. To get around this some manufacturers produce off-set cams which feature cams on one side being a size larger than the cams on the other.

Offset cams are mostly employed in aid climbing and it's unlikely they would find a permanent place on your free-climbing rack, though it's worth knowing about them in case one day you find a specific placement on a 'big lead' where they become a crucial piece of protection.

Protection

Orientating to the direction of load

As for all protection, cams need to be placed in the direction of load. In a vertical crack, this means placing the cam at an angle that anticipates the downward and outward force generated during a fall (*see page 65 for more on this*).

Try to avoid shallow cam placements where the stem 'sticks out' from the rock (*left*), as these place a greater than normal strain on the device and only loads two cams. Admittedly, sometimes this is all you have on offer!

Modern flexible-stemmed Friends are designed to bend when loaded - they can cope with horizontal placements like this without being over-stressed.

Rigid-stemmed devices

Back when rigid-stemmed cams were commonplace, there was a danger that a placement in a shallow break could bend and weaken the solid stem.

This was patched by tying-off the stem with some cord (preferably Dyneema), and clipping that when using a shallow placement. These days this problem is most readily solved by ditching those old solid-stemmed cams and getting some nice new flexible ones!

A placement with perpendicular orientation creates a mis-match loading to the cam. Try to point the cam in the direction of a fall if you can.

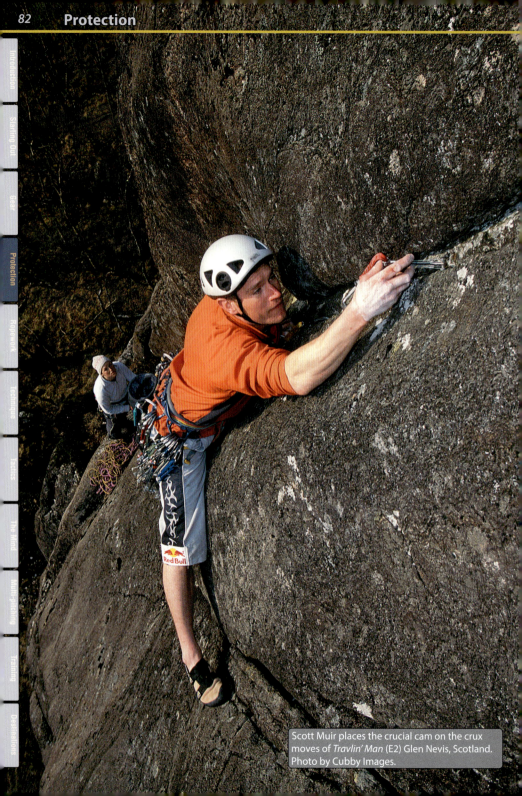

Scott Muir places the crucial cam on the crux moves of *Travlin' Man* (E2) Glen Nevis, Scotland. Photo by Cubby Images.

Protection

Reverse strength

Most cams now have what is known as reverse strength. This means that when the cams are fully open, 'cam stops' attached to the cams prevent the cams opening any further.

Cam-stops on a Wild Country Friend 5.

The theory is that this allows the cam to be placed like a piece of passive protection. In practice a single-axle cam used passively is highly unreliable. If placed in a crack, more often that not, a load will simply rotate the cams and pull it through. Things are a bit better with double axle cams which, due to their design, have much greater stability in reverse strength 'mode', though still not as reliable as a correctly sized cam or hex.

Walking

The failure of cam placements is very often due to the process of 'walking'. If you place a cam in a parallel crack and jiggle the stem up and down, you can see how, in turn, one side locks while the other side gets pushed into the crack. This results in the cam 'walking' deeper and deeper into the crack. Often, the cam will walk into a wider part of the crack where it will open up completely and become useless. Walking is particularly likely where a cam is placed at the limit of its range due to the reduced spring pressure. A cam that walks into a narrower part of the crack can easily get stuck, or walk so far back the you can't reach it to get it out.

The best way to prevent walking is to place your cam at the back of the crack where there is nowhere for it to walk, but this is often not possible. Extending your cam placement will reduce the chance of your rope's movement to cause walking.

While cams come with tape already sewn into them, this is rarely ever long enough, so it is wise to get into the habit of extending your cams with quickdraws or slingdraws as a rule rather than the exception. Some Cams have doubled-up tapes that are easily extendable and you should extend them in nearly all instances.

Micro-cams

The most recent innovation in cams is the development of very small cams. While these amazing objects provide protection where nothing else could, it is important to be aware that these units have lower strength than larger cams (typically under 10kn) and also that the very small cam range (as low as 2mm on each side). This gives very little margin for error when the rock is soft, or the cam walks into a slightly wider part of a crack. The very smallest cams are not rated to be used for anything other than direct aid and so shouldn't be used for protection (well, unless absolutely nothing else is available).

Testing your placement

When you've placed a cam, it makes sense to give it a test before clipping it and relying on it. With wires, a reasonably good test can be performed by giving it a good tug, it is initially better to pull at the cam more gradually and closely observe what the cams are doing. With a good placement, the cams will lock firmly into place and there will be no movement. If you noticed one or more cams move significantly each time you pull, there's a chance that the placement will fail.

Next, it is a good idea to test whether, and to what extent, the cam will walk (see previous page). Just give the stem a bit of a jiggle and watch what it does - if it immediately walks into a wider part of the crack and opens completely, then you will probably want to place a different cam, or find a better place to put it, or use an extra-long extender on it. Sometimes, a cam will walk into a better place where it can't walk any further. By 'pre-walking' your cam, it may find a more secure position that you hadn't noticed.

Once you're sure that the cams are all locking into position, you can then give it a good tug in the direction in which it is likely to be loaded. Any movement at this point may indicate that some rock has broken inside the crack, and the placement is worth re-examining.

Removing cams

Taking cams out can be hard work, especially if they have been over-cammed or have walked deep into a crack. A patient approach is always best - what went in must come out.

Stuck cams may need two hands to get out, so be prepared to sit on the rope or another close piece of gear. Nut keys are handy in that they allow you to move individual cams. If it's hard to use the trigger, take a pair of wires and loop one around each end of the trigger (mono triggers can be operated by your nut key). This will allow you to pull the trigger even in the tightest of placements.

When over-cammed, pulling the trigger doesn't actually help much and the only thing you can do is work on each cam individually. Use your nut key to flick the cams on one side while tugging the cam to put some tension on them. Then pull it the other way and flick the cams on the opposite side. By repeating this you can slowly reverse walk the cam out of its placement.

However desperate you get when trying to remove your cam, never break the rock to free it - better to leave it for someone else keen to toil for some precious booty.

Lucy Creamer, testing a cam on *Five Finger Exercise* (E2) Cratcliffe, The Peak District, England.

Alex Barrows on pitch one of *Diocese* (VS) Chair Ladder, Cornwall, England.

Protection

Using slings

Slings are the least technical of all climbing protection; maybe that's why we like them so much!

There are three main things that can be done with a sling. The most obvious is to drape it over a spike or a block. The result is a piece of protection that is very good - as long as the sling doesn't lift off. To keep it in place, use plenty of extension. If you are nearing the top of a climb, consider clipping heavy items of gear to it - items that you are fairly sure you're not going to be needing, in order to weigh it down. Slings are strongest without any knots in them and care should be taken not to use a sling that is too short. The angle created where the sling meets the karabiner should be as acute as possible - ideally less than 60°.

The second use of slings is in making use of natural threads (holes in the rock). These can be very good - there's no chance of them lifting off and they will take a pull in any direction. On many climbs, natural threads have slings *in situ*, though their condition should be inspected. Some natural threads take some effort to thread a sling through - a nut key can be really helpful in pulling the end of a sling through a hole.

The final use is in making use of trees and other significant plants. Trees are surprisingly common features, especially at the tops of climbs, and are about as secure as you could ever hope to find. Naturally, the smaller the plant, the weaker it is. If you ever find yourself belayed to a stem that is still green (like a cabbage plant), you know you're in a serious situation.

Main photo: Climber making good use of a sling placement on *Crack and Corner* (S), The Roaches, The Peak District, England.

Insert: a creative use of a sling on a pair of 'chicken-heads' in The Grampians, Australia.

Alex Hughes clipping some *in situ* protection on *Great Wall* (E4), Clogwyn d'ur Arddu, Snowdonia, Wales.

Protection

In situ protection

Pegs

Also known as 'pitons' and 'pins', pegs come in various sizes, and are usually placed with a hammer. Long gone are the days when they were routinely placed on lead, but there are many to be found on trad routes the world over. Some are ancient relics from the past, though others have been placed more recently, either to replace a rotten old peg or to protect an otherwise very bold new route.

Older pegs were made from mild steel, which owes much of its strength to the fact that it bends relatively easily. The problem with mild steel is that it rusts very quickly, especially on sea-cliffs. More recently placed pegs are made from stainless steel, which lasts much longer, even on the coast, though there are significant concerns about their strength with many cases of unexpected failure.

> In general, it is worth being very wary of in situ pegs, they *frequently* fail and even reasonably good looking ones can break under body weight.

A tied-off water-pipe (!) A clove hitch is best, but if you only have one hand free at a time, a lark's foot will do. Photo by Duncan Skelton

Tying-off pegs

Quite often you will encounter a peg that has not been hammered all the way into the rock, and the eye (the bit you clip) will not be in contact with the rock, as it should be.

Loading a peg that has not been fully hammered-in will place a great strain on it due to the much increased leverage. Pegs loaded in this way will bend even under body weight. Higher loads, such as short falls can easily snap the peg.

To reduce the chances of breaking a protruding peg, take a sling and 'tie it off' by placing a lark's foot, or clove hitch (with the 'cross' at the top) over the peg so that the peg will be loaded close to the rock, and will take a greater force before failing.

A peg on the famous Snowdonia route *A Midsummer Night's Dream* (E5). Just a twist of a karabiner (a good test) reveals the fact that the eyelet is completely snapped.

Bolts

Old bolts can occasionally be found on trad routes, some dating from the era of aid climbing, some placed as protection to create a hybrid sport/trad climb.

Working out whether a bolt is any good isn't easy without removing the hanger (the bit you clip), but there are some tell-tale signs to look for:

Firstly, the most obvious sign that a bolt has gone bad is rust: the more rust, the less metal is left, though a little discolouration is to be expected. A fresh-looking bolt with a rusty nut is probably OK, as the nut isn't responsible for the bolt's shear strength.

Secondly, the size of a bolt is a real indicator as to how old it is: older bolts where all you see is the head of the bolt are probably self-drilling bolts (from the era before electric cordless drills became common) and they come in two sizes: 8mm and 10mm. 8mm bolts have a distinctive, diminutive 13mm bolt size, whereas the more substantial 10mm bolt has a significantly larger 17mm bolt size. 8mm self-drilling bolts should not be trusted. There are even older bolts which measure only 6mm - or 1/4 inch!

Be especially suspicious of any bolts you find on a sea-cliffs. Unless it's stainless steel, it will probably be severely weakened by corrosion.

10mm

8mm

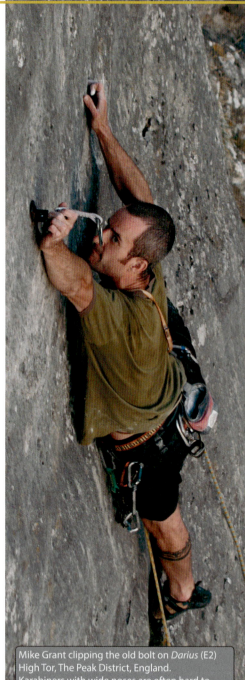

Mike Grant clipping the old bolt on *Darius* (E2) High Tor, The Peak District, England.
Karabiners with wide noses are often hard to get through home-made 'specials' such as this! A good trick is to place a wire down through the hole, using the nut to hold it in place - simply clip the wire as you would normally do.

Matthew Thompson leading *St. Peter* (E1) Stoney Middleton, The Peak District, England. The old peg in the crack can be easily backed up by a small wire below it and a cam in the break. Photo by Nick Smith.

Backing up

Often, old pegs and bolts were placed back in the days before much of the modern gear we take for granted was invented. It is not surprising to find alternative protection near an old peg or bolt, and due to the fact that much in situ protection is of dubious quality, it is always worth hunting around for some backup protection - even the tiniest wire could make the difference between a short fall and hitting the ground.

Protection

'Tat'

Old tape or cord (often called 'tat') is commonly found on trad routes, either making use of a natural thread in the rock, or extending an *in situ* peg. It's very hard to know how good a piece of tat is and it's always worth backing it up where possible.

To help determine its quality, here are four things to look for - in order of importance:

1) Look at the rock - some natural threads have very little rock to them. It doesn't matter that you're clipping a new 11mm piece of cord, if it's only attached to a wafer of rock, it's no good.

2) The material is important. The thickness of the tat is going to have a major influence on its remaining strength. Cord lasts longer than tape because the core is protected by the sheath, unlike tape where what you see is what you get. Dyneema (Spectra) has been shown to degrade more quickly than nylon.

3) Look for obvious damage along the full length of the tat. Tat can be severely damaged after being loaded over a sharp edge, or by simply being blown by the wind over rough rock over time.

Francis Haden eyeballing the faded *in situ* tat on *African and White* (E4) at The Castle, Pembroke, Wales. Photo by Ian Parnell.

4) Look for fading caused by the sun, there is no doubt that this will weaken tat over time, but it is unlikely that this alone will cause failure.

Replacing tat
When you come across a rotten piece of tat while seconding or at a belay, why not cut it out and replace it? Someone's got to and you might just save a life.

Protection

Wires

Stuck wires can be a big problem since they have a tendency to appear on crux moves, often after taking a fall which has securely 'welded' them in place. Subsequently several people may well have tried hard to get them which often leaves a mashed up mess of a nut in the crack. Obviously they tend to be solid placements but ultimately a stuck wire is only as good as the condition of the wire, which rusts quickly, especially on sea-cliffs. Clip them, by all means, but back them up as best you can with some more gear of your own. Also, try to avoid leaving stuck wires if you can, especially on hard and steep sections of the climb.

Karabiners

You sometimes find karabiners left on routes where someone has 'bailed off', or at belays where it's usual to abseil off. Karabiners fare reasonably well outside - though in salty air they corrode. The most important thing to check it that the gate closes properly - the strength of a karabiner is severely reduced if that gate can't be closed. Often, the opposite is true and the gate can't be opened. If you have to abseil from a karabiner where the gate is locked shut, it may be better to thread the rope through the karabiner, than bashing it open it at the risk of not being able to close it again.

Although the general rule is that any gear you find on a climb you can keep for yourself (within reason), be wary of claiming karabiners back off routes, especially harder routes - they may well be there for a good reason like a regularly used abseil or lower-off point.

Cams

Seized cams should be treated with caution - cams that don't move don't work! The most you can hope for is that the unit has seized so thoroughly that it will function passively. If you manage to retrieve a seized cam then it is usually possible to get them working again after a thorough cleaning and lubrication, but treat them with caution as they may still not function properly at a crucial moment.

An in situ wire and karabiner at Gogarth, Anglesey, Wales.

Bouldering mats

Bouldering mats can be incredibly useful in protecting situations where either there is no protection, or where the climber is so close to the ground that the protection serves little purpose.

When bouldering mats began to be used to help protect un-protectable short routes, there was a period during which climbers were divided as to whether they were ethically valid. Routes where falling could result in serious injury could now be protected by covering the landing area with pads and some cried foul. Today, the use of bouldering mats to protect routes is accepted and commonplace. The only real consideration is that many routes are graded for an ascent without mats. Climbing a short E6 with a massive gym mat beneath you does not make you an E6 climber - but if you enjoyed the route, then who cares?

How they work

Mats work in a similar way to ropes, it's just that ropes stretch to absorb a fall, while bouldering mats compress. Mats are not just expensive pieces of foam; a good mat will have two or more layers of foam of different densities. The surface you land on needs to be hard so you don't sink deeply into the foam and turn an ankle. The middle of the pad is made of a softer foam. Working together, the hard foam will distribute the force of your fall more evenly across the mat to absorb the force evenly.

Stack or spread?

If you have multiple mats, the dilemma is whether to stack one on top of the other, or place them side by side. While the answer will always come down to the exact circumstances, the biggest problem with mats is the fact that it is so very easy to fall off and miss them entirely. This is particularly so with routes that are dynamic, or wander around. In most circumstances it is better to ensure the widest area is covered, then if you have any extra mats, you can double-up the area you feel you are most likely to land on.

If you do feel you need to stack mats to make them more effective, you will get a much better result from taking a hard bouldering mat and a big chunk of foam, and placing your mat on top of the foam, rather than on top of another bouldering

Adrian Berry on *Enterprise* (V9) Burbage North, The Peak District, England.
For this new route, the mats were so big, it was decided not to give a route grade, but a bouldering grade instead. Without the mats it would probably feel around E8! Photo by John Arran

Protection

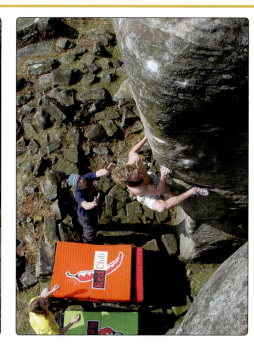

Miles Gibson making the first ascent of *Superblock* (E8 / V11), Moorside Rocks, The Peak District, England. There are a number of routes which are on the border between 'highball' boulder problems and miniature routes. For such climbs, the use of multiple bouldering pads can make the difference between guaranteed broken ankles and a soft landing.

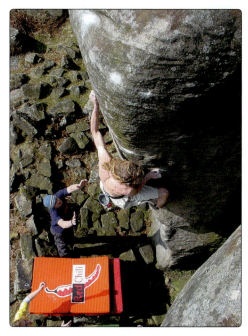
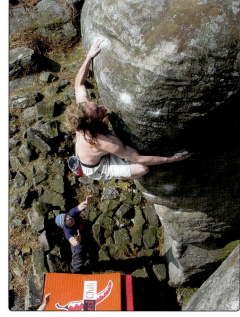

Steve Ramsden on *Fay* (E4) Lower Sharpnose Point, Cornwall, England.

Ropework

The greatest assets a climber can have in regard to ropework are a good dose of practical common sense and a healthy awareness of self-preservation. A trad climber should always be asking themselves 'what if?' and working hard to ensure that even if the most unlikely event were to happen (and even the most unlikely event *will* happen sooner or later) the consequences will be something that they can cope with.

Good ropework skills come as the result of a little bit of knowledge and a lot of experience. Knowing what to do is one thing, but making sure you do it in the heat of battle is another. This section will detail a little bit of that knowledge.

Ropework

Knots

Knowing how to tie knots is the first stage in becoming a self-reliant climber. There are many knots that are used from time to time, but you can spend a lifetime climbing safely knowing just a few. The following is not an exhaustive list of climbing knots but it is unlikely you will need to know any more.

The re-threaded figure of eight, with a double stopper.

The standard knot for tying-in and one that everyone should know.

The re-threaded figure of eight is used to attach the end of a rope to something without using a karabiner. It is useful in attaching fixed abseil ropes to trees and blocks, but is most commonly used to tie-in to the end of the rope, in which case the rope is threaded through both the leg loops and waist belt of the harness, but not through the belay loop.

A stopper knot is added as a means of ensuring there is enough spare rope to allow for slippage - it just keeps things tidy.

❶ Start by tying a figure of eight knot about 75cm from the end of the rope. Now thread the end through or around whatever you are attaching the rope to - in this case a the leg loops and waist belt of a harness.

❷ Now take the end of rope and follow the figure of eight knot back on itself exactly.

❸ When fully threaded back on itself and tidied up a bit, the knot will look like a two '8's on top of each other.

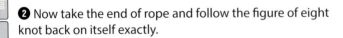 

❹ Now tidy up the end by tying a double stopper knot.

❺ The finished knot should look like this.

Ropework

The bowline

The bowline has the advantage of being easier to undo after it's been loaded which is quite useful if you intend to take some falls. The bowline is a very useful knot for fixing the end of a rope to an object such as a large boulder where it's hard to guess how big the loop formed needs to be.

❶ Thread the end of rope through or around the object you're tying the rope to.

❷ Now take the long end, and form a loop in it.

❸ Take the short end of rope and pass it up through the loop.

❹ Pass the end around the long rope.

❺ Now tuck the end back down through the loop and pull it snug. It should now have this distinctive appearance. If it falls apart, you have probably passed the short end around the wrong section of rope - in which case pull it apart and try again.

❻ When you're happy with your bowline, tie a double stopper knot as shown.

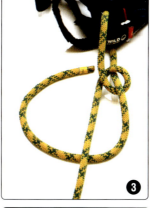

The double bowline

This is a variant of the basic bowline which produces a snugger knot that is less prone to working loose. The only difference is that a double loop is made at stage '2' instead of a single one.

The figure of eight on a bight

A 'bight' is simply a loop of rope made by folding the end of the rope back on itself. By tying a figure of eight knot in this bight, we turn it into a secure loop that can be clipped to something.

This knot is often used to attach the end of a rope to a belay where a karabiner is being used to connect. Where it is tied on the end of a rope, a double stopper knot is usually used. It is also a good way of quickly attaching something to the middle of a section of rope.

The overhand knot

The overhand knot is useful for joining two ropes to set up a long abseil (*see page 144 for more on Abseiling*). It is very similar to a figure-of-eight but has one less twist.

To join two ends of rope, simply tie a snug overhand knot about 60cm from the ends. The overhand knot has an advantage over other joining knots as it presents a flat profile on one side, allowing the knot to run over edges without getting stuck. It is not uncommon to see two overhand knots used to join a rope although in reality, only one of them takes any strain, it just looks a bit more reassuring.

The overhand works best when the ropes being joined are of similar diameters. Ropes of greatly different diameters should be joined by other means, such as a reef knot tied off with double stoppers.

Ropework

The reef knot

Handy for non-critical situations like attaching your chalk-bag - ❶. If tied off with a double stopper knot - ❷ it is secure enough to be used to join ropes, without jamming too tightly.

The double fisherman's knot

Essentially just two double stopper knots that allow two ends of rope or cord to be joined - ❸. When pulled tight it has a distinctive appearance with two crosses on one side - ❹. This knot is useful for joining two ends of rope that are of uneven diameters, or turning a piece of cord into a prusik loop. If you add one extra twist you get a triple fisherman's (recommended if you're using Dyneema/Spectra), one less twist and you get a regular fisherman's (worth knowing if you need to make a loop out of a very short piece of cord).

The tape knot

Not as essential as it once was due to the fact that all slings are now sold already stitched, the tape knot is the neatest means of connecting two ends of flat tape.

A tape knot is essentially an overhand knot followed through in the opposite direction by the other end of the tape. To allow for slippage, a good few centimetres should be left on either end after it has been pulled tight.

Tape knots can, and do, come undone over time, so remember to periodically check they are still tight. For slings you intend to use for a while, it is a good idea to lightly sew the loose ends to the main sling to prevent the knot slipping.

The French prusik

The French prusik is most often used to make an 'auto-block' to protect abseils. This knot is formed by simply rotating a piece of cord four times around the rope. The knot locks when pulled. Each end of the cord is attached to a karabiner, which is attached to the harness. As you abseil one hand grips the top of the knot and slides it down the rope with you. If you let go for some reason, the knot automatically locks onto the rope and stops you going any further. It is easier to release than other prusik knots.

The lark's foot / girth hitch

A simple knot which is useful for attaching slings to trees. To tie, simply thread a looped sling or piece of cord around the object so you are holding a loop of the cord in each hand. Now place one loop through the other and pull it snug - ❶.

It is generally best to thread the loop with the join (such as stitching on a sling) through the other loop. It's worth noting that, as with all knots, using a lark's foot does reduce the strength of the sling or loop of cord it's being tied with - so it should only be used where necessary.

The lark's foot is also a good way to attach a sling to your belay loop, or tie-in loops, to produce a quick means of attaching to a belay.

The prusik

The knot that gave the prusik loop its name. This is the most common way of ascending a rope, or pair or ropes. The prusik knot locks well, but it is important to ensure that the cord is thin enough to grab - this is especially true for skinny half ropes.

Start with a lark's foot - ❶ - but take the end and pass it around once more and through the knot - ❷. When loaded it will lock - ❸.

See page 34 for a basic description of a prusik and page 152 for how to use them to ascend a rope.

Ropework

The clove hitch

This is an amazingly useful knot for belays. It's simple, quick, adjustable and easy to undo afterwards. Once mastered, you will probably find yourself using it on every route you climb.

❶ Take a bight of rope and make two loops in it - one loop exits above the rope, the other below it.

❷ Slide the loop where the rope exits on top below the other loop until one is on top of the other.

❸ Clip the two loops.

❹ Pull tight to lock it.

The clove hitch is also good for attaching to belay stakes, in which case it is stronger if the knot is formed on the rear of the stake, reducing the tightness of the bends.

The Italian (friction) hitch / Münter hitch

If you drop your belay device, you will need to use one of these. They are best used with a pear-shaped karabiner - a large one if you want to handle two ropes.

To arrange an Italian hitch, place two loops into a bight of rope - exactly as for a clove hitch (❶ above) but instead of sliding one under the other, fold one loop onto the other as though closing a book. Now clip the two loops into a karabiner. These knots are tricky to use and have a habit of 'flipping' when loaded or paying out. It is a good idea to have a practice with one before you have to use it to get yourself out of an extreme situation.

Ropework

Coiling a rope

Strictly speaking the following isn't actually coiling, but *hanking*. Putting a rope into a proper coil tends to make it kink and can be a nightmare to undo - though it makes you look the part if you're hitch-hiking.

The Alpine / butterfly coil

This can be done with a single rope starting at one end, or with the rope doubled-up, starting with both ends. If your rope has a middle mark, you can start at the middle, with the advantage that you get rid of any kinks, but it is hard to get the ends to be even.

Start a couple of meters from the ends - ❶ - and pass the rope around the back of your neck and place the bight in your hand - ❷ - now simply pass it around your neck again, but in the opposite direction. Repeat this until you run out of rope - ❸.

Next, holding the rope at its bend - ❹ - wrap the ends of rope several times around the top - ❺ - then pop a bight through the hole - ❻ - and push the ends through that bight - ❼.

Now you can put the rope on your back by passing each end over a shoulder and crossing them around your back - ❽. Bring the ends around your front and tie them with a reef-knot - ❾.

Walking back to the campsite after a day at the crag at Arapiles, Australia. An Alpine coil is a great way of carrying a rope without needing a pack.

Ropework

Ropework hazards

Knot strengths

Having just looked at a range of knots, it is a good time to look at their relative strengths. A knot places a series of bends in the material being knotted and those bends reduce the strength of the material, often quite dramatically, though failure is incredibly rare. The gentler the bends in a knot, the stronger it is. There are a great many statistics on the relative strengths of different knots and these vary wildly between sources. However, they are consistent in the following assertions:

1) A knot can reduce the strength of the material it is in by over 50%.

2) The figure-of-eight, neatly tied, is stronger than the bowline (the figure of nine is stronger still).

3) A clove hitch is weaker than both the figure-of-eight knot and the bowline.

4) Ropes joined with a double fisherman's knot are stronger than when joined with an overhand knot.

5) Joining gear with sewn slings and karabiners is stronger than using knots. For example, a lark's foot between two slings will reduce the strength of those slings by up to 50%. It is much better to join them with a karabiner.

Sharp edges

The easiest way of cutting through a rope or sling is to load it over a sharp edge. The effect is even more dramatic if a sideways 'sawing' action occurs. The logical conclusion is that sharp edges should be avoided as much as possible.

It should also be noted that rough rock, such as granite, will also severely damage loaded nylon rubbing over it.

Nylon on nylon

When rope runs through a karabiner, it generates heat that is dissipated through the metal. Should you ever run a nylon rope over a stationary piece of nylon, such as a sling, the heat generated may be easily enough to melt through the stationary sling in seconds, causing it to fail. It should be pointed out that nylon has a melting point of 250°C, whereas Dyneema/Spectra only has a melting point of around 150°C, making it even easier to melt.

If you clip two lead ropes into a single karabiner and fall with more slack in one rope than in the other, a fall may result in one rope moving while the other remains still - nylon over nylon, causing damage to the still rope. This can be avoided by keeping to one rope per karabiner where possible.

The section of nylon tape above was removed from an *in situ* sling that had been used to lower-off. Only the facts that the sling was close to the ground and the terrain was slabby have prevented it melting all the way through.

Ropework

Badly loaded karabiners

Karabiners are designed to be loaded along their 'spines' - the continuous longest side. Loading a karabiner any other way will reduce its strength. Here are some examples of poorly-loaded karabiners:

Three-way pull

Always avoid a three-way pull on a karabiner - just use more karabiners.

Loading the gate/nose

Avoid orientating a karabiner so the gate or nose of the karabiner are loaded. Loading the nose of a karabiner reduces the strength to as little as 3kn - making it a likely point of failure in a fall.

Here, two wires have been clipped with the same quickdraw resulting in a three-way pull on the karabiner. Additionally the wire on the left has lodged in the karabiner's nose, further reducing its strength. The simple solution is to use a second quickdraw, or if one is not available, to clip just one of the wires.

Karabiner loaded over an edge

Karabiners should never be loaded over a rock edge as strength is severely reduced. The simple solution is to extend the karabiner (such as with a sling) so that it lies below the edge.

Karabiner with a gate open

Rock features can open the gate of a karabiner. If this is likely, turn the karabiner around so that gate faces the other way - or use a screw-gate. The strength of a karabiner with its gate open is severely reduced.

Too wide an object in a karabiner

Care should be taken when using old wide slings with modern karabiners as the strength of the karabiner is reduced because the load is applied away from the spine of the karabiner.

Here, a sling used as a runner around a tree has been joined with a screw-gate karabiner and the same karabiner has been used to connect the rope, resulting in a three-way pull and the possibility of the gate being loaded. The solution would be to use another karabiner to clip the sling to the rope.

Belaying

Belaying is a key skill on all roped climbing and should be the first skill you learn. When you agree to belay someone, you are literally taking their life into your hands. You are also playing a crucial role in your partner's climb. A good belayer instils confidence and adds to the enjoyment of the climb. A bad belay is at best a psychological drain and at worst a hazard.

As a belayer, we have three main responsibilities, these are to:

1) Hold your partner when they fall off. If you can't do this, your partner would have been safer if you hadn't been there at all!

2) Maintain a steady feed of rope to your partner. There's little worse for a leader than to go to pull up the rope to clip some protection only to find it tight. The leader should always have enough slack to move freely and should never have to pull rope through the belay device.

3) Give encouragement and confidence. Climbing is a team game and belaying is more than holding your partner's ropes. A good belayer will be able to reassure their partner when they can see they are not in danger and may be able to spot protection and holds that the leader has missed.

Belaying is a skill best learnt from an experienced climber or professional instructor and the following advice should be used in conjunction with plenty of monitored practice before you go it alone.

Belaying basics

Assuming you're wearing a harness and have a belay device with the rope threaded through it. You will see that the rope leads out of the belay device from one side to the person you're belaying and from the other side to the slack rope on the ground. The rope leading to the climber is called the **live rope**, the other end is the **dead rope**.

When belaying, we keep one hand on the live rope and one on the dead rope. The live rope hand helps feed rope through the belay device, the dead rope hand arrests a fall: **one hand must always be holding the dead rope**.

The angle at which the dead rope exits your belay device is crucial in determining how much **grab** (or friction) is applied - the sharper the angle, the more grab. When the rope is held at a sharp angle, it is referred to as being **locked off**. The dead rope should be held in the locked off position whenever possible.

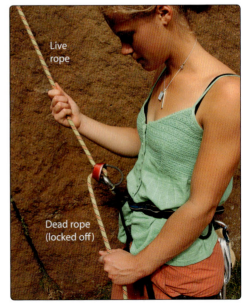

Live rope

Dead rope (locked off)

Ropework

Taking in

This is the basic method of taking in slack and one that you would learn to belay somebody on a top-rope. By repeating this action, rope is taken in without ever loosening your grip on the dead rope.

❶ Start off with your dead rope hand close to the belay device and your live rope hand at about half an arm's length away.

❷ Pull and push the rope through the belay device with both hands. When you've pulled about half a metre through, lock off the belay device.

❸ Now let go of the live rope and place that hand on the dead rope, a hand's width away from the belay device.

❹ Next, move your dead rope hand to its original position on the dead rope next to the belay device and return your live rope hand to its starting position.

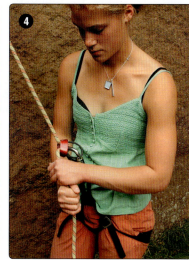

Ropework

Paying out

To belay someone on the lead, you need to be able to pay out rope while keeping one hand on the dead rope at all times. It is difficult to maintain a firm grip on the dead rope and pay out rope quickly enough so you will naturally adopt the 'sliding method' for paying out slack.

❶ Start with one hand on the dead rope about half a metre away from your belay device and the other hand on the live rope right next to your belay device.

❷ In one movement, pull out the live rope and feed in the dead rope.

❸ The dead rope hand locks off the device when rope isn't being paid out.

❹ To return your hands to the starting position, first move the live rope hand back to its position next to the belay device.

❺ Now, maintaining good observation of your partner, relax your grip on the dead rope and slide your hand down the rope.

❻ Continue to slide your hand down the rope to the start position where you are able to pay out more slack when needed.

Ropework

Using the sliding method to take in

The 'sliding method' used to pay out rope can be used in exactly the same way to take it in (just in reverse). As you become more confident in your belaying, you will naturally adopt the sliding method for both paying out and taking in.

Lowering

To lower someone, simply relax your grip until the rope feeds out smoothly. By adjusting the angle of the dead rope, you can increase or reduce friction as desired. If you are struggling to lower a heavy climber, you may find it easier to place both hands on the dead rope and feed the rope through, ensuring one hand is gripping the rope at all times.

Using a magic/guide plate

A number of belay devices on the market have the additional functionality of being used as a 'magic plate' or 'guide plate'. With these you can attach the belay device directly to the belay (at point B) and then simply pull the rope through. If your second loads the rope, the belay device will lock. These devices are popular with guides who then can easily belay two climbers simultaneously. To use a magic plate, the belay needs to be beyond doubt and the attachment point ideally at around chest height.

Lowering a fallen climber is a tricky business when using the 'magic plate' method. The idea is to make point A take the force rather than point B. This is best achieved by clipping A with a sling, passing that sling through the belay, and back down so you can clip into it and load it with your body-weight. Bear in mind that this will release the rope completely and so you will need to be able to maintain control of the rope through another belay device, or a friction hitch. The ATC *Guide* belay device has a third attachment point specifically for this job.

Ropework

Tying off a belay device

There are a many instances in which you may find the need to tie-off a belay device: your partner may be sitting on the rope and you're tired of holding them, or you may need to free your hands up to sort out a tangle in the rope without taking your partner off-belay. The method shown to the right is quick and allows you to release the device easily when needed. It basically involves tying a lark's foot, then adding a half-hitch for security.

Escaping the system

Escaping the system is simply being able to tie-off your partner directly to the belay so you can move away. A typical example would be if your partner has fallen and injured themselves. If you can't simply lower them down, you may need to get help. It is not something you should expect to do regularly, indeed, it's unlikely you will ever have to do it, but it's worth knowing about.

First you need to find a point in your belay that will withstand a pull in the right direction and is beyond doubt. You may need to add to your belay, and naturally, if you are belaying from the ground without a belay, you will need to build one. If you can't reach your belay and are belayed with your lead rope, you will need to attach to that with another prusik.

When you have done this, it is simply a matter of putting a prusik (or other similar device) on the live rope, connecting it to the belay with a sling, getting it as snug as possible, then releasing the belay device gradually until the force is applied directly to the belay through the prusik. Next, be sure to back-up the prusik by tying the rope into the belay.

Photos by John Arran

Ropework

Using double ropes

In trad climbing, double ropes are very popular, especially in the UK. By using two ropes, it is possible to access protection over a much wider area without suffering from rope drag and other problems.

Double ropes also allow you to place and clip a high runner on one rope without exposing yourself to a huge fall due to the slack required to clip since you are protected by a runner on the other rope.

Another under-used advantage of double ropes is the ability to place two pieces of protection next to each other with a rope clipped in each. In the event of a fall, the impact will be shared evenly between the two pieces, potentially halving the force they need to withstand - great for marginal placements.

Double ropes also allow full length abseil descents to be made and so are very useful should you need to descend unexpectedly.

Where double ropes are used, it is usual to use thinner (half) ropes than the fatter (single) ropes used when only one rope is being employed. When you are new to climbing, it is a good idea to learn the basics using a single rope. As you become more confident with your rope-work, you can switch to using double half ropes. On pitches shorter than half the length of your rope, you can simply use one rope doubled and lead on both ends of the same rope, saving carrying the extra rope, although the problem of them being the same colour will arise.

Most belay devices are designed to work with double ropes, but it is worth checking that your device is designed for use with thinner, half-ropes, when you come to move over to half ropes.

Learning to belay with double ropes takes a bit of practice, so make sure your partner is familiar with the required techniques before you set off.

Ian Parnell on *Harlequin* (E3), Kinder, The Peak District, England.
Double ropes are particularly useful when a pitch changes direction, such as here where a traverse leads to a vertical section; one rope protects the traverse, while the other is kept free until the final vertical section. Doing this with one rope would have increased rope drag and risked unseating runners. Photo by John Arran.

Ropework

Belaying with double ropes

If you are happy with belaying with a single rope, then you should easily be able to progress to belaying on double ropes.

To make things as simple as possible, start by separating the ropes onto the ground with the 'left' rope in a pile on the left and the 'right' rope on a pile on the right. Now place the ropes in your belay device with the left on the left and the right on the right - ❶.

Treating two ropes as one.

One of the advantages with using two ropes is that you can reach up with slack to make a clip with one rope while the other rope is nice and snug between you and the last piece of protection.

When your partner requires slack on just one rope, it is a simple matter of selecting the right rope to pull through the belay device on the **live** side. Note, both ropes are still securely gripped on the **dead** side - ❸.

For most of the time, both ropes can be treated as one, with one hand holding both dead ropes and one hand holding both live ropes at the same time - ❷. Slack can be paid out or taken in exactly the same way as you would employ if you were belaying with a single rope (*see page 109 and 110*). Of course, there will be times when you wish to adjust just one rope and this is where things get just a little more complicated.

Paying out one rope only - note the break hand on the dead rope is securely covering both ropes.

Taking in one rope while paying out another

When it comes to evening up the ropes, a quick trick is to pull one rope in while paying the other one out. To do this, cover both dead ropes with one hand, but firmly grip the one you want to pull slack in on. With your other hand grab the live end of the rope want to pay slack out with - ❹.

The left hand pulls out the orange rope, the right hand pulls in the blue rope while covering the dead orange rope.

Now, with one movement you can pull out slack with one hand and pull it back in with the other. It takes a little practice, but soon becomes second-nature - ❺.

Al Mason on *Void* (E4) Craig Bwych Y Moch, Tremadoc, Wales.
Pulling through the blue rope to clip the peg, it's comforting to know that the red rope has no additional slack in it.

Clipping protection

Gates away

When clipping protection, always aim to orientate the karabiner with its gate facing away from the direction of your travel.

Protection clipped correctly. The gate is facing away from the direction of travel. Because of this, the gate is not rubbing against the rock.

If you are using a quickdraw, you will want to apply this rule to both the karabiners (for this reason you should choose to arrange your quickdraws with both karabiners facing the same direction).

This rule is most applicable when making a traverse. If the line is straight up, it doesn't matter which way the karabiners face - though if there is a risk of them opening against the rock, it makes sense to orientate them so as to reduce this risk. This may require you to turn them.

Back-clipping

When a karabiner is situated so that it is flat against the rock, it is important to clip the rope through it in the correct direction to avoid 'back-clipping'. The karabiner has a front and a back - the front faces out and the back faces the rock. Always clip your rope so that the lower rope enters the back of the karabiner and the upper rope exits the front.

Here, the gate is facing the direction of travel. Because of this, the gate is facing the rock. It would have been better to flip the karabiner upside down so that the gate faces the other way, however, unclipping is still unlikely in this example.

Here, the cam has been back-clipped. While this isn't desirable, in this instance there is little chance of accidental un-clipping.

Ropework

When clipping, ensure that the rope enters the karabiner through the back and exits through the front. To do otherwise (to back-clip) places a twist in the protection, adds rope drag and in extreme circumstances, can cause the rope to run across the gate and unclip itself.

Here the cam has been back-clipped. The way the rope is exiting on the left, across the gate, then pulled to the right presses it against the gate, making accidental un-clipping a real possibility.

It should be noted that self un-clipping is very rare and in the vast majority of situations, if you are running out of strength and have mis-clipped, it may well be better to carry on rather than to use the last of your strength re-clipping before slumping onto the rope. As always, it's your call!

Z clipping

This is surprisingly easy to do when clipping a series of pieces of protection that are close together. When we clip a piece of protection, we take the section of rope between our harness and the previous piece. Z clipping occurs when we inadvertently grab the rope that is below the previous piece of protection, and clip it into the higher piece of protection.

'Z' clipped protection caused by grabbing the wrong bit of rope to clip the higher piece.

This creates a distinctive 'z' shape in the rope and will be instantly recognisable as you will have so much rope drag, you won't be able to move. Even if you can still move, you may well lift out the lower of the two runners.

Undo the 'z' by un-clipping the upper piece of protection (or the poorer runner of the two) and re-clipping it with the right bit of rope.

Building belays

A belay is a secure means of anchoring something - usually ourselves - to the rock. A belay will usually consist of two or more belay points - usually consisting of pieces of gear or slings - that are arranged so the load is divided equally between them. If any one point fails, the remaining point(s) should not be shock loaded.

The actual number of belay points will depend on how many the rock presents, how much gear you have to make use of them, and how many you need to be safe. The better the belay points, the fewer you need. If at the top of a route you found a fat tree, you wouldn't need to search for anything else, whereas if all you could find were micro-wires and loose blocks, you'd want to use as many as your remaining rack would allow.

Belays and screw-gates

The use of screw-gate karabiners in belays is best practice, but they are only strictly necessary where there is a chance that the gate may be opened by pressing against the rock or ground. Where a karabiner is 'in space', a snap-link is fine. If you need a screw-gate, but don't have one, used two snap-links with the gates facing opposite directions - *below*.

Direction

Just like when placing protection, belays should be arranged in anticipation of the direction in which they are to be loaded. Usually this is a simple matter, but sometimes, especially on multi-pitch belays, you may need to take account of pulls from more than one direction.

Attaching / equalising

The way we attach to a belay is also the same way points of protection are equalised - so as to receive an equal share of the load. There are basically three methods, the one you choose will depend on:

1) what gear you have available;

2) how close you are to the belay points;

3) whether you are going to want to allow someone else to use your belay, without having to completely re-arrange it.
The latter is a useful practice if you are on a multi-pitch route and intend the lead the next pitch as well as the previous.

Ground belays

There are good reasons to set a ground belay at the the base of a route, but also a few good reasons not to.

The most obvious reason to belay to the ground is if there is some hazard that the belayer needs to be protected from, such as a cliff-edge or a sea-washed gully. A belayer who is pulled into a gully may suffer an injury which could result in them releasing their grip on the rope.

Having a belay arranged at the base will also make life a little easier should the leader need to escape the system since the belayer will be able to tie the leader off and release themselves from the system more easily.

Another scenario where a ground belay makes sense is where the belayer is a lot lighter than the leader, though care should be taken to allow some 'give' in the belay.

The biggest reason against attaching to a ground belay is that, should any loose rock rain down, the second will be unable to jump out of the way. The seriousness of rock-fall avoidance is sufficiently high that ground belays should be avoided unless the reasons above come into play.

One other reason for avoiding ground belays is to allow some slack in the system to soften a fall - see *Dynamic belaying on page 140*.

Jill Croskell and Wendy Robson climbing at Porth Clais, Pembroke, Wales.
Photo by Nick Smith.
The belayer has taken a ground belay to avoid being pulled into the wave-washed gully at the base of the route.

Belay method 1 - close belay points

If the belay points are easily within reach, you can very simply use your lead ropes to attach to each one with a clove-hitch. This is a very quick and effective way of attaching to belays.

Dave Jennions belaying on *Valediction* (HVS), Stanage Edge, The Peak District, England. Double lead ropes attached to separate belay points allows a simple and quick belay to be arranged. Photo by Nick Smith.

❶ If you have more belay points than ropes, you can simply connect the additional points to your harness using screw-gates and clove-hitches. In the illustrated example, the climber has connected three belay points to his harness using two ropes - one point has a rope to itself, the other two points share a rope.

❷ Things are a bit simpler if your belay points can be arranged in a straight line, as you can just clove hitch them all in a row. Tie the closest ones first so as to get the length right.

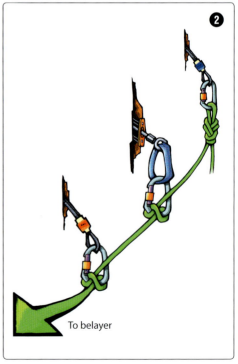

Ropework

Belay method 2 - distant belay points

Often you need to hunt around for belay points and you won't be able to adjust the lengths if your clove hitches are at the belay points out of reach when back at the top of the climb. To get around this, simply clip your lead rope into the belay points and return to the spot where you are going to belay, attaching the rope to your harness with a clove-hitch - ❸.

If there is not enough rope to reach the belays and allow you to get back to the cliff edge, you may have to untie, and tie the end of your rope(s) to the belay points. You can then re-attach to your rope(s) at your desired belay spot. Obviously ensure you're either on safe ground, or otherwise protected (such as by using a prusik) at all times.

Using your ropes as a sling

If your belay is a large block or tree, you can simply walk around it and clove hitch it as you would with any other distant protection. This is very useful when you've run out of long slings. The only down-sides to this method are that it may the wear on your rope and, because there is more friction than using a sling and karabiner, it is harder to get the length just right.

Paul Evans belaying at the top of *Thirst for Glory* (HVS) at Curbar Edge, The Peak District, England. Photo by Nick Smith.

Ropework

Belay method 3 - using slings

This method keeps your lead ropes out of the equation. Instead you can use a series of slings to equalise the belay points.

A *cordelette* is a very long sling, designed specifically for arranging equalised belay. Simply clip the cordelette into the various belay points, equalise the lengths and then put an overhand knot to lock them together. You can clip directly to the knot with a screw-gate, though it is likely you will want to extend it with a another sling to get into a comfy position. The advantage with using a cordelette is that should someone else want to take your place at the belay, they can simply clip into the same place without any fuss.

Steve Ramsden belays Al Mason leaving the belay on Vector Buttress, Craig Bwych-y-Moch, Tremadoc. This belay consists of a cordelette plus one additional sling. Note how the rope has been stacked to avoid it getting snagged below.

Ropework

Equalising with short slings

Often you will have two belay points close to each other. In these situations it can be quicker to simply equalise them with a couple of slings - ❶ - and treat them as a single belay point. As there are no knots, this is the strongest method of equalising, though care should be taken not to exert a three-way pull on the karabiner: aim for an angle of less than 60° where the slings join at the karabiner.

If your sling is long enough, you can use it like a cordelette, but with shorter slings you may not have enough material - in which case simply tie an overhand knot (dividing the sling into two 'halves') where you want to clip the sling and clip with the karabiner passing through each 'half' of the sling - ❷.

Avoid equalising two pieces of protection with a single, un-knotted sling - ❸ - the downward pull is converted into sideways forces on the protection, which in this case consists of pegs that could be pulled out. In addition to this, the wide angle (greater than 60°) created when using a sling which is too short amplifies the force on the protection to an even greater extent.

If you must use a single un-knotted sling, it is tempting to simply attach one end of the sling to the two belay points, then clip your attachment karabiner around both strands of the sling in the middle but, if one piece fails, it will pull through this karabiner. This can be rectified by clipping the lower one with a loop.

Real world belays

In practice, your belays will naturally involve a mixture of all three methods. As long as the belay points are secure, equally loaded, and won't be shock-loaded should one or more fail - anything goes.

See page 70 for more ways on equalising belays.

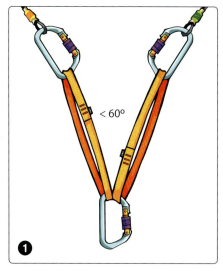

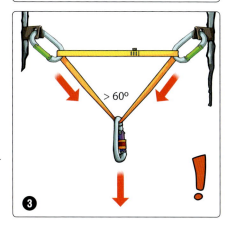

Where to belay

Deciding where to take a belay usually isn't a difficult question. At the top of a route, the belay is taken at the end of the easy ground where it will be safe to untie. However, there may be options such as how far back to belay and which position to take on the edge of the cliff.

How far back?

The important consideration here is to ensure good communication between yourself and your partner even though it may be tempting to belay back away from the edge to get out of the wind. By belaying too far back, there is also going to be increased friction generated by the rope running over the edge - with the associated risk of damage to the rope and the chance that some loose rock may be dislodged.

Protecting a traverse

There are some routes where the danger in seconding is greater than that of leading. For example, if a traverse has a hard move followed by an easy section with no protection, a bomb-proof runner placed before the hard move will protect the leader, but will have to be removed by the second before attempting the move, with the potential for a huge swinging fall.

Often, such hazards can be avoided by thoughtfully placing gear not just before hard moves, but also after them, with a view to protecting the second.

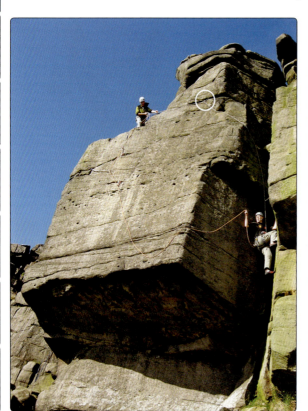

Another good trick, as shown in the photo on the left, is to place a side runner level with the belay with the aim of protecting the second. In this instance, the leader has placed a cam (marked by the circle) several meters to their left. This will protect the second for the crux move onto the arete after they have removed the runners from the groove. Failure to have done this would have exposed the second to the risk of a big pendulum fall, slashing the ropes across the lip of the overhang - far scarier than leading!

Rob Owen and Graham Hassall on *Wuthering* (E2) Stanage Edge, The Peak District, England.
The marked cam isn't a runner on the route - it has been placed solely to protect the second as he makes the crux moves onto the arete.

Sensible belaying on a windy day, *Paucity* (HVS) Stanage, The Peak District, England.
Photo by Chris Craggs.
Belaying close to the edge is sometimes a little uncomfortable but it has the advantages of giving you a good view and enabling better communication with your second.

No belay?

It's quite rare, but does sometimes happen: you get to the top of a route and there simply is nothing to belay to. If there really is nothing to belay to, the best thing you can do is to inform your partner of the situation and look for a natural 'stance' where you can sit and brace your legs against something. A good braced stance is surprisingly effective, as long as you don't allow slack to build up, the amount of force you are likely to have to deal with is quite low. The friction generated by the rope running over the edge will take much of the strain.

If you can't find a belay, and all you have got is flat ground (look for stakes - they are often buried in the grass) all you can do is walk back as far as you can, sit down, and take in by shuffling back. The friction generated by the rope running over the edge, plus your weight sat on the ground will probably be enough, but keep the rope snug to avoid shock loading yourself. By moving back as far as you can, you will introduce the maximum amount of rope into the system, thereby reducing the impact force should your second fall, though communication will naturally suffer.

Fixed belays / abseil belays

It is very common to find a fixed belay at the top of a route where the descent is by abseil. Fixed belays can consist of pegs, bolts, threads, and stuck wires, all equalised by pieces of tat. There is usually one central attachment point, usually a karabiner or *maillon rapide* (like a chain link with a screw closure).

Fixed belays should always be checked to make sure they are up to the job. If necessary add to or replace *in situ* gear.

Lowering off

There are trad routes which don't reach the top of the crag. This may be because there is only uninteresting scrambling to the top, or because the rock becomes loose or turns into soil. Lower-off belays are fixed belays that are usually no more than half a rope-length (assumed to be 50m) from the ground. In some areas, belays may consist of a couple of bolts, as found on sport climbs.

If there are *in situ* karabiners, you can simply clip the belay and lower to the ground. If the karabiners have seized, or there are fixed rings, you will need to attach to the belay with slings, untie, thread your rope(s) through the lower off. Then remove your slings and lower down. Naturally, it makes sense to check you have enough rope to make it back to the ground.

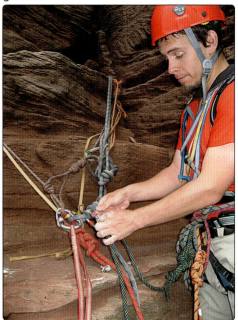

Kai Green deciphering the mess of tat at a belay on The Old Man of Hoy. Photo by Duncan Skelton.

Ropework

Sitting or standing?

This will usually be dictated by the position of your belay points and whether you can find somewhere comfy to sit.

Standing
Requires high belay points.

- \+ May give a better view of the action
- \+ Allows limited movement
- \+ Allows you to provide a little more assistance if necessary
- \- May become tiring

Sitting
Necessary if your belay points are low.

- \+ Less strenuous and more comfortable
- \- May give a poorer view
- \- Take care not to run ropes over your thigh which will get squashed if your partner falls

Belaying through the top piece(s)

This is not a popular technique in the UK, but it has some real advantages over belaying straight from a harness. For a start, if your second falls, holding them directly from your belay device is usually awkward and it's not uncommon to sandwich your leg between the rope and the ground. Secondly, if you are taking a belay mid-route, the inevitable rope tangles are almost always due to the fact you have been belaying through your harness. Thirdly, if you ever find yourself having to escape the system, most of the hard work is already done if you are belaying via a high piece of protection.

By belaying through a piece of protection that is higher than the belay device, the force of your partner falling will mostly

be taken by the top piece rather than directly by yourself, making it far easier to hold them as they rest and re-compose themselves. Because this will produce an upward force on the belayer, it is important to ensure the belay is set up to handle it. It should go without saying that a lot of trust is being placed in this top piece and it needs to be beyond doubt - if possible, add another and equalise with slings.

Belaying direct

This is very different from belaying through the top piece. In a direct belay, the belay device is attached directly to the belay, not the belayer. Belay devices with a 'guide mode' functionality are designed to be used this way. Direct belaying places a total reliance on the belay, requires re-arrangement if your partner leads through, and is not commonly used in British trad climbing.
See page 111 for more on Direct Belaying.

Ropework

Understanding forces

While there are plenty of accepted methods for doing things in climbing, mastering ropework is about moving beyond 'rule based thinking' to 'objective based thinking', and having an intuitive understanding the forces involved is of vital importance in making this step.

We're going to start off with some ideas that may be familiar, then we're going to show how many of them, though helpful, are some way from the truth.

Force is measured in Newtons (N). In climbing, we often deal with quite large forces, so rather than work with lots of '00s', we deal in thousands of Newtons, or Kilonewtons (kN). All climbing equipment is rated by the maximum force it can withstand, so for example, a standard snap-link karabiner should expect to hold no more than 25kN (which is equivalent to 2.5 tonnes).

A much greater force is generated during a fall than when gear is loaded more statically - such as when abseiling. Simply hanging off the end of a rope produces a force on the rope of just 0.7kN (for a 70 kilo person staying perfectly still). Even someone abseiling in a stop-start manner is unlikely to generate much above 3kN.

In contrast, a typical fall might generate between 5-10kn. While a lot more than when abseiling, the gear still has plenty in reserve, though as we have seen in the previous section, the weak link is often the rock, so it is always important to reduce the forces generated in a fall as much as possible.

Examples are reproduced by permission of The BMC and Beal Ropes.

Forces and falling

The pulley effect

To arrest a fall, the force of the falling climber needs to counterbalanced by the belayer. In the example below, to stop a falling climber with 4.2kN of force, the belayer applies 2.5kN of force to balance the fall. This results in 6.7kN (both their forces combined) being transmitted to the top piece of protection. These values are not identical because of the friction generated by the karabiner resulting in the climber feeling more of the force than the belayer, as can be seen in the illustration below.

In arresting a fall, the force of the fallen climber will be converted into a myriad of other forces: the belayer will be jolted into a different position, gear will bite into the rock, the climber's knot will tighten, and the rope will stretch. Ultimately, the force of the fall will be converted into heat - most evident if you touch the karabiner through which the rope has been running.

Paul Evans and Meilee Rafe on pitch two of *Vector* (E2) Tremadog, Wales.

Fall factor

The piece of equipment that contributes the most to absorbing the force of a fall is the rope. The more rope *freely* available to stretch, the safer the fall. The 'fall factor' is simply the distance fallen divided by the amount of rope available to absorb that fall. The lower the fall factor, the safer the fall. You'll notice that the distance fallen isn't important on its own and in many situations longer falls are safer than shorter ones, which is contrary to what most people might expect.

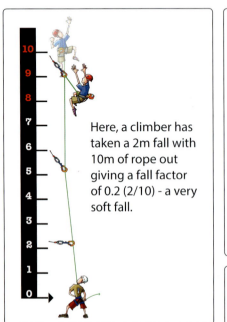

Here, a climber has taken a 2m fall with 10m of rope out giving a fall factor of 0.2 (2/10) - a very soft fall.

In this example, the climber has once again fallen 3m, but is had only just moved above the belay, and so only had 3m of rope out - giving a high fall factor of 1.0.

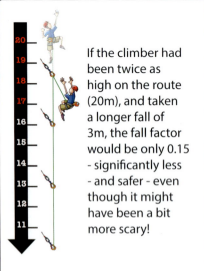

If the climber had been twice as high on the route (20m), and taken a longer fall of 3m, the fall factor would be only 0.15 - significantly less - and safer - even though it might have been a bit more scary!

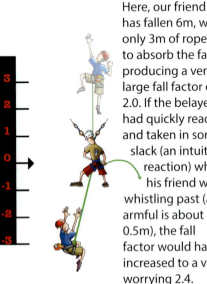

Here, our friend has fallen 6m, with only 3m of rope to absorb the fall, producing a very large fall factor of 2.0. If the belayer had quickly reacted and taken in some slack (an intuitive reaction) while his friend was whistling past (an armful is about 0.5m), the fall factor would have increased to a very worrying 2.4.

Ropework

Real world fall factors

The fall factor is a very useful way of understanding just how the forces of a fall are dissipated and the role of the rope in not just stopping a fallen climber but stopping them gradually.

The examples on the previous page are highly simplified, and in each example the rope is running perfectly free. In practice, each time the rope runs against either a karabiner or the rock, it reduces its ability to absorb force through its full length.

In the example on the left, the presence of only four twenty degree bends in the rope caused by runners is enough to more than double the fall factor from 0.3 to 0.6 due to the added friction in the system.

A more severe point of friction, such as a ledge where protection has been placed at the back, or the lip of an overhang, where protection has not been sufficiently extended, can as much as double the force on the top piece of protection - taking it into the realm of failure.

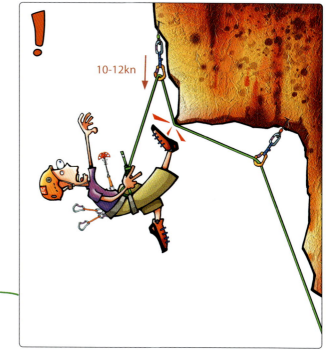

Ropework

Keeping ropes straight

The hallmark of a leader with good ropework is a rope, or pair of ropes, that lead in a straight line from their belayer, regardless of the quantity and positions of the protection they've placed.

Here are three reasons to keep your ropes as straight as possible:

1) Straight ropes = soft falls

We've already seen on the previous page that putting bends in a rope reduces the amount of rope available to absorb the force of a fall, increasing the load on the top runner. Falling onto straight ropes is always going to be softer for the fallen climber which means less risk of gear failure.

2) Reduce rope drag

Another reason for keeping rope straight is the reduction of drag. Every time a karabiner puts even a slight bend in your rope, it causes drag. While you can easily live with a little bit of rope drag, over the course of a long pitch, little bends back and forth quickly can add up to a situation where you can hardly move. It's not unheard of for rope drag to build to such an extent that the climber has had no option but to untie a rope and climb to the top on one rope, or even no ropes in extreme cases.

The added strain caused by rope drag will, of course, increase the likelihood of falling which will be the last thing you want.

Ropework

3) Prevent sideways pull on protection

We've already seen in the previous section that it is preferable to load pieces of protection in a limited range of directions

Badly clipped ropes may well cause protection to be pulled to the side, when it was placed to withstand a downwards force. This is very likely to unseat the protection and send it sliding down the rope. Wires placed in horizontal cracks are particularly susceptible to this.

An example of where double ropes might have been a better idea. Two climbers on *Accessory Chimney* (Diff) Stanage, The Peak Disrtrict, England
Photo by Chris Craggs

Ropework

How to keep your ropes straight

Use double ropes

The most effective way of reducing zig-zag ropework is to use double half-ropes. With two ropes in use, protection may be sought from a wider area without suffering rope drag.

As a general rule, one rope is used on the left and one on the right, though on traverses this becomes a system where one rope take the high ground and one rope takes the low ground. On routes that follow straight lines, such as cracks, it is best to simply alternate the ropes. There is a temptation sometimes to clip both ropes

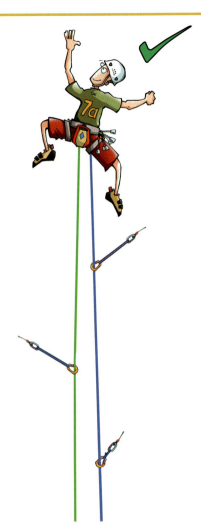

Ruth Taylor on *Just Another Day / Scorched Earth* (E5), Huntsman's Leap, Pembroke, Wales.
With a single rope, the spread of protection that has been clipped would have either generated a huge amount of rope drag, or would have required a lot of very long extenders.

into each piece of gear. In practice this is usually very fiddly to carry out, plus it can result in badly loaded karabiner and less elasticity in the rope system should you fall.

For routes which are mostly 'up', but with a minor traverse, it makes sense to use one rope for the section below the traverse, and the other rope for the section above it. Any protection placed on the actual traverse section should be thoroughly extended or not placed at all.

See page 113 for more on double ropes.

Kiwi Wendy leading *Clean Head Blues Band* (E2) St. Govan's, Pembroke, Wales.
This is a perfect example of how to use double ropes.
Photo by Nick Smith.

Ropework

Extend, extend, extend

Extending your protection is a bit of a pain when you just want to clip and go, but it will save a lot of grief higher up. Extending is particularly necessary if you are using a single rope and the line is anything other than dead straight.

While we're used to extending wires, it is nearly always a good idea to extend other pieces of protection such as cams. Extending a piece of protection should be the rule, rather than the exception and your rack should contain a sufficient number of quickdraws and slingdraws

Nick Smith taking air off *Tippler Direct* (E3), Stanage Edge, Peak District, England.
Notice how the karabiner on the red rope has been completely opened by the edge of the overhang. An open karabiner has less than half the strength of a closed one, so it would have been worthwhile putting a longer quickdraw on the right-hand cam.

to allow you to extend at will without worrying about running out of gear - *see page 46 for more on quickdraws and slingdraws.*

Extending your protection reduces rope-drag, prevents lift-outs and reduces the impact force of a fall, which means there's less chance of your gear ripping. Also, by extending protection on a route that is vertical or steeper, you move the pivot point (the karabiner in your top piece of protection) away from the rock, reducing the force with which you swing into the rock during a fall.

Finally, if you like short quickdraws because they mean you don't fall so far, ask yourself this: isn't it better to fall 30cm further on gear that stays in? Only in the rarest of situations where protection is very low does over-long extension pose any danger. *If in doubt, extend it out!*

Ropework

Extending gear in breaks

An easily overlooked hazard is caused when we place protection, typically cams, in the backs of horizontal breaks. It is crucial to extend such placements so that the karabiner is over the edge of the crack.

If the karabiner is on the edge of the break, the gate could easily open and there is a chance that a fall could break it. A deeper placement produces drag and risks locking the rope between the rock and the karabiner, resulting in a fall with a very high fall factor and risking damage to your rope.

This problem is easily avoided by extending the protection over the edge and therefore ensuring that the karabiner is not loaded across the edge.

This Camalot placement is fine and is not in need of any further extension since the karabiner is hanging free allowing the rope to move smoothly.

The problem here is that the karabiner is over the edge. This is one of the few situations in which a karabiner can actually break.

A fall onto this piece will trap the rope, creating a high impact force, risking damaging the sheath, and generally producing an unpleasant fall.

Clipping the cam's sling with a long slingdraw extends it well over the edge, reducing the risk of a high impact fall by allowing the rope to run freely.

Here, clipping the cam's sling would have still placed a karabiner over the edge. By looping the sling through the device itself, the hazard is avoided.

Ropework

The art of redirection

In a perfect world we'd all manage to keep our ropes straight at all times, there'd be no rope drag, and there'd be no chance of gear popping out because it was pulled the wrong way.

Back in the real world, there are many routes where your ropes are never going to run straight. The art is in knowing that a change of direction is taking place and placing a piece of protection that will handle it.

Unzipping - the redirectional base runner

The most common example of a change of direction is at the first piece of protection where the belayer is unable or unwilling to position themselves directly beneath the route. The rope then forms an angle at the first runner which can exert a big outward force on this runner. If this runner 'pops' out then the rope then forms an angle on the next runner up which may then also pop, and so on up the route. There are accounts of climbers who have fallen safely onto their last piece of protection, only to find that all the protection beneath has 'unzipped' from the ground upwards, leaving them hanging from a single piece!

Protection that can take an outward and upward force is needed in this situation. Cams, especially in horizontal breaks, are ideal, as are natural threads. If an angle change is looking likely, it is an excellent idea to place a redirectional piece of protection as soon as you find one, even if it's at waist height and useless as a runner. If you're using double ropes - you will probably want to clip both ropes into the redirectional piece, but using separate karabiners.

Luke Roberts starting up *The Arrow* (E1), St. Govan's, Pembroke, Wales.
In this case the belayer is unable to get close to the base of the cliff due to the series of ledges. The danger is that the direction change will 'unzip' the lower protection. The best solution is to place a solid redirectional piece of protection at the start.

Left: The DMM Revolver: the drag caused by a redirectional runner can be reduced by using a pulley - this clever piece of gear combines a pulley with a karabiner and is ideally suited to this task.

Ropework

Placing a redirectional base runner is often a good idea, even if you think you don't need it. Here are four good reasons for placing one wherever you can.

1) It keeps all the rest of your gear in place.

2) It makes your position as belayer largely irrelevant, allowing you to belay somewhere with a better view of what is going on, out of the way of potential rock-fall, or even just somewhere where it's nicer to sit.

3) If you find yourself belaying someone on a route where they face the possibility of a big fall, maybe hitting the ground, the only thing you can do if they fall is run for it and take in as much slack as possible. Placing a redirectional base runner makes this process *significantly* more efficient and can literally make the difference between ending the day in the pub with a good story and ending it in casualty.

4) It makes dynamic belaying much easier to achieve. *See page 140 for more on Dynamic Belaying.*

Here are three points of caution:

1) The redirectional base runner can increase the drag experienced by the leader, particularly if the redirection runner is low in the route. For this reason you may choose to remove the runner once the leader is high on the route.

2) The piece of protection you place as a redirectional base runner needs to beyond suspicion. You may wish to place more than one piece.

3) A low base runner will result in the belayer being pulled inwards rather than upwards, in the event of a fall. The belayer should anticipate this and consider a ground belay, or at least be ready to use a leg to prevent being slammed into the rock.

A redirectional base runner in use on *London Wall* (E5). The cam, placed at the base of the crack ensures that the subsequent wires are held snugly in place even when the belayer moves away from the base of the route to gain a better view of the climber. Climber: Miles Gibson.

Dynamic belaying

Knowing that your gear is going to stay in should you fall on it is crucial to having the confidence to 'go for it'. We've already looked at how to place protection to get the very most out of both the gear and the rock, but the story doesn't end there.

We looked at ropes on page 38 and discussed how ropes with low impact forces stretched, absorbing more force and subsequently putting less of a strain on our gear placements. Stretchy ropes work because the force of the falling climber is absorbed more gradually as it takes more time for a falling climber to come to rest on a stretchy rope than a stiffer one. Naturally, this will make us look out for ropes with a low impact force, but before you do, read this:

> *Through dynamic belaying a large part of the fall's energy is dissipated and so the impact force is reduced. Measurements by Mammut of typical sport climbing falls show that with dynamic belaying the difference in impact force between two different ropes is barely discernable. It's therefore important to provide a truly dynamic belay.*
>
> From the Mammut Rope Guide
> www.mammut.ch

This is rather like a car manufacturer telling us that the latest safety features on their top-of-the-range model are of very little value compared to driving more skilfully!

Dynamic belaying is a skill that few climbers are ever taught, yet it will significantly reduce the chances of your partner's gear failing and of them injuring themselves after slamming into the rock. Dynamic belaying has become more common in sport climbing. In trad climbing, potentially less secure protection means dynamic belaying offers real benefits.

The objective

The objective is to lengthen the amount of *time* taken to bring the fallen climber to rest. A fall absorbed very quickly may sound less scary, but it generates a high maximum force.

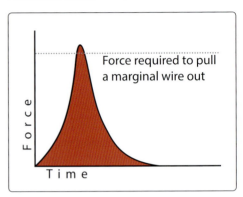

Force required to pull a marginal wire out

By lengthening the amount of time taken to absorb the fall, even slightly, the result is a reduction of the maximum force. This will almost certainly mean the climber falls further, but can be more sure that their protection will hold.

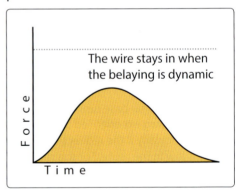

The wire stays in when the belaying is dynamic

Avoiding hazards first

The fact that dynamic belaying makes the climber fall further may make it unsuitable if there is a hazard such as a ledge or the ground, that the climber has a chance of hitting.

Ropework

Analysis of a fall

In the photo sequence below, the climber falls low on a route, protected by a well-placed and correctly extended wire, and yet ends up inverted with her head close to the ground. Why? Is this an advert for wearing a helmet - or could this have been avoided?

The position of the belayer is often crucial, but no more so than when a fall is short and close to the ground. In this instance, the belayer has positioned himself in a standing position a little way out from the base of the route. This is a very typical position and would have been fine were the climber to have fallen from higher on the route. However, in this instance, the position has resulted in the rope inverting the climber. A much better belay position would have been at the base of the route - one step to the side (X marks the spot).

Things are made worse by the fact that the belayer has not moved position. By belaying in a crouched position (see next page), the belayer would have introduced more live rope to absorb the force of the fall and given themselves the opportunity to move to a standing position to further reduce the force of the fall.

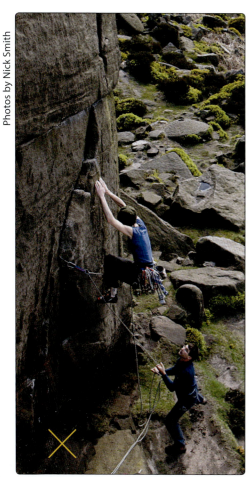

Photos by Nick Smith

Dynamic belaying: how it's done

Dynamic belaying, as its name suggests, is all about moving. The first time we hold a fall, we react naturally to hold our position - and try to stop the fall as quickly and as suddenly as possible. Dynamic belaying requires us to re-learn this instinct.

Ground belays

As a belayer, we can't move around if we're tightly attached to the ground or to the base of the cliff, so the first thing is to ensure we only take a ground belay if there is a hazard - such as when the route starts from a ledge above a drop. Even then, if possible, we should aim to clip in with some slack in the system which will keep us safe from tumbling over a cliff, but at the same time allow us some movement.

Giving in to the pull

When holding a fall, the instinct is to react *against* the pull by pulling in the opposite direction. Fighting this instinct by letting the pull take you with it is the essence of dynamic belaying.

A question of weight

If you are significantly lighter than the person you are belaying, then you don't have to do much other than hold tight and expect to get pulled off your feet. This may sound alarming, but in truth you're giving the best belay possible. If the weight disparity is very great, then consider attaching to a ground belay with some slack in the system.

If you are heavier than, or of a similar weight to, your partner, you are going to have to work a bit harder to give a dynamic belay. The key skill here is observation; it's important that you can react the moment you know a fall is imminent. The following three techniques are ways of providing a dynamic belay.

Method 1: Crouching/standing

If you are standing, belaying at the bottom of a route and you expect your partner to fall, immediately crouch down. Keep your eye on your partner, and when they fall, the moment the force of the fall begins to transmit to you, move to a standing position, letting the force pull you upwards. This method is particularly useful where the climber falls low and there isn't much rope out, or where there is not much room to manoeuvre.

Method 2: Walking in

With a redirectional base runner, there's no reason to stand directly under the base of the route. By belaying three or four paces away from the cliff we can give in to the force of a fall by simply walking in. It is important to start walking at exactly the moment the force is transmitted. This can allow a degree of control over the fall, and can be used to 'steer' a falling climber away from hazards like ledges by letting them fall past the hazard before arresting the fall.

Ropework

Method 3: Controlled slippage

Non auto-locking belay devices inherently allow a degree of slippage that all adds up to a more dynamic belay. It is tempting the think that the perfect dynamic belay can be achieved by simply letting some rope slide through the belay device, but in practice this is quite difficult.

The best way is to take a firm grip on both the live and dead ends and, at the moment the force is transmitted, lock-off and force some rope through the belay device. This way you will maintain complete control over the rope.

Mike Grant starting up *The Smile* (E1) Lower Sharpnose Point, Cornwall, England. By positioning himself a few metres from the base of the route, the belayer is able to give a dynamic belay - and has a better view of what is going on. As stated in the main text, it is vital that a redirectional base runner is used in this situation. Photo by Duncan Skelton.

Abseiling / rappelling

Abseiling (or 'rappelling') is the term used to describe descending down the rope after, or before, we climb a route.

Setting an abseil belay

The most crucial part of an abseil is setting up the belay. If you place a bad piece of protection on the lead and it fails, there's a good chance that the one below will hold. Arrange a bad abseil belay and you will probably die. Look for at least two belay points that are beyond doubt and secure the abseil rope to them so that they are loaded equally.

There are two arrangements of abseil belays: fixed rope and retrievable rope.

Fixed rope abseil belays

A fixed rope abseil belay will usually involve a single rope - preferably static - that is left in place, as long as it is required. It is most often used when approaching routes from above like on sea cliffs. The advantage of having a fixed rope is that it is always there should you decide to escape - *see ascending ropes on page 152*. The main disadvantage is that you need to carry an extra rope. If you arrive at a cliff to find a rope already in place, and its owners are not within earshot, it is commonly understood that you may use it, though it is worth checking the setup first!

When an abseil rope is fixed, it is usual to make use of the rope itself in equalising the belay, though take care not to use too much rope if you're about to make a long abseil with a rope that is only just long enough! If you are concerned about using too much rope - use slings instead.

An important consideration once you've set up your fixed abseil belay is the presence of any sharp edges that may dangerously abrade the rope. This may not present a big problem in getting down, but if you find yourself ascending the rope later in the day, you will be pleased to know that it is not rubbing over any sharp edges and grinding away to nothing.

One solution is to use one or more rope protectors. These are made from tough, flexible material, and work by enclosing the rope at its vulnerable points. They are held in place with metal clips, cord and velcro fastenings. Alternatively, you can try to use a backpack, camping mat, jacket, or similar items; just be sure that they are securely fastened in place, otherwise they may fall away when your weight comes off the rope.

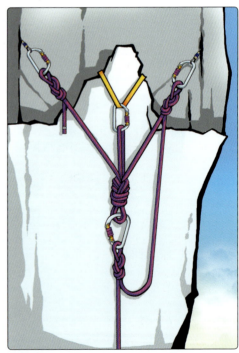

A solid three-point belay equalised using the abseil rope itself.

Ropework

Retrievable rope belays

A retrievable abseil allows us to abseil on two ropes (or, less commonly, one rope), then pull the rope down afterwards. This can be done with a single rope (if you're only going half its length) or a pair of ropes tied together (*see page 147*).

There are a number of reasons why you may need to arrange a retrievable abseil: you may not have a spare rope you can leave in place, you may be retreating from a climb, or you may need to make multiple abseils to reach your destination.

The belay for a retrievable abseil is very different from a fixed rope abseil. The first big difference is that the rope or ropes are not tied to the belay, they are only looped through it. Because of this, the ropes can not be used to equalise the belay, and we need to use slings instead. The second major difference is that, because the ropes need to be pulled afterwards, friction generated by running over any edge could well lead to your rope getting stuck. This means the belay must extend over any edge at the top, allowing the rope to run free, even though this often makes getting yourself into position to abseil awkward.

Belay points are arranged in the same way as any other belay, with at least two points that are beyond doubt. Equalising must be done using slings and any spare cord you may have. If there is an edge that the rope is going be running over, keep adding slings until the ropes are running freely from a sling or slings over the edge.

To get onto a retrievable abseil where the rope is clipped to the belay at a level below your waist, you will need to pull up the rope, attach your abseil device and an auto-bloc (*see page 148*) and then climb down to it - grabbing hold of the belay until your weight comes onto the rope. You will be glad you did this when it comes to pulling the rope down later.

A two-point belay equalised with slings and arranged for a retrievable abseil.

Leaving gear

If you are setting up a retrievable abseil to escape from a route, you are not going to want to leave all your best gear behind! To leave the minimum amount of gear, you can dispense with using karabiners - while it's not best practice to tie nylon to thin wire, the low forces involved in an abseil make it more acceptable (so you could, for example, tie a sling to a wire, or peg).

Running your rope through a karabiner rather than through a nylon sling will allow it to run more freely when it comes to pulling it rope down. Lastly, you may choose to place 'back-up' gear for the first (and heaviest) person to abseil, which, once the belay has been tested, can be removed by the last person.

Ropework

Retrievable sling belay

There are many objects (large blocks and trees, for example) you can abseil from simply by putting your rope over, or around, the object and pulling it down when you're done. There are a few problems with this: firstly you are likely to get a lot of resistance when it comes to pulling the rope, secondly you are likely to damage your rope, and thirdly, if you are doing this to a tree, you can easily damage the tree.

A solution is to leave a sling behind, but if you have enough rope, a good way of avoiding leaving the sling is to arrange the belay so you can pull the sling down after you. If you have only one rope, you can abseil 1/3rd of the length of your rope. If you have two ropes, you can abseil 1/2 the length of your rope, and if you happen to have three, you can abseil the length of your shortest rope.

How it's done

1) Assuming you are sure about the quality of the belay, pass a sling around the object.
2) Take one end of rope and pass it through the ends of the sling.
3) Feed it through until the end reaches the ground.
4) Assuming you have just one rope, take the other end of the rope and tie it to one loop of the sling. If you have more ropes then use one rope to tie to the sling and the other one (or two) to abseil on.
5) Drop the rest of the rope and check that the rope touches the ground with both an end and a loop - there should be three ropes dangling now.
6) Abseil on the ropes that are looped through the sling - be sure to double check you're abseiling on the right ends!
7) When everyone is down, simply pull the abseil rope through the sling, then pull the end/rope attached to the sling to release it from the object. Check that you haven't damaged the sling in the process.

Alex Hughes abseiling from a tree using a retrievable sling belay. The third rope running from the belay is not loaded and is used to pull the sling down once the rope has been pulled through.

Ropework

Joining ropes

Most retrievable abseils will require you to join two ropes. The best way of doing this is to tie a simple overhand knot about sixty centimeters from the ends. The overhand knot has the advantage over the double fisherman's knot (traditionally used in abseils) in that it presents a flat edge, which is much less likely to catch when you pull the rope. The double fisherman's knot is still used where the two ropes being joined are of greatly different diameters.
See page 100 for more on these two knots.

Single rope abseil with two ropes

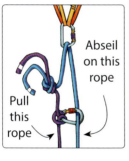

There may be the need to arrange a double rope abseil so that you only abseil on one of the ropes - possible scenarios include having one rope with a serious cut in it, or having a single-rope-only belay device. To do this, tie a knot such as a simple clove hitch into the end you are pulling (and not abseiling on) and clip this via a screw-gate karabiner to the end you're abseiling down.

Hazards

Having set up your belay, checked it all, and attached your rope to it, you need to get your rope down. Before you toss it recklessly over the abyss, bear in mind two things that could slow you down:
1) Ropes like to get snagged - any little bush or spike of rock will attract your rope like a magnet and the resulting mess can take a lot of effort to untangle, particularly if you are dangling in mid-air!

2) One of the most common abseiling accidents is to abseil off the ends of your ropes - although this speeds your descent up remarkably, it is greatly undesirable!

To avoid these two dangers, tie a knot in the doubled rope end and clip it to your harness before you throw your ropes down. Now you know that you have got a knot in the end, plus by throwing down a loop, there is significantly less chance of the rope getting stuck (strange, but true). This is particularly useful if you are abseiling in over water and don't want to get your rope ends wet. The only disadvantage of this method is that it's not as easy to tell if your ropes will reach the ground. If you are unsure then you will need to throw your ropes down with a knotted end to test the length. Aim to throw them out, away from the cliff as much as possible, and into the wind.

Remember to check for people below before lowering your ropes down - and always shout 'rope!' as a warning, giving people time to take cover before you drop rope (and anything else) down on them.

Try to get in the habit of telling your partner which colour rope to pull before you set off abseiling. Do this each time you abseil since the rope will change on multi-pitch abseils.

On windy days, lowering your ropes down is asking for trouble. If your ropes are carried off far to the side and wrapped around even the smallest bush, you can get into a really tricky situation. In this situation, don't lower your ropes down, instead coil them up, or stick them in your pack, and pay them out as you descend. Alternatively you can clip some heavy things to the knot in the end and lower it.

Missiles

Falling rocks are a constant hazard in climbing, but often the chances of being hit are small. When abseiling, however, the thing that is most likely to cause a rock fall (your rope) is nearly always directly above you. The hazard is often at its greatest when you have reached the ground and take your weight off the rope.

As always, prevention is better than cure, so, after checking that no-one is below you, give the rock that your rope is going to be running against a kick. If anything seems loose, it is a good idea to get rid of it safely before you find yourself below it.
Make sure your abseil rope itself is well out of the way if cleaning loose rock before you abseil off. Attaching the ends to your harness (*as described on page 147*) is a good way of ensuring against this problem.

A helmet will provide a degree of protection against falling rocks - but avoiding in the first place is better still.

Creating an auto-bloc

There are occasions when you might want to take both hands off the rope when abseiling and not plummet to the ground. You may need to disarm a loose block, clip the rope into some protection to keep in contact with steep rock, untangle the ends of your rope from a bush, or you may have been knocked unconscious by a falling rock.

An auto-bloc is a means of arranging your abseil device with a prussic loop so that it will lock up automatically should you let go. The simplest setup is to attach a French prusik (*see page 102*) to the rope *below* your abseil device. Placing it below the abseil device makes it more effective, as it does not require so much force to lock the system. You will need to place it above if you are expecting to pass a knot in the rope (*see page 151*). The best place to clip your prusik to is your leg-loop, as shown below. You can clip it to your belay loop, but this will require extending your abseil device so they are kept apart.

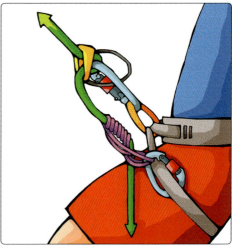

If you expect to do a lot of abseiling, a Petzl Shunt will prove more user-friendly and less prone to wear (prusiks used in this way should be regularly inspected, as they will wear out eventually). If you use a Shunt, you will probably need to extend your abseil device as show here:

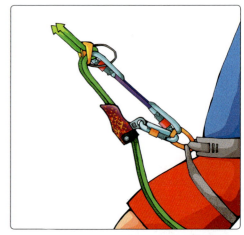

Ropework

Simultaneous abseiling

It is very, very unusual to *have* to do this, but one day you just might. A simultaneous abseil is a way of abseiling off a two-sided rock - even if there is no belay.

Abseiling in tandem, each climber counterbalances the other. The rope must be lodged in a natural niche to avoid the possibility of it rolling off.

Only when each climber is on the ground, and is sure that their partner is too, can they take their weight off the rope.

A simultaneous abseil off the middle fin of Lower Sharpnose Point on the North Cornwall Coast.

Abseiling dramas

The rope doesn't reach the ground!

If you think your ropes won't reach the ground then the key is to act early. Don't wait until you are dangling in space 5m above the ground, below an overhang you can't reach!

If your ropes are close, but not actually touching the ground, then you may well find that you will reach the ground on rope stretch. The closer to the ends of your rope you get, the more stretch there is, but a rope will also get less stretchy with time, both through its life, and at the end of a day where you have made multiple abseils. Use your own judgement based on the circumstances. If the lower section of the crag is slabby with ledges, then you may be able to swing across to a relatively safe position from where you can scramble down.

If you are sure your rope is too short then try and spot a belay point you can use to make a second abseil from - a tree, or crack for example. This can be to the side of your abseil line since you will normally be able to swing across quite a distance. Take a second belay and set up a second abseil from this point. You may well end up having to leave some gear in these circumstances.

Abseiling with a pack

If you need to carry a heavy pack while abseiling, you will find it pulls you off balance. The best way to counteract this is to take the pack off your back and suspend it from your belay loop using a short sling. If you must keep the pack on your back, an improvised chest harness using a sling will keep you upright.

Alex Klenov and Miles Gibson descending from Angel Falls in Venezuela.
Miles has clipped his sack to his belay loop to reduce the strain on his stomach muscles and reduce the risk of turning upside down.
Photo by John Arran.

Ropework 151

I need to pass a knot!

Passing a knot is something you may occasionally have to do - for example when two ropes have been tied together to make an extra-long abseil rope, or if the rope has a cut that has been removed from the system by means of a knot.

To pass a knot you need to have an auto-bloc set up with the prusik/Shunt above the abseil device (i.e. completely the other way around from the way ordinarily recommended). *See page 148.*

As you approach the knot, lock the auto-bloc securely - you are about to rely heavily on this, so it is worth tying into a backup knot below the knot you're passing just in case there is some slippage.

Now, take your abseil device off the rope and put it back on under the knot you're passing, add an auto-bloc, or if you haven't enough prusiks, tie off your abseil device - *see page 112.*

Next, you need to release the top prusik. This is usually where things get awkward and you may need to use another prusik with your foot (*see ascending for details on this on page 152*) in order to get the weight off.

Now you can untie your back-up knot and carry on down.

Anne Arran abseiling down Lembert Dome in Tuolomne Meadows, California, USA. Photo by John Arran.

Ascending ropes

It's not often you have to ascend a rope, but sometimes it's the only way home. Ascending ropes isn't technically difficult, but without a lot of fairly specialised gear and plenty of practice, it is usually a very slow process and very hard work.

Ascending a rope requires two devices that are able to lock onto the rope. The cheapest and lightest are prusik loops. Increasingly more elaborate devices that make ascending quicker and easier are available. It is possible to ascend one or two ropes, though it is worth bearing in mind that only prusik loops and Petzl *Shunts* are capable of handling two ropes, although belay devices with auto-bloc functionality (such as the *Reverso/ATC Guide*) can be used as the lower device at a push.

Prusiking

The basic setup involves attaching two prusiks to the rope(s), one about 50cm above the other - *see page 102 for how to tie a prusik*. One prusik is attached to your belay loop via a screw-gate karabiner, and the other is simply used as a foot loop. Height is gained simply by stepping up on the foot loop, and holding onto the rope with one hand, sliding the other prusik up the rope until it comes tight and you can sit on it.

Because this method places a lot of trust in a single prusik loop, it is a good idea to tie into the rope as a backup, re-tying periodically. Clipping your harness into the lower prusik with a sling (not shown in the diagram) is also a good backup. If you are ascending using mechanical devices you will need to use slings or daisy-chains to attach to the devices. You may wish to attach your harness to both devices as a backup.

Ropework

Ascending (jumaring) with a croll

If you know you are going to be doing a lot of ascending, especially on free-hanging ropes, then you should use this method. You will need a chest croll attached to your belay loop, and held up by some cord (bungy works well) around your neck - or a chest harness if you have one. Your foot is attached to a handled ascender via a foot-loop (or etrier) and the handled ascender is positioned above the croll. For a backup, you can attach your harness to the handled ascender via a daisy chain (a long sling securely sewn into small loops so that you can clip into it at various points).

To make upward progress, it helps to have a bit of weight on the end of the rope - although after a while, the rope itself will suffice. Height is gained by grabbing the handled ascender with both hands and standing up in your foot loop. The croll will automatically slide up the rope, just repeat this - with practice you will gain height quite quickly. A similar but more strenuous technique uses a second handled ascender attached directly to your belay loop, instead of using the croll. If you are using an etrier (a mini ladder made of nylon) you can stand up with both feet, making it easier still.

Ascending ropes using a jumar, a chest croll and a daisy chain

Using two handled ascenders

On slabby ground, or if the rope isn't running straight up, you will be better off using a pair of handled ascenders. Simply clip each to the rope, put a foot-loop (or etrier as you choose) on each ascender, and clip each ascender to your belay loop with a daisy chain. You will need to experiment to get the lengths just right. To ascend, simply alternate between standing on one foot-loop while raising the other ascender.

Ascending with a pack

If you are carrying a heavy pack, it is better to clip it to your belay loop via a sling than have it on your back where it will un-balance you. Better still, put it on the end of your rope and haul it up when you're at the top.

Ropework

Top-roping

The term 'top-roping' is commonly used to refer to the practice of protecting a climb by having a rope from the climber to a belay at the top of the climb, then back down to the ground, where the belayer is situated. Instructors often refer to this as 'bottom roping', using the term 'top-roping' for when the belayer is at the top. Most climbers use the term top-roping for both.

To arrange a top-rope, a belay needs to be built at the top of the route. A top-rope belay is no different from a retrievable abseil belay (*see page 145*). The belay needs to attach to the rope via a screw-gate karabiner, below the edge of the cliff in order to avoid damage to the rope and the rock. The parts of the belay that do extend over the cliff edge will be subjected to wear and it is important that rope protection is used, particularly if several people intend to top-rope the route.

Top-roping is a good way to improve your technique, but keep in mind the fact that it can spoil the satisfaction you may get from a subsequent lead of a route - it is always easier to lead a route when you have practised the moves. Because of this top-roping is commonly employed to 'work' routes with a view to headpointing - *see page 204*.

While climbers who are top-roping have every bit as much right to be at the crag as climbers who are leading, leaving top-ropes in place for longer than necessary creates a cluttered atmosphere at the crag and frustrations can surface at busy crags when climbers wishing to lead a route find a large party taking turns at top-roping it.

Marie-Claire Haddock top-roping *Brooks' Layback* (HS), Burbage North, The Peak District, England.

Ropework

Self-belaying

Sometimes when you can't find a climbing partner, or you just want some time on your own working a project, it's useful to be able to climb with a self-belay.

While there are exotic devices that enable you to lead with a 'mechanical belayer', a far more common scenario is where a rope is fixed at the top of a climb, removing the need to place protection on-lead.

There are several devices that can be used to 'top rope self-belay'. The most common is the Petzl *Shunt*. In fact, self-belayed climbing is often referred to as 'Shunting'. There are, however, a number of serious safety issues with using Shunts for self-belaying: firstly, if you instinctively grab the Shunt when you fall, it will not lock-up and you will fall until you let go or hit the ground. The second issue occurs on steep ground where a weighted rope can easily squeeze the Shunt against your body, holding the device open and liable to failure. While these problems can be overcome, it is far better to use a device designed with self-belaying in mind - the most commonly available being the Petzl *Mini Traxion*, which Petzl actually endorses as a self-belay device (unlike the Shunt!).

After you've fixed a (dynamic) rope and abseiled down to get to the start of the route (cleaning any loose rock off as you go), it is a good idea to weight down the bottom of the rope. Often, the easiest way of doing this is to coil up the remaining rope and using that to weight the climbing rope.

Attach the Mini Traxion onto the rope and ensure that it's the right way up and the teeth are engaged - give it a test to ensure it locks when pulled down. Now clip directly into the Mini Traxion with a screw-gate karabiner. The device must be held in a safe position so that, when you fall, you don't shock load it. A top tip is to thread some bungy cord through the hole on the Mini Traxion and tie it around the back of your neck - this holds the device much higher and the connection to your harness will be under constant tension so when you fall, the device will engage more rapidly - *see photo below*.

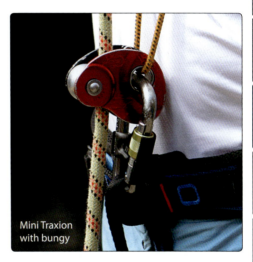

Mini Traxion with bungy

Working projects on self-belay

If you are working a route on self-belay, you will probably wish to work a sequence of moves repeatedly. This is where the Mini Traxion is less than ideal because if you want to move back down - you need to transfer to an abseil device, then back again - holding the cam open and hand-over-handing down the rope is not advised!

While there is no perfect solution, using an auto-locking belay device such as a Grigri in conjunction with a device such as a Shunt attached to a second rope via a long sling can work reasonably well.

Ropework and falling off

Leader falls

Taking a leader fall is commonly viewed with a certain dread, but aside from placing protection well, arranging your extensions, and having an alert belayer, there are things you can do, or avoid doing, to make your 'flight' a more pleasurable one.

1) Keep your belayer informed

Under dynamic belaying, your belayer can greatly influence the safety of a fall. If your belayer knows you are more likely than normal to fall, they can be more ready to react - steering you away from hazards (tell them about them) and being ready to provide a more dynamic belay to reduce the force on the protection - and on you. If your belayer can't see you, a tug on the rope (you falling) could easily be interpreted as a request for slack - "TAKE!" usually does the trick.

2) Try to stay upright

If at all possible, stay upright. This will greatly reduce the chances of injuring your head and will allow you to absorb much of the force of the fall with your legs.

On vertical or steep climbs the natural instinct to grab the rope will go a long way to keeping you upright - though if possible, keep one hand free to protect your head should you swing into the rock. On slabs, stay upright by 'running' downhill.

One of the biggest culprits for flipping us upside-down is getting the rope caught under our thigh. Always be aware of where the rope is running, especially when starting a traverse.

Above: it is easy to get the ropes caught behind a thigh, especially when moving into a traverse. This will flip you upside-down in the event of a fall.

Below: much better.

3) Avoid outward motion

If you fall semi-deliberately, try to fall in as downward a direction as possible. Only push-off outwards if there are hazards such as ledges that you want to avoid. The greater your outward force, the greater the chance of popping out wires and you will only swing back in with greater force.

4) Stay alert

Keep your eyes open and be ready to slam into the rock. Many fall-related injuries are caused by slamming into the route, whereas it is rare to hit the ground. If at all possible, use your legs as shock-absorbers and bend them as they strike the rock. This can make the difference between feeling a little disappointed to have fallen off and getting a broken ankle.

Getting back on the rock after a fall

Firstly, be wary of getting back on the rock too quickly - take a moment to calm down and evaluate your situation. On vertical or slabby rock, getting back on is rarely a problem, but on steep rock, or when a climb traverses over steep ground, a fall can put you in the middle of nowhere. In such situations, there are two options:
1) if you are within range, you can lower to the ground, pull your ropes and try again:
2) if you are not within range of the ground, you will have to ascend the rope(s) until you reach your top piece of protection - *see prusiking on page 152.*
If you use the latter, you may choose to ascend one rope, leaving the other rope to be taken in by your partner as you ascend. Once you arrive at the protection, you will need to clip into it to allow your partner to take in the slack before you can continue - up or down.

Dave Johnson falling off *The Rasp* (E2), Higgar Tor, The Peak District, England. Photos by Nick Smith.

Ropework

Retreating mid-pitch

If you get to the point where you cannot continue, your options will depend on how long your ropes are and how far from the ground (or last belay) you have gone.

1) Lower-off

If you have good protection the simplest thing to do is lower off. You will need to be sure your protection is good enough, and that your ropes will reach the ground, especially on a steep route where you can't stay in contact with the rock. If you are stripping your lower pieces of protection, it may be worth leaving the higher pieces as a backup for the protection you are lowering from.

2) Down-climb

If your protection is poor, your only option is to reverse the climb, or reverse to your next solid runner. You may want to retrieve your protection, or leave it in if your partner is intending to try the route. If you haven't actually loaded your protection, you may decide to down-climb and preserve your onsight for a future attempt.

3) Take a belay and bring up your partner

If you are committed on a long climb, and have enough good protection, the best bet is to take a belay, bring up your partner and let them try to continue.

4) Arrange a belay and abseil off

If you haven't long enough ropes to reach the ground by lowering, you will need to arrange a belay to abseil from. This may well mean that you have to leave some gear behind.

Albie Niedojadio considering the options on the traverse of *Great Western* (HVS), Almscliff, Yorkshire, England.

Ropework

Spotting

The technique of 'spotting' was developed originally to make bouldering safer. The objective when spotting is to protect a climber falling a short distance onto the ground by ensuring they fall feet first and guiding them away from obvious hazards.

In trad climbing, spotting is a very useful way of helping to protect short unprotected 'micro' climbs which may be little more than 'highball' boulder problems and where a bouldering mat would be of use. Spotting can, however, be used on just about any climb where there is a chance of the leader falling before placing their first piece of protection.

When spotting, the first thing to do is take your hands off the belay device - there's no sense in holding ropes when no protection has been placed. Now, adopt a stable position where you aren't going to be easily knocked over yourself - you may choose to build a ground belay for this purpose.

The part of the leader's body you aim to guide will very much depend on how steep the climbing is. On very steep starts, your priority will be to prevent injury to the head and back: to do this, aim to make contact with the climber's upper back and try to keep them upright when they fall.

On a more gently angled start, the best part of the body to make contact with is the climber's bottom - much easier to grab than a waist.

Cara-Lyn Reynolds being spotted by Dave Jennions, on *Marble Arete* (HS) Stanage, The Peak District, England. Photo by Nick Smith.

The objective is to keep the climber upright, guide them away from bad landing areas and take a bit of the force.

When spotting, always consider your own safety first. There will be a point where the leader is so high that a spot will be of little use and could cause greater injury to the spotter. The part of the body most at risk when spotting are your thumbs - try to make contact with the palms of your hands and keep your thumbs out of the way.

Al Mason on *High Neb Buttress* (VS) Stanage, The Peak District, England.

Technique

Technique is what defines a good climber. You can go a long way with strength, fitness, composure, flexibility and a host of other attributes, but all the physical prowess in the world can be rendered useless in the face of a technical move you can't work out how to do. The best part is that the effect of applying good technique to a VDiff will be just as striking as applying it to an E10.

Technique gives you something for nothing. With the same strength and fitness a better technical climber will climb the same route much more easily and may well use significantly less energy in doing so.

Technique

Trad technique

Trad climbing technique shares a lot in common with sport climbing and climbing indoors, but there is no doubt that trad climbing tends to favour certain techniques that you'll rarely have chance to practise unless you spend time on trad crags.

When a climber fails on a trad route they're often too pumped to do the next move. It's tempting then to think that the 'being pumped' is the sole cause of the failure and, hence, that more training is needed. While this may be true, it's important to look into ways of minimising the strain by using better technique. Better technique will mean your body doesn't need so much strength or fitness to pull through the same moves and it isn't limited by genetically determined aspects such as your muscle mass.

Use your feet

In our everyday lives, tasks requiring skill are mostly related to our hands and our eyes. Our hands and eyes collect a huge amount of information - seeing something and then touching it is innate human behaviour, but often one that let's us down when we attempt the un-human act of climbing up rocks.

Watch someone climbing for the first time and you will see how their visual focus is almost entirely on their hands. Meanwhile, their feet blindly hunt out holds. When encased in climbing shoes, you get very little sensory information from your feet, so we need to learn to move our visual focus from our hands - which can take in a surprising amount of information on their own - to our feet.

If you ever get the chance to watch a really good climber, notice how every foot placement is calculated and often they make two foot movements for every hand movement.

Adam Long keeping his focus on his feet on *Artless* (E5), Froggatt Edge, The Peak District, England.

Technique

Put your weight through your feet

Feet are amazing things: you can stand on them for ages without getting tired and with a good pair of climbing shoes you can put lots of weight on even the tiniest of edges. Use the same holds with your hands and you'll be pumped before you know it and that's if you're strong enough to hold on at all. So the key, wherever possible, is to keep lots of weight on your feet and as little as possible on your arms. Many of the techniques in this chapter have the aim of taking the weight off your arms and onto your feet.

When moving between footholds, especially on steep ground, it's tempting to pull hard on whatever handholds are available, taking weight for just long enough to move your feet up to different holds. While this often works - and occasionally may be the only option - it's very inefficient and you'll have problems as soon as the handholds aren't quite good enough.

To keep your weight through your feet when moving from foothold to foothold, you need to transfer the weight that was distributed between both feet so that it is directly above the foot that you aren't moving, only then should you attempt to release the other.

The wider apart you place your feet, the harder it is to un-weight one of your feet. Because of this, as a *default* position, it is better to keep your feet directly below you and to avoid having them any wider than shoulder width apart.

Steve Ramsden on *Bella Lugosi is Dead* (E1), Rainbow Walls, Llanberis Slate, Wales.
By extending his left arm and leaning to the left, Steve shifts his weight over his left foot, putting himself in a more balanced position to stand up and move his right foot.

Do try this at home!

Stand on the floor with your feet shoulder-width apart. Now lift your right foot *slowly* off the ground. Notice how you shifted your body so all your weight was over your left foot.

Try it again with your feet twice as far apart. You'll find you have to bend your left leg before you can get all your weight over onto it.

Now see how far apart you can place your feet and still be able to lift one of them *slowly* off the ground. Try extending both arms out left as a counter-weight and pointing your right toe to get maximum extension.

Understanding and harnessing this balance is invaluable when you're on rock, because if you can keep in balance purely by shifting the weight between your feet, any handholds you have will be a luxury!

Technique

Handholds for balance

On all but the steepest ground, handholds should be used to stay in balance - that is to say your hands are principally to reposition your body so as to make the best use of the footholds. Upwards progress should be made by using the muscles in your legs to push down on footholds - rather than the muscles in your arms to pull down on handholds as much as possible.

Use the correct part of your feet

There four parts to your foot that are useful in climbing: your inside edge, outside edge, toe and heel. Different footholds will require a different part of your foot depending on your body position.

A common mistake made by novice climbers is to step onto a hold with the middle of their foot - as if it were the rung of a ladder. Using the edge of your shoe gives you much greater precision when using smaller holds and allows you to use your calves to gain extra reach or to help you balance.

Use the correct part of the foothold

When using large footholds, place your foot comfortably near the edge of the hold rather than at the back. While this may seem insecure, the further out your feet are, the less steep the rock will feel, and the easier it is to get your weight over your foot.

Benjamin Harding resting his right foot by standing on his heel on *Kitten Claws* (E3) Carreg-y-Barcud, Pembroke, Wales.

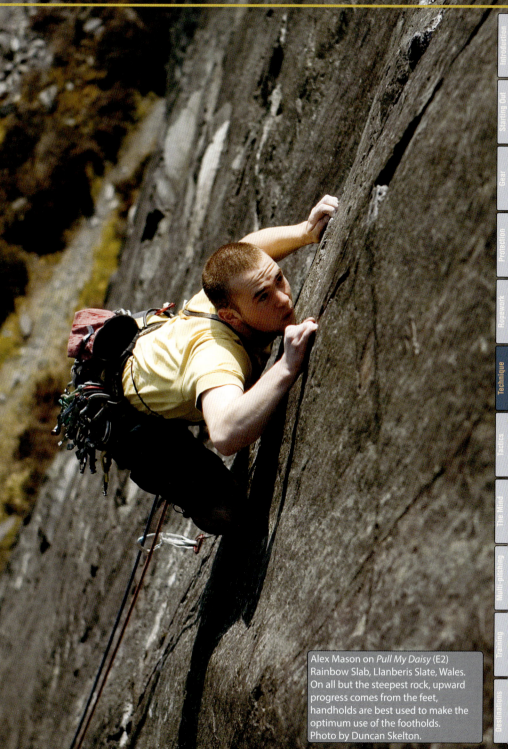

Alex Mason on *Pull My Daisy* (E2) Rainbow Slab, Llanberis Slate, Wales. On all but the steepest rock, upward progress comes from the feet, handholds are best used to make the optimum use of the footholds. Photo by Duncan Skelton.

Technique

Slabs

A slab is a section of rock on the friendly side of vertical. When you find a good foothold on a slab, it is easy to stand in balance (while you contemplate how fierce the next moves look and how far away the last protection is!) At this angle precise and effective use of your feet will make the most difference because the hard moves will tend to have small or nonexistent handholds.

Keeping your weight directly above your feet on a slab means keeping your upper body some way away from the rock, so avoid the temptation to 'hug' a slab as that will usually make it harder.

Bear in mind that falling from a slab is often more dangerous than falling from steeper rock since you are inevitably going to make contact with the (hard and abrasive) rock as you fall. The chance of tumbling upside down is relatively high, so wearing a helmet is more of a consideration.

Rab Anderson padding with straight arms up *The Pause* (HVS) Etive Slabs, Scotland.
Photo by Dave Cuthbertson.

Padding

If the angle of the slab is particularly low, you can sometimes climb by 'padding' up the blank rock, using just the friction generated between your shoes and the rock.

To achieve good padding technique, point your toes directly up the slab and drop your heels in order to distribute your weight over as much of the front of your shoe sole as possible. Pick a line that is roughly straight to keep in balance and keep going!

Small steps are best to help you stay in balance and keep your feet rooted. All your weight should be on your feet: your hands are for balance only. Keeping your arms straight and outstretched will help ensure your weight is directly over your feet. Avoid grabbing holds and leaning into the rock (an easy reaction when you're gripped!) as this will take weight off your feet and increase the likelihood of them slipping and you making an ungraceful slither back down the slab.

Smearing

On slightly steeper slabs, friction alone won't be enough; you'll have to find ripples or other features and place your feet very carefully to gain the best advantage from these tiny changes in angle.

Placing your instep (the front of your inside edge) diagonally on the flattest part of a smear is most effective, as you can apply pressure through the strongest part of your foot, though it is equally important to fit your foot position to the hold. Once you have placed your foot on a smear, weight it gradually, but firmly and avoid re-adjusting your foot once it's been weighted. It is the pressure you place on a hold that keeps your foot 'stuck' to it. You will find that keeping your foot roughly horizontal is the best orientation for maximising the contact area and ensuring your weight is evenly distributed over the hold.

Be careful not to over-reach from a smear, as the resulting change of angle of your foot on the hold will reduce the friction.

The most marginal of smears demands a good clean contact between rubber and rock. If your head is level with a smear you are going to be using, blow off any dust that may have settled on it and give your shoe a wipe on your trousers to make sure it is clear of dirt - this can be a real confidence booster!

Smears don't make good handholds, but pushing (palming) down with the palm of your hand can help make best use of it.

Smearing can be scary since you feel your feet can 'pop' at any moment. If you get nervous try and focus just on the rock immediately in front of you for just a moment while you compose yourself.

Cecile Rittweger climbing the unprotected *Great Slab* (E3) at Froggatt, Peak District, England.

Technique

Edging

An edge differs from a smear in that it is square-cut, often offering the possibility to get your weight comfortably over your foot. Edges usually also make good handholds so make the most of them, both for upwards progress and for resting between moves.

On easier routes you will normally find plenty of good-sized edges. As you progress through the grades you need to develop your technique to make the most of the smaller edges you encounter.

To stand on the smallest edges, you need to make sure the rubber edges on your shoes are nice and sharp. Stiff shoes will give a greater degree of security on small edges over softer shoes, but will be lacking in sensitivity should you find yourself having to smear.

Small edges are best used with the side of your big toe (inside edge) or the side of your little toe (outside edge) and keeping your foot nearly parallel to the rock.

Edging can be tiring on your calves. When you have chance try shaking out each leg in turn, just like you would shake out your arms on a steeper route. On a larger edge, you can get a good foot rest by switching to standing on your heel for a bit, or if you

Steve Ramsden checking the footholds on *Bella Lugosi is Dead* (E1) Rainbow Walls, Llanberis Slate, Wales.

can't do that, try consciously dropping your heels, your calf muscles will relax significantly and you will also find yourself calming down a bit.

Often, very small edges are hard to spot on slabs, so it's worth making sure you've put a little chalk on them when you are level with them. This is particularly useful if you find yourself retreating in a bit of a panic.

Technique

Walls

Walls range from almost vertical to radically overhanging and the technique you choose will depend very much on how steep the rock is. It's usually not possible to stand in balance on a wall so it's important to move decisively between rest positions and to think carefully about where to stop to place protection.

Balance

Balance is about keeping your centre of gravity directly above your feet. Your centre of gravity is a point that usually lurks somewhere in the middle of your torso, between the tops of your hips.

When wall climbing, we spend much of our time in an off-balance position simply because our footholds are close to the rock, and our centre of gravity is a little way out. The reason we don't fall is because we use handholds to take the strain. The more off-balance we are, the more effort our arms must expend.

Whilst the steepness of the wall is a major factor in how balanced we are, our choice of technique is also important. The following techniques all aim to bring our centre of gravity in closer to the rock, with the main goal being to keep our hips as close to the rock as possible.

Adrian frogging on *The Grim Jim* (E2) Dinas Cromlech, Wales.   Photo by Duncan Skelton.

Frogging

As we've already seen, upwards progress should come from leg power as much as possible. To achieve this we have to bend our legs: keeping your hips parallel to the rock and bending a leg naturally pushes your body away from the rock, putting strain on your arms. Frogging solves this with a little flexibility by simply turning both knees outward. The more flexibility your hips have (turnout) the closer you can bring them in to the rock. This technique works particularly well when your legs are fully bent, especially on aretes where your hip flexibility is less of a factor.

Dave 'Cubby' Cuthbertson hanging off his arms on the first ascent of *Thunderbird* (E3) Seanna Mheallan, Torridon, Scotland.   Photo by Cubby Images.

Technique

Dave MacLeod climbing side-on and crimping hard on *HoldFast* (E9) Whale Rock, Glen Nevis, Scotland. Photo by Dave Cuthbertson.

Adrian flagging on *Cockblock* (E5), Clogwyn Y Grochan, Snowdonia, Wales. Photo by Duncan Skelton.

Climbing side-on

When things get steeper than vertical, the best position to adopt is usually with your pelvis at ninety degrees to the rock. This position requires less in the way of body tension and gets your weight closer to being over your feet. When making a reach from a side-on position, arrange yourself so you are reaching with the arm that is closest to the rock: so if you are facing right, the left side of your body will be facing the rock, and you will be in the position to move up with your left arm. This is also known as a twist-lock.

Swapping and flagging

To keep in balance when there aren't many footholds around, you may find yourself frequently swapping feet on holds. Sometimes this is the best plan, but to save a couple of moves, consider passing your free foot between your supporting leg and the rock and flagging for balance (inside flag).

Alternatively, if there is not enough space to pass your leg on the inside, pass your free foot behind your supporting leg and flagging (outside flag).

Drop knees and Egyptians

Dropping a knee is a good way of bringing your hips closer into the rock. At its mildest, this is simply turning one leg so your knee faces inwards - towards the other knee. This will turn your foot slightly so that the side of your inside edge is on the hold rather than the toe - a position that allows increased purchase. A more extreme position can be useful on steep rock, ideally with high, 'side-pull' footholds that face each other. The aim is to take a side-on position and 'bridge' between the holds. This position requires the knee to be 'dropped', the closer the holds are to each other, the more the knee must be dropped - at its most extreme, the knee will point directly downwards. This move is often referred to as an 'Egyptian', owing to the characteristic shape of the legs. This can be particularly useful when the handholds are very sloping.

Technique

Adrian using a drop knee on *The Grim Jim* (E2) Dinas Cromlech, Snowdonia, Wales. Photo by Duncan Skelton.

Straight-arming

One objective of good technique is to reduce the amount of weight on your arms. The less your arms have to do, the longer you have before the dreaded forearm pump sets in - this is when your arms become solid with lactic acid build-up and in extreme cases you can't even hold on anymore. Much of the time, however, you have no option but to hang from your arms. The goal then becomes to ensure your arms have the best blood-supply possible. By helping the heart pump blood through your arms you will allow the lactic acid that causes your forearm pump to be removed in the blood.

When we bend and tense our arms, the blood supply to our forearms is reduced, resulting in a more rapid forearm pump as well as the fact that you are using up your arm strength. The simple solution is to hang from straight arms wherever possible when you're on steep ground. Of course, it is also important to be able to see what you're doing - you may want to look inside a break to check out gear placements, or to find better holds, in which case by all means pull up, have a good look, then return to straight arms as soon as possible.

Shaking out

Shaking out is a recovery technique that helps your blood supply remove lactic acid from your forearms. To do this, blood must enter your forearms, collect the lactic acid, then exit. You can help your body do this by relaxing your arm and shoulder muscles, and alternatively hold your arm above your head (blood flows out), then letting it hang straight down (blood flows in). Hold each for between five and ten seconds. Shaking your arm and hand makes it feel more effective. The fitter you are the quicker you will recover.

Dave 'Cubby' Cuthbertson straight armed and shaking out on the first ascent of *Thunderbird* (E3) Seanna Mheallan, Torridon, Scotland. Photo by Cubby Images.

Technique

Handholds

When people first start climbing they tend to regard only large solid holds which you can pull down on, or hang off, as actual handholds. As you progress in climbing the variety of rock features that you can utilise with your hands increases dramatically. Here are a few of the different handholds that you may encounter and the best way to make the most out of them.

Side-pulls

A side-pull is a vertical edge usually off to one side. Whenever you need to use a side-pull remember that you'll need something to oppose the force you're applying. If there isn't an ideal foothold for this then often pushing a foot against a blank bit of wall will help prevent you rotating.

Undercuts

An undercut is a downward pointing hold which can be incredibly useful if you need to reach past a blank section. By pulling hard with one arm and getting your feet high you can sometimes make really long reaches to better holds above.

Arun Brenner on the notorious sloping finish of *Strapiombante* (E1), Froggatt Edge the Peak District, England. Photo by Nick Smith

Slopers

Sloping holds can fell okay when you're below them but as you get higher they suddenly start to become worse and worse. Try to keep your weight low and your elbows in close.

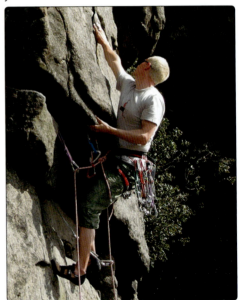

Above: Nick Smith uses an undercut to make a long reach on *Auricle* (E2) Bamford, The Peak District, England. Photo by James Rowe
Left: Alex Barrows side-pulling towards the crux of *Kafoozalem* (E3), Bosigran, Cornwall. Photo by Duncan Skelton.

Technique

Special techniques

Manteling

Manteling (or 'mantelshelving') involves pressing down on one or both palms - usually on a ledge or a big hold - until your elbow locks straight, then by getting a foot on the same ledge you can take a hand off and reach a very long way. If the footholds beneath the ledge are poor it'll test your triceps strength, and you'll need reasonable hip flexibility and abdomen strength to lift your foot high enough, but when it works it can feel almost like levitation.

If the ledge is quite long consider heel-hooking on it before pressing up into the mantel. It can be easier on the triceps and your leg can help pull your weight closer to the rock.

If there's only a small place for your heel you'll have to take great care in placing it precisely. Remember that even though you may start off hanging from the back of your heel (with your toe pointing upwards), as you gain height your foot will roll until you're standing on the under-side of your heel (with your toe pointing horizontally). So make sure you leave enough room on the hold for your heel to roll onto.

Another useful foot trick when your heel is flat on a ledge or hold is to hook your toe under any available projection. Pressing upwards on your toe can help lever your weight up over your heel.

Topping-out with a mantelshelf

For many climbers, especially those used to clipping bolt belays and lowering-off, topping out on a route with a mantelshelf

A classic gritstone belly-flop. Anna Sherratt topping out on *Right Unconquerable* (HVS), Stanage Edge, The Peak District. Photo by Nick Smith.

is an object of dread. Typically, a mantleshelf top-out will go wrong when we're most stressed. The reasons for this is simply because when we get stressed we tend to focus on getting handholds when we should be paying attention to our feet. The result of this is we follow handholds back over the top, to the point where we can no longer see our feet, and then finally we 'beach' ourselves in a position where we can't even bend our legs.

The solution is to keep our hands on the lip of the top and resist the temptation to reach back for what may be better holds. Keep your eyes on your feet and build the height up gradually until you can step onto the top. If there are no footholds to build up on, you will be best off placing a heel-hook over the edge and using this as a third arm - in such an instance, holds set further back may be of use in allowing you roll sideways over the top.

Rockovers

A rockover is a move where you find yourself trying to stand up on a high foothold especially one that's off to the side. It's a great way of gaining plenty of height especially when there is an absence of handholds. At its most basic a rock-over is just applying the footwork ideas that we discussed at the beginning of this chapter - *page 162*. When pushed to the extreme rock-overs on footholds that are level with your hands can allow you to bypass a completely blank section of rock.

The aim in doing a rockover is to move your pelvis (and therefore your centre of gravity) so that it is directly above the foothold and as close into the rock as possible. Your body should be facing directly into the rock but your knee will be turned out so it projects horizontally.

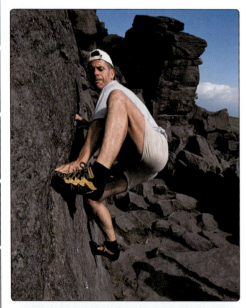

John Arran setting himself up for rocking over on *Ash Tree Variations* (VS) Burbage North, The Peak District, England. The trick is to get as much of your weight over the high foot as possible. Hip flexibility is a real advantage here.

Once you've got your weight directly over the foothold, your weight will come off your arms and onto your leg. Pressing up on your leg from this position is one of the few occasions in which strong legs are a real advantage in trad climbing. The important part is to keep your weight directly over the foot you are rocking onto. As you begin to straighten your leg your trailing foot will slide up directly underneath. On a slab you may reach a point where you are able to straighten your leg completely and stand in balance.

On steeper ground the rockover position will become harder to hold the higher you press up from it. Your trailing leg will need to be pushing ever harder against the flat wall and the friction of this foot against the wall may actually make it harder for you to press further up. Entering the rockover move with your trailing foot already higher (but still directly in line) can help, as can pushing up in a series of 'udging' movements rather than exerting constant pressure.

Rockover rests

Not just a great way of passing a blank section, a good rockover can also provide a welcome no-hands rest on steep rock.

If you have a large hold on a vertical wall, stand on it on one heel or on the ball of one foot, then lower yourself, dropping your other foot directly beneath you (don't put it on any holds) until your higher heel is tucked up by your crotch. By pressing your lower foot directly against the blank wall below, you may now be able to take both hands off completely, all your weight being on the single large foothold. Bear in mind that this technique places a considerable strain on your knee, especially on very steep rock!

Technique

Laybacking

A layback is where you pull with both hands on one side of a crack and push with both feet against the other. It's often dismissed as a technique for those who can't jam, but there are situations where it's by far the best approach.

The principle is that, if you exert enough outward pressure to both sides of a crack, the friction will prevent you sliding down it.

The art of laybacking is to optimise the distance between your hands and feet: when placed close together, you steepen your body position, use more arm strength, but push your feet directly into the rock making your foot placements very secure. By increasing the distance between your hands and feet you will be in a more balanced position, you will reduce the strain on your arms, but at the cost of making your foot placements more dependant on friction and face holds. Good judgement as to what you can trust with your feet will, therefore make laybacking a less tiring affair.

Laybacking is a wonderful technique for making upwards progress, but be warned, it can take a lot of effort, even to stay still, and taking a hand off for long enough to place gear may be all but impossible. Try to find jamming or bridging possibilities before committing yourself to a strenuous layback.

If you really have to layback, place gear as high as you can beforehand. If you think you need to place gear half way through, consider getting the piece ready before you start pulling. If it is a crack of consistent width then the right sized cam could be the quickest thing to place. Once you start climbing, try and get it over as quickly as possible before your time is up and your arms give way.

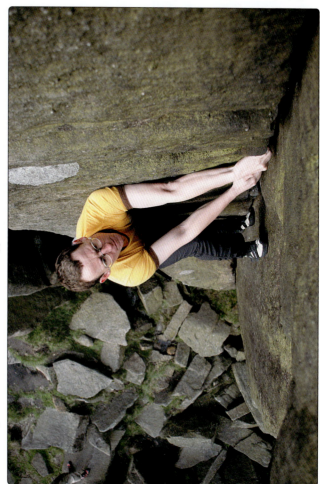

Jamie Veitch soloing *Brooks' Layback* (HS) Burbage North, The Peak District, England. Photo by Nick Smith.

Technique

Climbing different rock features

Corners and grooves

You are likely to encounter corners and grooves throughout your climbing career - they are natural lines of weakness in the rock so climbers have always aimed for them when establishing new routes.

As with many of the techniques we have discussed in this chapter, your footwork is key when climbing corners and usually your legs should be more tired when you get to the top if you have climbed one correctly.

Many corners have a crack at the back which is obviously useful for both your hands and your gear but utilising the walls and holds on either side of the crack for your feet is often the key to making progress. On vertical or even overhanging rock you can often stand in balance, 'bridged' across a corner using one foothold on each wall. By transferring your weight over each foot in turn, maybe using your opposite hand to push against the wall, you should find you can move upwards with few handholds or even none at all. Using one foot and one hand on either wall will feel the most natural, but depending on the availability of holds you should be prepared to vary this for each move.

Using both hands on one side while you move a foot is common and if the footholds on one side run out you may be able to walk both feet up the same side, while pressing down on a palm-hold on the other to complete the bridge. Leaning with your shoulder or your back against one wall of the corner can give a welcome rest while you place gear.

Another technique you can often use in corners is a layback - see page 179.

Meilee Rafe on the classic slate test-piece *German Schoolgirl* (E2), Rainbow Walls, Llanberis Slate, Wales.

Aretes

An arete is the opposite of a corner in that it is where two walls meet projecting from the face rather than being recessed within it.

At first acquaintance it's hard to see how such a blank feature could possibly be of any use, until you realise it's a huge side-pull to use whenever you choose. Indeed, if the arete edge is good, and the angle not too steep, you may be able to layback up it with no 'real' holds at all!

Their blank nature tends to make aretes quite hard to climb with limited possibilities for protection. This means they usually only occur on harder routes. If you do find one on an easier climb then enjoy it, since they offer exposed climbing often in a great position.

Once on the arete, keep a look for toe or heel-hooks to keep your balance while you move your hands between holds. Consider reaching your lower foot around the other side and hooking the arete with your heel.

When laybacking use your whole hand as usual but press hard on your fingertips rather than taking the strain on the base of your fingers. This will subtly change the direction of pull and may by just enough to stop you rotating - try it on a doorframe!

Adrian bouldering out the right-hand variation to *Crescent Arete* (E1), Stanage Plantation, The Peak District, England.

When things get steeper you'll often find yourself 'barn-dooring', which is when you aren't quite able to stay in balance on the arete and you start pivoting around and off it - swinging like an open barn door. Because of this, steep aretes are often climbed dynamically, laybacking with one hand and slapping the other between holds on the wall.

Technique

Overhangs

The problem with overhangs is that they're steep! There's no way to keep your weight over your feet so your arms have to take much of the strain. Hanging foot-loose will see even top climbers pump out quickly, so it's vital to find ways to keep weight on your arms to a minimum. Having said that, sometimes cutting loose momentarily to reposition your feet can be quicker and more efficient than a series of complicated foot movements.

It can help to split the problem into two: reaching the lip and turning it. Reaching the lip is often easiest from an undercut in the roof itself; even a very poor one can feel far easier than leaning out a long way from a good edge. While you're reaching out try to curve your back to the shape of the overhang so your centre of gravity stays as far in as possible. This back flexibility is often overlooked and can make a massive difference to your climbing.

Once you have holds on the lip of the overhang, a common problem is that of swinging wildly once your feet let go of the back wall. A big swing can send you straight off into space! In this case try to keep one hand under the roof until after you've released your feet, ideally not letting go with your trailing hand until you have a heel-hook on the lip.

Once your hands are on the lip try to throw a heel over as soon as possible to take some of the weight, as you gain height this can be changed to a toe which you should aim to get your weight over as soon as possible.

Pressing down into a mantelshelf on the lip is often a good solution, especially if there aren't any heel-hook options.

Cecile Rittweger using a heel as a third arm on *Flying Buttress Direct* (HVS), Stanage Edge, The Peak District, England.

Technique

Cracks

Cracks are almost synonymous with trad climbing, since without them there would be few opportunities for placing protection. Indeed it's no coincidence that the parts of the world where trad climbing is most popular are those where the rock offers more cracks.

But it's not just wires and cams that fit snugly in a crack; fingers, hands, arms and whole bodies can be stuffed in too and developing crack climbing skills is crucial to becoming an all-round trad climber.

Lee Meadows at the very top of *Tody's Wall* (HVS), Froggatt Edge, The Peak District, England. Photo by Nick Smith

Technique

Jams and locks

Finger locks

Thin cracks are rarely perfectly parallel and as the width of a crack varies you can often find tapered slots of just the right size for your fingers. These are called finger-locks which offer some of the most useful holds you will ever find. Because your fingers are mechanically wedged, your fingers don't need to be pulling at all to stay in place, which can even feel restful. The only real decision you'll have to make is whether to place your fingers in thumb-up or thumb-down position.

Thumb-down is often more secure - especially in small or shallow jams - but if you need to reach a long way above it will be far easier from a thumb-up jam.

Finger jams

In slightly wider or more parallel cracks your fingers won't lock by themselves. Thumb-down is the order of the day here and the two things to try are pulling your elbow down (so each finger gets more horizontal) and curling your fingers inside the crack, both of which make your fingers wider and wedges them more securely. Bracing your thumb under your forefinger can help too.

Finger-crack foot placements

The hardest thing about climbing thin cracks is often the dearth of footholds. You're never going to be able to insert your whole foot into a crack you are finger-jamming, so be prepared to smear on the edge of the crack - and keep an eye for any face holds which will make a massive difference. If one edge of the crack projects further than the other, or you're in a corner, you will probably find that laybacking with your feet while finger jamming with your hands is the best combination.

Having a shoe with a narrow toe profile will help and turning your foot through 90° - so your big toe is directly above your little toe - will help you get as much of your shoe in contact with the rock as possible.

Above: a thumb-down finger lock.
Right: a twisted toe in a thin crack.

Technique 181

Ring locks

Ring locks are used on cracks that are too wide for finger jams, but too narrow for hand jams (a.k.a. off-fingers). They are not nearly as secure as finger and hand jams but sometimes, you have no choice.

❶ To place a ring lock, start by placing your thumb on the inside of the crack. This will serve as the base of the lock.

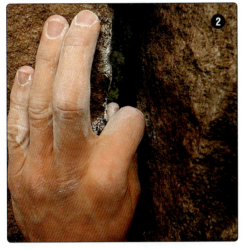

❷ Now place your index finger in the space between your thumbnail and the opposite side of the crack.

❸ Now stack the remaining fingers on top and with a bit of fiddling around you should be able to get it to lock.

Ring locks are easier on cracks with sharp edges than they are on cracks with rounded edges. If the crack has very rounded edges, you will probably be better of sticking your hand in as far as you can and making do with a very poor flaring hand-jam. Ring locks require space for your hand to the side of the crack, so in these photos it is clear that it would not be possible to place ring locks with the right hand.

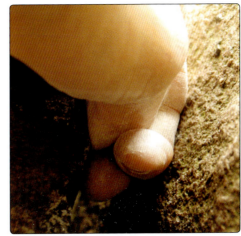

Hand jams

You either love them or you hate them, depending on whether you ever learned to do them properly! Hand jamming is not only an essential technique for crack climbing, it's also a great way to rest on many other routes, as it only takes one good jam and you may be able to completely rest your fingers.

Hand jams work by expanding the width of your hand to fit the crack. This is achieved by two separate actions: most importantly the muscle at the base of your thumb is moved towards the centre of your palm, this is all that is needed for tight hand jams and creates the most restful and secure jams - the thumb itself does very little. Secondly, the fingers can be pressed down to create an opposing force between your finger-tips and the back of your hand. This is more crucial on wider jams where your thumb-muscle is unable to produce enough width.

When you have placed your hand jam, weight it gradually until the skin on the back of your hand is fully stretched. You're now ready to pull hard on the jam without it feeling like it's going to slip out. If it hurts, hunt around for another placement, there's usually a better one if you look for it.

Jams can be placed with your thumb pointing upwards or downwards: thumb-up jams are preferred when the crack is a comfortable size. A thumbs-down jam will work better in narrower placements but you won't be able to reach far above it with your other hand. Corner or diagonal cracks are usually best jammed with one thumb-up jam and one thumb-down jam.

Foot jams

As with all climbing techniques, the feet should be doing all the work. Foot jams work simply by inserting your foot into the crack and with the 'big toe' side of the shoe pointing upwards. The foot is jammed in by rotating it as far as necessary until it sticks. You don't need to shove your whole foot into the crack, just enough to stand on, too much and you'll struggle to get it out again! Foot jamming can be painful in soft shoes or slippers, so a stiff shoe is recommended.

Above: a solid hand jam.
Right: a twisted foot jam.

Technique

Fist jams

Fist jams are less useful than you might imagine and often painful. A clenched fist can be wedged so that the edges of your index finger and little finger touch the sides of the crack. Some people prefer to hand jam cracks of fist-size, even though such wide hand jams feel relatively insecure and strenuous.

It's often best to keep your thumb outside your fist but experiment and see what works for you. The expansion range of a fist jam is very small so it's critical to place it very carefully in exactly the right place in the crack. If the crack is too wide for good fists, try twisting to the side to get more purchase on the crack - doing this with both fists together can be enough to move your feet up - which should take most of the strain - the one consolation for climbing fist-sized cracks is that they tend to offer the best footholds.

Off-fists

When cracks are just too wide for fist jamming, you can be sure you're going to be suffering. The first option is to cheat and tape your hands up (*see page 184*) until they are wide enough to jam securely. You will need to pay particular attention to taping the sides of your fists to make this work for you.

There are a couple of techniques available that allow jams to be placed in cracks slightly too wide for fists. The first is known as a **teacup jam**, this involves extending the width of your fist by pushing out your thumb as though it were the handle of a teacup. It would certainly be a good idea to tape your thumbs for this - and prepare for some discomfort.

A less painful method is to expand the width of your fist jams by placing them in the crack, then rotating them in the crack until they stick. The approved method here is to place your upper fist jam with your palm facing down, and you lower fist jam with your palm facing up. Now rotate both fists (top fist anti-clockwise, bottom fist clockwise) and you should be able to get enough purchase to build your feet up and shuffle the jams up the crack.

It is also possible to enlarge a fist jam by rocking it to the side - though your body position will be more crucial in getting them to lock securely.

Jams and cams

A top tip for climbing cracks is to relate your jams to cam sizes. For example, a good finger jam may equal a Number 1 Friend or a Camalot 0.5, a good hand jam may equal a Friend 2 or a Camalot 1. This way you will always know what cam to reach for depending on the type of jam you can place. Similarly, if someone tells you that a certain crack takes, size 1.5 Friends for its full length, you know that there's a good chance you're going to be trying to climb it on insecure finger jams.

Technique

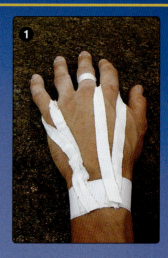

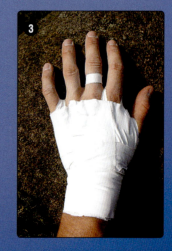

Matt Goode, Cookie Cliff, Yosemite. Taping-up is essential if you're heading off on long granite cracks - unless you have skin like a rhino. Photo by Alex Messenger.

Technique

Taping

Once dismissed as only for the soft or for those without technique, the practice of taping your hands for hand jamming cracks is now much more common - maybe because it makes jamming easier and less painful, and enables you to do it for longer.

For both these methods you will need a wide roll of climbing tape - a knife or scissors will help too.

Tape gloves

This method creates a 'tape glove' that can be removed and re-used. It is well suited to situations where you are going to be doing a lot of jamming.

Start off with a band of tape around your wrist. Then run two thinner strips of tape from your wrist, down your hand, around your digits and back to the wrist - ❶.

Run these thinner strips for your index and little fingers - include your thumb if you expect to fist jam - ❷. Now all you have to do is tape over the spaces and keep adding tape until you're happy it's thick enough - ❸.

You want it thick enough to protect, but not so thick that you can't use the jams! To remove, just snip through the wrist tape and pull off - hairy guys may wish to *depilate* before starting!

Palm taping

A quicker method is to simply tape around the base of your palm. Starting on your palm - ❹ - wrap the tape around the base of your hand so that your knuckles are just covered - ❺. It is important to clench your fist while taping the back of your hand or the tight tape will prevent you from bending your fingers. Continue wrapping the tape around your hand passing alternately past each side of your thumb to help keep the tape in place - ❻ - and - ❼.

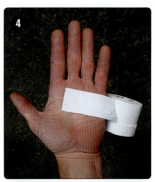

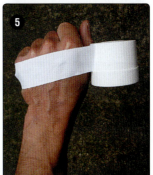

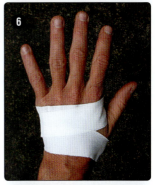

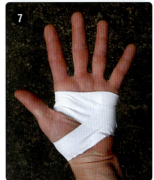

Off-widths

An off-width is any crack too wide to fist jam but too narrow to crawl into. They've long been the stuff of nightmares in Yosemite, where top climbers often turn to jelly when faced with an off-width pitch, even though its grade may be much lower than that of the rest of the route. Thankfully they are now easily protected with large cams.

Off-width climbing can be improvisation at its finest, it's rarely fast or pretty and it's usually exhausting. Here are some suggestions:

A chicken-wing: the palm pushes to lock arm into the crack by forcing the elbow in the opposite direction

Photo by Alex Messenger

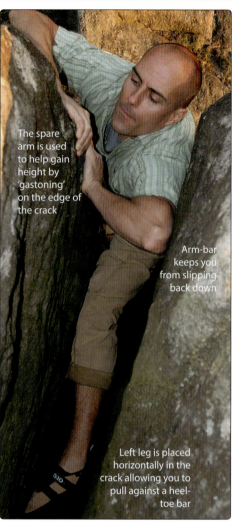

The spare arm is used to help gain height by 'gastoning' on the edge of the crack

Arm-bar keeps you from slipping back down

Left leg is placed horizontally in the crack allowing you to pull against a heel-toe bar

Chicken-winging

The technique for cracks not much wider than your arm is to put your straight arm deep into the crack and then try to make your arm wider by pushing hard against opposite sides with your palm and your elbow. It never feels secure but it may be just enough.

Arm-barring

Arm-barring is for slightly wider cracks. Put your bent arm in as deep as possible elbow-first, such that your palm lies against the inside of the crack, next to but facing away from your chest. With the right size crack your arm will cam across the crack and take almost no effort to hold you in. Moving up though is a different matter!

Hand-stacking

There is also a technique called stacked-jamming, where both hands or fists are placed side-by-side to create a single, much wider jam. A nice idea, but moving this jam is virtually impossible unless your feet are wedged above your head!

Technique

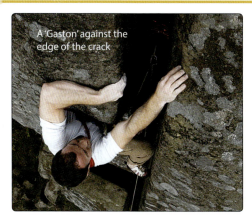
A 'Gaston' against the edge of the crack

Pull toes back to lock heel-toe in the back of the crack

Gastons

A 'Gaston' is where you use a hand to pull against the side of the crack. You can only chicken-wing or arm bar with one arm at a time, so these techniques are often best used with a gaston. If this technique fails entirely, you may find yourself using opposing gastons - good luck!

Leg jams

If the crack is just the right size for you, you should be able to get a good jam by inserting your knee deep into the crack and bending your leg - jamming securely into the crack. This can be a solid and secure position but as with many jams, upwards movement is a struggle.

Pushing down against a heel-toe does most of the height gaining

Off-width footwork

For off-widths you're best off wedging your foot across the crack - toe and heel. You will probably find it easier to pull against a heel-toe than to push against it, in which case place one foot deep into the crack, and as high as you can, set a heel-toe lock and use your leg as if it were a third arm.

A stiff shoe here can make it feel like you're standing on a ledge, whereas a soft shoe may mean pain and insecurity.

Gear and clothes

Off-width cracks require big cams, but before you set off, decide which way you're going to face, then place all your big cams on your outside gear loop so they don't get in the way. Some off-widths come with rocks jammed in place (chockstones) which you can thread with a sling. On a long off-width you will probably want to shift a cam up the crack as you climb - if you decide to do this it is a good idea to clip it with a sling so it doesn't drag the rope up each time you move it above your head. Lastly, the more bare flesh you show to an off-width, the more it will eat you alive - thick clothing like jeans will make life a lot more bearable, as do long sleeves.

Chimneys

By now you've probably realised that all jamming is just pushing outwards on both sides of a crack at once, so what better way than to get completely inside a crack and use the strength of your legs to do the pushing? Naturally the crack has to be of monstrous proportions, but once snugly in place you can achieve an almost foetal-like security.

The classic chimney position is to have your back against one wall and both feet against the other wall, pressing your hands behind you as you shuffle your back up the wall - this is generally called 'back-and-footing'.

If the chimney gets tight you'll be better off tucking one foot on the wall behind you and bracing with your arms while you shift both feet up at once.

Very wide chimneys will need to be bridged with one foot on either side. Face in to find gear, face out for the view.

Above: Alex Mason putting up a good fight against *Tower Chimney* (E1), Stanage Edge, The Peak District, England.

Right: once the cracks start getting really wide things get far less claustrophobic and the climbing also gets easier.
Photo by Duncan Skelton

Which technique when?

Initially it may be difficult to know which combination of techniques will work best for any given route. Indeed deciding which holds to use, and exactly how to use them, provides much of the technical challenge of climbing. With experience you'll find you are able to do quite complex moves instinctively, simply by having encountered and learned from many similar situations in the past.

Try to concentrate on your technique whatever grade of climb you're on and however hard you're finding it. Sometimes your technique will suffer when it gets hard, and sometimes it will do so on easier climbs when you're not concentrating, but only by practising can you expect it to improve.

Bouldering is a great way to work on technique, as your judgement won't be clouded by fear. Try repeating problems you've already done in as many different ways as you can and think carefully about why some ways work better than others. If you are really keen you could try videoing yourself and your friends doing the same problems and analysing what you're each doing differently.

Also remember that the easiest way through a sequence is not necessarily the best way when you're facing the prospect of a leader-fall. Dynamic moves can feel great on a boulder problem but terrifying on lead!

Use the jams in the crack or the holds on the face? Decisions, decisions... Maria Michails on Wicker *Cranium* (5.9) Squamish, Canada.

Paul Evans climbing *Comes the Dervish* (E3) Llanberis Slate Quarries, North Wales.

Tactics

To improve your climbing standard you can train many things. You can get stronger, fitter, and more flexible; learn to read moves better, place gear more quickly and learn to cope with the stresses of the sharp end. But when you arrive at a crag with a route in mind it's too late for all that. You are not suddenly going to get better as a climber but there are still many things you can do to improve your chances of getting up your target route.

Tactics are ways of making the most of your current ability and turning it into success on your chosen route.

Tactics

Styles

Trad climbing has no real 'rules'; this is one of the reasons many people are attracted to it. You are largely free to choose what you want to climb and how you want to climb it. What matters most is that you don't spoil it for others, such as by chipping holds or hogging a route for hours on end. Beyond that it's largely up to you to choose how you want to climb.

While many people would agree that the most fulfilling way to climb a route is to start at the bottom and work it out as you go up, there are occasions when sticking rigidly to this approach will limit the range of great climbing experiences available to you.

As a result, a great many terms have evolved to describe the style in which climbs are done. What's more, these terms and definitions are continually adapting, with the result that very few climbers ever seem to agree on their precise meaning at any one time. But climbers are a competitive bunch, always striving to succeed on routes in the best possible manner. When they share their experiences in the pub or café afterwards, you'll often hear them use (or misuse!) the following terms to describe the way they climbed.

Free

A free ascent is one where no gear has been weighted. For an ascent to be free, you can't have rested on gear, or used direct aid by pulling on gear. Reversing to the ground to rest or re-think is fine, as is coming back another day if it doesn't feel right the first time. The term 'free' is also often mis-used by non-climbers to mean solo climbing without ropes.

Onsight

An onsight ascent is one where you had no knowledge as to how to do the climb prior to your successful ascent. Of course you can get a good idea of what to expect by studying it from the ground, or by climbing other routes nearby, and sometimes the guidebook will offer helpful advice.

Flash

If you get to the top of a route first time without falling, you've flashed it. You can't have top-roped any of the moves or failed on a previous attempt. A flash is distinguished from an onsight by the presence of 'beta' - helpful information about the climb: if you've watched other people on a route to see how they climb it, or asked people who've done it for specific advice, then your ascent will be considered a flash rather than an onsight.

Yo-Yo

If you fall off a route you may choose to lower to the ground (or the last hands-free rest), leaving your rope in place and trying the route again. This is called 'yo-yoing', and it isn't widely practised now that top-rope rehearsal has become accepted as a legitimate - albeit less than ideal - tactic.

Headpoint

The term headpoint comes from its sport climbing equivalent: redpoint, which means climbing a bolt-protected route from bottom to top in one go regardless of the amount of top-rope practice required. On a successful headpoint all protection will be placed during the ascent. The very hardest trad climbs have only ever been headpointed, as they are so dangerous that a fall may be unthinkable.
More on headpointing on page 204.

Tactics

Pre-placed gear

On many climbs, particularly multi-pitch routes, there is no convenient way to get the gear out after a fall, as you cannot easily run around to the top and abseil. In these cases it is common to lower to the belay, pull the ropes and try again with some of the gear in place. While it certainly 'taints' your ascent somewhat it's often a better option than failing completely. Routes that have only been climbed in this style still await a truly clean ascent.

Many routes have been climbed after protection has been pre-placed on abseil. While such ascents are still free ascents, the general consensus amongst climbers is that deliberately pre-placing protection is a style that can and should be improved upon, and that routes established in such a way should be clearly reported as such.

Soloing

Soloing means climbing alone. In free-climbing terms it usually means climbing without using a rope or any protection, although there are ways to self-belay, in which case it is usually called roped-soloing.

John Arran soloing on gritstone during his record setting ascent of five hundred routes in one day.
The route is *High Flyer* (E2) Burbage North, Peak District, England.

While many climbers choose to solo - particularly on shorter crags where the rock is solid like gritstone - it is not usually considered better style, even though it may be more impressive. Of course there are some routes that are soloed by necessity, having no options at all for placing protection. Soloing such a route is in fact no different from leading it and the route will have been given a grade that reflects this.

Tactics

Choice of style

There are some who would argue that onsight is the only real way to climb and that anything else is somehow cheating! While it is true that many of your most memorable climbs are likely to be those you've climbed onsight, if you stick to this rigidly you will miss out on many great climbs, and may well develop your climbing skills less rapidly than you otherwise might.

To onsight or not to onsight?

If you really want to try a hard climb ask yourself whether you ever will feel able and confident enough to try it onsight. If the answer is yes or maybe, consider saving it for later. Otherwise, rather than never climbing the route, a bit of inside knowledge or some top-rope rehearsal may be enough to convince you to go for the lead after all. Afterwards you could end up regretting you didn't try it onsight, if it wasn't as hard or as scary as you'd feared, but equally you may have found it desperate and really enjoyed the challenge of a headpoint or even top-roped ascent. Even if you do headpoint routes you wished you'd onsighted, your ascent will have taught you a valuable lesson, and will probably give you the confidence to try other routes onsight.

... or to flash?

Would it lessen the experience for you if someone told you the best way to do the crux and what gear goes in best just below? Or are all such tips welcome? Will you be you happy to trust that thread you've heard is getting quite old now, or should you abseil down and replace it beforehand? Getting some useful information may lose you the onsight - but it could still be a very satisfying way of climbing something hard, and as with headpointing, it will probably boost your confidence so that next time you may be willing to try another route onsight. Sometimes limiting yourself to just 'gear beta', is a good way of preserving the onsight climbing experience, and yourself at the same time!

Adrian Berry headpointing *Diazepan* (25), The Grampians, Australia. Photo by Carole McGloughlin

Tactics

Conditions

The term 'conditions' refers to the external factors affecting the difficulty of a climb. With experience, you will find that the level at which you can climb is strongly affected by conditions.

Heat

While it's pretty obvious that wet rock is not good for climbing on, fewer climbers are aware that climbing in the heat makes everything feel much harder. When it's hot the rubber on your shoes softens making it harder to stand on poor footholds, your feet swell making your shoes feel too tight, your hands sweat making sloping holds much harder to use and necessitate hanging on longer so you can chalk-up. The heat also saps strength and if you start to dehydrate your energy levels will plummet.

Cold

Climbing in the cold makes sense for climbing styles such as hard slabs and rock types such as gritstone where friction is all important - the important thing is ensure you are fully warm, cold fingers give very little tactile information and are prone to injury.

A good tip to test if you're fingers are warm is to touch them to the back of your neck - if your neck feels warm, your fingers are too cold. If you're heading out in the cold, remember to take plenty of warm clothes, pay extra attention to warming up and keep moving.

Avoiding poor conditions

Getting on a hard route when the conditions are not right is often a demoralising waste of time, so do all you can to make sure your route will be in condition; maybe ask around to see if other climbers have been on it recently and if it was dirty or damp in places. If you arrive at the base of your route and you can see wet rock, or if it's hot and sweaty, consider returning after a dry spell, or later in the day when the sun has moved around. Other things worth bearing in mind are distractions from other climbers. For example, if someone is having a mini-epic on the route next-door, maybe it would be wise to return when it's quieter. Lastly, make sure you choose a day when the weather is right; you'll have enough on your hands already without worrying about it raining when you're half-way up.

Your condition

In addition to getting the conditions just right, it is of course at least as important to be in good condition yourself! To climb at your best, you will naturally want to arrive at the crag well rested. This doesn't necessarily mean that you should have had a rest day just beforehand, but it does mean your forearms shouldn't still be aching from having overdone it the previous day!

Matt Heason soloing *Taurus Crack* (VS) on a cold Stanage Edge, The Peak District, England.

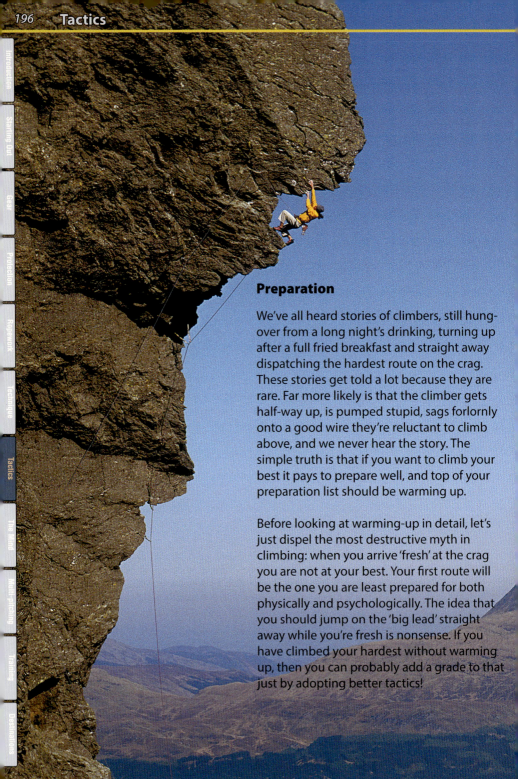

Preparation

We've all heard stories of climbers, still hung-over from a long night's drinking, turning up after a full fried breakfast and straight away dispatching the hardest route on the crag. These stories get told a lot because they are rare. Far more likely is that the climber gets half-way up, is pumped stupid, sags forlornly onto a good wire they're reluctant to climb above, and we never hear the story. The simple truth is that if you want to climb your best it pays to prepare well, and top of your preparation list should be warming up.

Before looking at warming-up in detail, let's just dispel the most destructive myth in climbing: when you arrive 'fresh' at the crag you are not at your best. Your first route will be the one you are least prepared for both physically and psychologically. The idea that you should jump on the 'big lead' straight away while you're fresh is nonsense. If you have climbed your hardest without warming up, then you can probably add a grade to that just by adopting better tactics!

Tactics

Warming up

An effective warm-up will ensure you have:
1) Muscles that can pull as hard as possible and for as long as possible
2) Your best range of mobility
3) The lowest chance of injuring yourself
4) The best possible familiarity with the type of rock and the type of moves expected
5) A positive and confident frame of mind

The psychological benefits of a good trad climbing warm-up may be at least as beneficial as the physical ones, since how relaxed and confident you are can make an enormous difference to how easily and efficiently you climb.

The first part of any warm-up should be exactly that: getting warm. Often the walk-in to the crag carrying a backpack full of hardware will have you peeling off layers to avoid overheating, but for roadside crags you may need a little more. Jogging on the spot can work well, as can a brisk walk or jog to each end of the crag to re-acquaint yourself with possible options for the day. In cold weather try to get your body warmed up before leaving the house, and keep the car heater on higher than usual to give yourself a head start.

Once your body is warm it's safe to stretch. Stretching will not only allow you to contort into odd positions, it will help prevent all sorts of tweaks and strains when you suddenly ask a lot of a particular joint near the limit of its extension.

As well as stretching at ground level it can also be useful to continue stretching on your first route. The grade should be very easy for you, and it's a good idea to deliberately seek out or exaggerate any bridging, high-step and shoulder-extension moves as you climb.

The number of routes you climb before being fully warmed up will vary a lot, but three decent-length pitches is probably a good average. Try to climb pitches of similar length to your goal route so you're using the same energy systems. Ideally you will start with a route many grades lower than your maximum and work up gradually. Where possible start on large holds first and move on to longer reaches and smaller holds. If you're climbing a long multi-pitch route you may be able to warm up on the lower pitches, but if the crux is very low down consider doing a couple of other pitches before you start, maybe even at a different crag. Failing that try to simulate it by traversing the bottom for a while, or even climbing up and down the first section of your route until you feel it's starting to flow more easily. If all the routes at the crag are too hard to warm up on, you can traverse around the base keeping your feet on the ground so you can vary the force on your fingers - also if you have a home wall, consider warming up before you set off assuming the crag isn't that far away.

Your warm-up pitches should, wherever possible, reflect the type of climbing you're expecting on your goal pitch. If you're aiming for a hard finger-crack try to find easier finger-cracks to warm up on. Not only will you prepare your muscles and joints well for what they are to expect later but you'll also prepare your head. A very thin bridging corner will look a lot less intimidating if you've just cruised up a slightly easier one, and you'll waste a lot less time and energy worrying.

Dave MacLeod on *Dalriada* (E7), The North Peak of The Cobbler, Arrochar, Scotland.
Photo by Dave Cuthbertson.

Tactics

Eat, drink and be merry

Making sure that you have enough glycogen (food) in your muscles is key. As is being sufficiently hydrated, since performance decreases significantly even before you realise you're thirsty. Eating small amounts regularly throughout the day is best, high G.I. foods such as bananas and white bread are rapidly absorbed, whereas lower G.I. foods such as flapjacks and dried fruit release energy more gradually. G.I. stands for *Glycaemic Index*, and there is a wealth of information on this subject available online.

Watch what you wear

There are few things better at putting you off trying a hard lead than getting cold belaying. While you're doing your warm-up routes it's better to get too hot climbing than to freeze at the top bringing your second up. Maybe clip an extra fleece to the back of your harness to belay in, alternatively, compact wind-proofs can make a huge difference to your warmth in a breeze - they often pack up to next-to-nothing and can be clipped onto the back of your harness.

Hats and gloves are easily carried too and can make a big difference in preventing numb fingers. Maybe consider hauling the clothes up after pulling a rope free - or leaving them at the top of the route if you start at the top.

When it comes to your target route, be careful not to overdo the warm clothing. You'll probably be working very hard and generating a lot of heat, so focus on lightweight clothing that gives you good mobility. If you make it up the pitch you should be happy enough not to mind getting chilly at the top! Aim to feel a little cool when setting off.

Clean your shoes

The soles of your shoes are your main contact with the rock and with the evolution of rubber technology we now enjoy a level of friction that would have been unthinkable a few decades ago. However, this advantage will be completely lost if you start with wet, muddy or sandy shoes, and even a little dust can make a big difference on friction-dependent smears and laybacks.

Before you start, check that the soles of your shoes look black, clean and dry. If they need cleaning give them a good wipe, then apply a little water (spit works well) and rub until 'squeaky' dry.

Remember also that clean, sticky shoes will pick up dirt again while you're climbing, so when you get to a good ledge or resting place use the opportunity to give your soles a quick wipe again, so you have maximum confidence in them at all times.

Paul Dyson taking time for a quick snack between routes at Arapiles, Australia. Next stop: *Kachoong*!

Tactics

Learn by looking

When you're on a climb you'll rarely see more than three or four moves ahead very clearly, and if you can't spot a gear placement or place to rest it can be very hard to commit yourself with that level of uncertainty. Having spent some time 'reading a route' from the ground can make a huge difference to your chances. Knowing there's a crack just beyond that bulge, or that the roof you're approaching has a big jug on its lip, will make you feel a whole lot better about continuing.

Route reading

There are three things to look for when viewing a route from the ground: moves, gear and rests. Working moves out from a distance is never easy, but with practice it's surprising how much you can learn in advance. Try standing well back and walking left or right to look from different angles. You may get a much better idea as to whether that blank-looking section will be a thin, hard crux, whether it has a big hold in the middle you couldn't spot from underneath, or whether you'll be better off traversing a little and climbing around it.

If it's a popular route there may be chalk on the holds people use the most, and if it's a hard route there may also be tick-marks next to critical handholds or footholds that are particularly useful and hard to spot on lead.

Cracks usually mean gear and if you've been warming up on similar routes you'll have a good idea of what type of cracks will take what type of gear. Make a mental note of what you're likely to need where and make sure you don't use your last piece of that size before you get there! If you know you'll be able to rest afterwards you'll be that much happier to run it out through a committing and strenuous section. Apart from obvious ledges, look for small corners you can bridge across, big holes or pockets you may be able to crawl into, or knee-bar across, and big flakes you can stuff your whole arm behind.

Break a route into sections

A long and tiring pitch can be a daunting prospect, but if you can identify probable rests and good gear you can reduce the problem to a series of smaller challenges. Focusing on each section in turn can stop you getting disheartened when you're already mega-pumped and still less than halfway up!

Route reading at the top of Huntsman's Leap, Pembroke, Wales.

Tactics

Tailor your rack

While a standard rack may work well for most routes, when you're pushing your grade you should question very carefully what you carry with you. Taking too much gear has three negative effects: firstly it weighs you down, making everything more strenuous than it needs to be, secondly it makes you feel encumbered, and thirdly, the more gear you have, the harder it can be to locate the piece you want.

Racking up is very closely related to route-reading. You can't choose what gear to take with you on a climb until you've had a good look at the route. It's usually better to err on the side of caution, as getting to crucial runner placements that you can't make use of will have more of a detrimental affect on your climbing than carrying a couple of extra pieces that you don't use.

Looking at the route, the first thing you need to work out is what size range to take. If the route is a series of wide cracks then you are naturally going to want to take some big gear. Alternatively, if your route is a thin slab with hairline cracks, you'd be better off taking plenty of small wires and micro-cams, leaving the big stuff in your sack. It is generally better to leave out big stuff that you don't envisage using, than small stuff simply because big gear placements are easier to spot, and the weight saving is greater with big stuff than small stuff. Lastly, don't forget you'll need some gear for the belay!

Once you've decided what sort of gear to take, you need to work out roughly how much to take. Once again, err on the side of caution as it's better to top out with a couple of extra quickdraws than it is to run out with ten metres of protectable hard climbing remaining.

Take the length of the route and the distance at which you'll be happy (or forced) to run it out, and divide the former by the latter to know how many placements you are likely to be using. So if your pitch is forty metres, and you are expecting to place a piece every two metres, that's twenty pieces. Of course there will be instances where you run it out on easy ground, or stop and place several pieces together, but on average you should be expecting to be able to place twenty. This may well translate to taking three sets of wires, a set and a half of cams, and fourteen quickdraws. Needless to say if you only have eight quickdraws, you're very likely to run out - in one way or the other.

Tools of the trade in Indian Creek, John Varco sorting out a typical monster rack of cams for a desert crack-line. Photo by Ian Parnell.

Tactics

Optimising your rack

There are some good tricks to optimising your rack so you don't carry unnecessary gear. Much of the gear we carry is wasted, even when we place it. For example, a cam placed then extended with a quickdraw. Often the cam will be placed with its own racking karabiner, then extended with a quickdraw, using three karabiners in total. A cam with an extendable sling may avoid using those extra karabiners. Alternatively you could just place a sling through the cam's own sling, joining the ends to the rope with the karabiner from the cam - saving a quickdraw and allowing you to save two karabiners from your rack for each cam you extend.

A good way of saving weight is to optimise the number of screw-gate karabiners you carry. While, ideally, belays should be built with screw-gates for optimum safety, if a karabiner is under tension, and not in contact with anything that could interfere with the gate, it won't be a problem. A couple of belay screw-gates is probably all you need.

Another area is how gear can be used for multiple jobs. We've already looked at how slingdraws can remove the need to carry extra short slings, and how using a prusik loop to attach your chalk-bag ensures you've always got a spare prusik without taking up harness space. Consider also things like the karabiner you carry your nut key on. If you like to take a nut key when you lead (can be very useful for threading slings through holes and cleaning out dirty cracks), it may seem good strategy to rack it with a non-load-bearing 'accessory' karabiner to save weight, but if you use a screw-gate instead - you'll be able to use it to build your belay as well as carry your nut key - saving some weight and space.

Tactical racking

Reducing the clutter on your harness makes it easier to find the items you're looking for. While on slabby, low grade routes you can stand around for ages looking for things, when you're hanging off your arms you need to be able to locate the right piece as quickly as possible. Whichever way you rack, consider placing size-critical pieces at the front of your harness where you can see them, and non size-critical pieces at the back (such as quickdraws), put other gear such as your belay device, prusiks and screw-gates at the back of your harness out of the way.

It is always a good idea to rack items according to size, this will help you quickly identify the right size. Wires are best racked according to size, so you might have one karabiner with small wires, one with medium, and one with large - oval karabiners seem best for racking wires - again, use full-strength karabiners for racking gear as you will probably find yourself wanting to clip it one day.

Too much gear?

If, after optimising your rack, you still find your harness struggling to fit all your gear - firstly consider changing your harness to one with more gear loops - five or more is ideal. Next, you can make a lot of space by Yosemite racking your quickdraws - simply clip the first to your gear loop, then clip subsequent *identical* quickdraws to the top karabiner of the first. Lastly, consider an over-the-shoulder bandolier, purpose made ones are much more comfortable than a thin sling.

Tactics when climbing

Be prepared to adapt

When you're on the route things can look very different from what they appeared from the ground and you should be prepared to make some fast decisions. One common problem is that you've misjudged the scale of the wall from a distance, and all the cracks are much bigger than you expected, in which case you'll have to be careful not to use up all your biggest cams too soon.

Hopefully your expected resting places won't disappoint, but the length of time you hang around at each will vary. Unless you're on a big ledge there'll be a limit to how long you can 'milk' a rest before some part of your body starts to get pumped or painful. Look for ways to vary the resting position and try to get a feel very quickly for how long you'll be able to hang around, so you can be mentally prepared when the time comes to move on.

While you're resting use your time to make certain your gear's as good as it can be and have a good look at the holds and moves above so you're ready to launch into a sequence without hesitation when the time comes.

Tactics

When the going gets tough ...

... Go for it!

As long as the gear keeps coming, and the potential fall would be safe, there should be few reasons to back off, even if you're completely pumped. Try to think rationally. Have you even seriously tried the moves, or have you been too preoccupied with getting (or failing to get) gear in? After all, the next hold might be a jug then you'll have done it! And what's the worst-case outcome? If your top runner fails, is it really a big deal to fall onto the previous one? If you can't find a convincing reason to back off, don't!

... Run away!

Sooner or later you'll find yourself in a situation where you're unsure about the gear, the moves above feel desperate, you'll have run out of ideas and you'll wish you were no longer there. This is the time to take a few deep breaths and consider your options. Climbing down is best if you can; not only will this mean not testing the gear, but if you make it to the ground without weighting the gear you won't have blown the onsight and you can come back another day to finish where you left off.

Lowering off is the other option and whether you're down-climbing or lowering you should think very carefully about your ropework. Assuming you're climbing on double ropes, and that the gear at your high point isn't the best, consider equalising it and clipping it all into only one rope. That way as you descend, your belayer can take in on the free rope and any gear you have in lower down on that rope will become more useful as you get closer to it.

To fight another day

Whether you're successful or not on a hard route, if you're pumped afterwards the best way to recover is to climb more! Whether you're wanting to try another hard route later in the day, or to be as fresh as possible for tomorrow, take a break then warm down on one or more easy routes or alternatively do some gentle traversing. This will stimulate the blood flow to your muscles and help clear any remaining lactic acid, actually speeding up the recovery process. Some light stretching can help too. Just make sure any climbing you do is very, very easy!

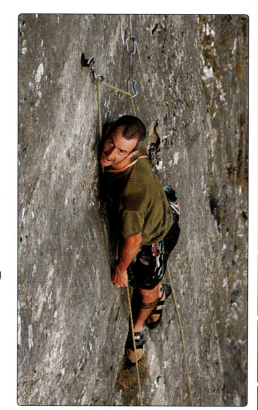

Both photos: Mike Grant on an onsight attempt at *Darius* (E2) High Tor, The Peak District, England.

Turning failure into success

If you are onsighting routes near your limit, inevitably there will come a time when you fall or have to hang on your gear. Disappointing as it may be, at least it shows you were being ambitious in your choice of objective. The question then becomes: what to do next?

One option is to rest, boulder out the moves you couldn't do, and continue to the top. This may be convenient but 'dogging it' (as this is termed) means you won't get the satisfaction of having successfully led the route, since you were using aid while you were hanging on the gear.

Ground-up

An alternative is to lower off, pull your ropes and try it again. Knowing how to climb the lower section you should be able to climb to your high-point more efficiently this time, giving you a better chance of continuing.

In an ideal world you would take all the gear out and re-place it on each attempt, but in reality this is often impractical. Besides, doing so would usually mean having to abseil the route, and that could take away much of the fun of working out the higher moves onsight. A 'ground-up' ascent can be an ideal choice if you've slipped unexpectedly low down on a route. You'll still keep much of the onsight experience, and it'll be a whole lot more rewarding than having aided it.

Headpointing

Headpointing is climbing a route after any amount of rehearsal. Having perfected the moves and knowing the best gear placements, climbers can usually headpoint routes up to three grades harder than they can onsight. Remember though that the adjectival (E) grade describes the difficulty of onsighting a route and isn't intended to assess headpoint ascents.

An obvious way to start is to try headpointing a route you failed to onsight; particularly one you didn't feel able to commit to because you weren't sure whether the gear would be good enough. After a quick session on top-rope you'll know the best way to do the moves and you'll know exactly where the best gear is. Leading it may then feel like a formality. This can do wonders for your confidence when you come to try onsighting another route at that grade. Be careful not to use this tactic too often though or there's a danger of your mind becoming conditioned to expect top-rope rehearsal before committing to any hard-looking climbing.

The greatest intrinsic rewards from headpointing come on routes you find very hard indeed, such that you wouldn't even dream of trying them onsight. A hard headpoint ascent will push both your mental and physical limits in a way that onsighting rarely can. Because the level of difficulty is much higher and the danger involved can be much greater, you'll need to do everything possible to control the risks you're taking and reduce them to an acceptable level.

Optimum protection

With no limit to the amount of preparation possible, you should try every available gear placement option and decide what works best. Because you're not restricted to a standard lead rack, this could include anything from tied-down skyhooks to hand-placed pegs. Indeed, anything you're able to place while you're leading that isn't going to cause any damage. In extreme cases a hard headpoint can be as much of an engineering challenge as a physical climbing one!

A big swing can often be reduced by using a second belayer stood well to one side and they can help even if the rope they're belaying you on isn't clipped into any runners.
If you're not sure whether a piece will hold, or whether it's high enough to prevent you decking out, try dropping a rock-filled backpack from the crux. If the highest piece is just too low, place a bomb-proof outward-pulling low runner and get your belayer to practise running from the base of the route to take in vital metres of slack as the rock-filled bag falls. All this may seem like a lot of effort and time that could otherwise be spent climbing, but if the route is hard enough you'd be foolish to commit to it without the best possible detailed knowledge.

A sawn-off peg used to protect the first ascent of Soul Doubt (E8) Froggatt, Peak District, England. The peg was cut to exactly the depth of the placement to ensure the optimum protection. It was hand-placed on the lead. Top: a skyhook.

Optimum confidence

The only way to be sure you won't fall is to practise. Even then you may find you can't succeed on every try, especially if the climbing is insecure, involving fine balance or marginal friction. With enough practice you'll learn every tiny nuance that can help. Placing a foot slightly differently on a crucial hold - even half a centimetre or less - could be the difference between reliable success and certain failure, and it's far better to find this out while you still have the security of a rope from above.

The big day

Once you're confident you have the perfect sequence there are still two important variables to consider. The first is you. Some days you feel great and climb well, other days things just don't feel 'right'. Top-roping the route just before a possible headpoint will tell you how 'right' it feels; but don't overdo it, as the moves will probably be near your strength limit so you won't be able to do them many times before your strength begins to fade.

The other essential factor is conditions. Get to know when it's too warm, too cold or too humid. If you've worked a route for a long time you may be tempted to seek closure on it. But imagine how bad you'd feel (not to mention how injured you'd be) if you fell off trying it on a warm day. The route will still be around when the conditions are right. The important thing is that you're still around too! Cooler conditions are nearly always the best for climbing at your limit - you will have to chalk-up less, and the rubber on shoes will be harder and less prone to creeping off marginal holds. Bear in mind though that *you* still have to be completely warmed-up to perform.

Max Adamson on *The Butcher* (E2) St.Govan's Head, Pembroke, Wales.

The Mind

Before we start, let's get one thing established: you don't have a problem with your head! If you think your head stops you as soon as you get above your gear, or you've reached a grade where everything above seems to be an impossible dream, don't worry, you are perfectly normal. Your mind, like your muscles, will strengthen as your experience draws a distinction between rational and irrational fears. The harder you push yourself, the more useful experience you have and the quicker your mind will strengthen.

The human body is a survival machine; it avoids danger, but at the same time it has evolved to frequently expect to come into danger, either unwittingly, or in pursuit of a greater goal. Whereas our ancestors may have put aside their fear of being injured in order to put some much-needed mammoth steak in their bellies, modern man seldom has such an imperative. Unless we put it there ourselves ...

Goal setting

In any human endeavour, a goal is vital. While the experience you have accrued in the past may give you the power to move forward, it is your goal, planted in the future, that gives you your direction and the motivation to keep on going. Having a goal is the single most important thing in the mental side of climbing. Without one you have no way of evaluating how well you are doing, there will be no focus for your training and you will quite simply not achieve the level you are capable of.

There are a number of goals we can set in climbing, ranging from ambitious, long-term goals, to modest short-term goals. Goals should be definite - you need to know when you've achieved one. Goals should be ambitious, yet achievable. Goals should push you, but should be things you do actually want to do!

Leah Crane on *Three Pebble Slab* (HVS), Froggatt Edge, The Peak District, England.

The Mind

Goals vs. means

Goals should always be distinguished from their means. Here are some examples of goals:

To lead a route.
To climb an E5.
To do all the *** E3s in Pembroke next week.
To lead Three Pebble Slab.

These are all quite different from each other, but they are all quite definite, you would certainly know it when you'd achieved one of them.

The following may look like goals but really they aren't.

To place better protection
To sort out my head
To improve my technique
To not worry so much when above my gear

While these are all laudable aims, they are means, not ends. One lofty goal - such as 'to lead *Three Pebble Slab* within a year' for a climber operating at, say, VS, may well demand all four of these means in order to achieve the goal of leading that particular route. Remaining focused on the goal will reveal our shortcomings, give us the incentive to work on them and will communicate to us whether we have achieved it.

Making your goals work

Most of our goals exist only in our heads, often as secret goals, and having such goals is far better than nothing, but you can improve the effectiveness of your goal setting by making them more public. By telling others about your goals you are more likely to follow through on them. If you've told your climbing partner about a particular goal, they will be in a better position to help you achieve it. Also, stating a goal adds some social pressure, which can be a very powerful way of staying focused if for no other reason than not losing face.

To maintain your awareness of your own goals, it is a good idea to write them down. Make a list of your goals, or, if you have a route-goal, put a glossy picture of it up where you can't ignore it - and picture yourself doing it.

Photo by Nick Smith

Ben Heason, Miles Gibson and Anne Arran hanging out on the first free ascent of Angel Falls, Venezuela. Photo by John Arran.

Lifetime goals

Having the longest time in which to achieve them, lifetime goals will naturally be the most ambitious. In setting a lifetime goal, ask yourself where you would like climbing to take you and what sacrifices you are prepared to make in order to get there.

If your lifetime goal is to climb The Nose on Yosemite's El Capitan, in traditional style, then you should expect to be able to achieve it after a few years of regular weekend climbing and the odd trip to increasingly larger venues. On the other hand, if your goal was to make a much harder 'all free' ascent of The Nose, then you would need to seriously ask yourself whether you are prepared to put in many years of hard training and take long breaks from paid employment - would you be prepared to organise your life around your climbing goal? Do you have family commitments that would allow this? If you set a goal that you don't believe in, then it isn't going to motivate you, it will only get you down.

What next?

When you do finally achieve your lifetime goal, it will be time to set another. No-one said you can't have more than one lifetime goal - even if you can't have more than one lifetime. If your initial goal was achieved quite easily, then you will probably want to set a harder one.

The Mind

Annual goals

On the way to your lifetime goal you need to set some mile-posts: subsidiary goals that tell you you're heading in the right direction. Here, the objective is to make gradual improvements, that leave lasting increases in ability. Setting a goal of reaching a new grade each year is a sound way of staying focused, without placing undue stress on yourself to make great leaps through the grades. Giving ourselves a grade goal for the year takes some pressure off. Having done our first E2, for example, we would have the remainder of the year to consolidate that grade across a variety of styles, knowing that E3 is for next year.

Having a route as a goal is a good idea. After climbing a couple of years, you may set yourself a goal for the year of climbing E2, plus the goal of climbing *Left Wall* - a benchmark E2. Having a route as a goal makes sure we don't 'cheat' by finding a soft-touch E2 that ticks the goal, but rather misses the point.

Trip goals

Going on a climbing trip is a great way of applying short-term goals. Setting a goal, or goals, for a trip gives the trip a sense of purpose. Your trip goal could be your annual goal if you feel it is achievable, or your purpose could be to consolidate a lower grade. So, for example, you may wish to climb your first E1 as your annual goal, but in an early spring trip, you may set yourself the goal of climbing at least one HVS each day to consolidate the goal you achieved the previous year.

Day goals

As for trip goals, having a goal for your day gives your day a greater sense of purpose. Goals for a day can be looser than those for longer periods. A typical goal for the day may be to climb one or two routes that you are fairly sure aren't going to be a problem and then set yourself the goal that you will try such-and-such route if you feel you're climbing well that day. A looser goal like this will still have a powerful effect in focusing your efforts, but doesn't heap on too much pressure to try something you may not be ready for.

Route goals

Goal setting may be a good way of getting you to the base of a route, but it doesn't end there. Breaking a route into sections, each being a goal in its own right, is a great way of taking some pressure off, rather than mentally digesting the route as a whole.

Kate Lawrence leading *Walrus* (S), Lundy, England.
Photo by Nick Smith.

The Mind

Fear of falling

Back in the old days, when falling off was always a dangerous business, there was a mantra 'the leader doesn't fall'. These days, climbing equipment has come a very long way and falling is often not nearly as serious as we expect it to be.

When we fail on routes, it is more often the fear of falling that stops us, rather than the difficulty of the route. Sometimes our fear is justified, often it is not. As mentioned at the start of this chapter, the instinct to avoid injury is innate, being afraid of falling down a cliff is not unnatural. Fear of falling cannot be 'cured' by any mystic mumbo jumbo - you are an intelligent survival machine, and need to know that the protection system, from the buckle in your harness, to the protection in the rock, is reliable.

Sport climbing for confidence

Before we look at the reliability of protection, let's take a look at the other aspects of the system. When we fall, we entrust our lives to our partner and to the ropes that connect us. If we cannot trust in that part of the system, then it is worth stopping right there and working on that first.

Sport climbing is rock climbing with *in situ* bolts for protection - it is as safe as leading can be, and so is a great way of building confidence with your partner. Taking falls on sport climbs (or on indoor leading walls) removes, almost entirely, the risk of protection failing. If you find you are afraid of falling on sport climbs, then it is worth dealing with this before moving on to the more complex game of building your confidence in trad protection.

Taking deliberate falls will build trust in your climbing partner and will remove some of the mystery of what it is like to fall off. Much of the fear of falling is linked with our need for control, if you can only climb in absolute control, you will be severely limiting what you can do. Sport climbing helps us learn to climb without having to be fully in control, and goes a long way to removing the irrational side of the fear of falling.

Luke Roberts falling from *The Butcher* (E2) St. Govan's Head, Pembroke, Wales. Photo by Nick Smith.

The Mind

Falling on trad protection

Much of the fear of falling is borne out of wanting to be in control and a lack of trust in the system is due to a lack of experience. Falling onto bolts, of course, is one thing, falling onto the protection we have just placed, is another.

Confidence in your protection can only truly come from falling onto it, and having it hold. Someone telling you that you're protection is fine is nothing compared to the experience of falling on it and knowing it's fine. There really are no painless short cuts to this and if you are looking for them, you will be disappointed and may find it hard to progress.

Evaluating your gear

If you are suspicious of the holding power of the protection you place, there are some exercises you can do to build your confidence.

Abseil inspection

Usually, after we've led a pitch, we take a belay and our partner follows. By the time our partner has reached the belay, they will have largely forgotten about your placements and would have been more concerned with getting them out than evaluating whether they were any good. A good exercise is to leave the protection in place and abseil down the route to check it, doing this in tandem with a more experienced climber can be a real confidence booster. Conversely, if your protection isn't that great, you may learn something even more valuable. Usually, you will find that your protection looks better from the safety of an abseil rope than it did when you placed it and this can be encouraging.

Setting up a fall

A good way building confidence in your protection is to stage a fall. Find a route which is free from obstacles and offers good protection. Now arrange a totally reliable batch of runners high on the route, lead up to these runners, clip them, then climb past and place a piece of protection, move higher and jump off. The fall should be positioned so that even if you rip the last piece, you will be safe.

Ben Wilkinson placing gear on the crux of *Fool's Gold* (E1) Bus Stop Quarry, Llanberis Slate, Wales.

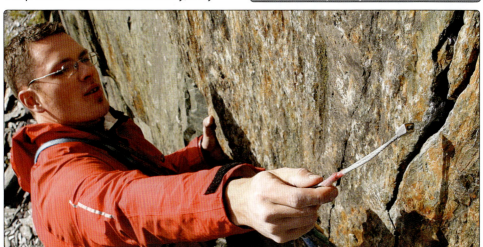

Boldness

There are many routes where the protection is spaced, poor, or even non-existent. While some climbers shy away from bold routes, others thrive on the excitement of the ultimate test of their ability as climbers. Experiences overcoming bold sections of climbing are often the most memorable, and treasured of all climbing memories. Over time, what may start off as something you try to avoid may turn out to be an unstoppable addiction.

To climb bold routes requires a real sense of determination and the ability to focus technically on the climbing without being distracted by the risk. These two factors result in what we usually refer to as 'boldness'. To develop your ability to climb bold routes, requires experience. A good way to get a feel for climbing bold routes is through headpointing (see page 204) and seconding more able climbers on routes you are not ready to lead.

As you get into bold situations your mind fights to keep its concentration on the climbing, but often the situation takes over and you end up thinking only about the negative consequences of failure, rather than the task at hand: completing the route. There is nothing like the experience gained from success in such situations to boost your confidence and ability to do it again next time your are out there, above the gear.

Better technique

The better your technique, the 'bolder' you can afford to be, simply because you know you are less likely to fall. The techniques you need to climb in bold situations need a different approach to the techniques used on boulder problems where you can afford to fall several times before succeeding. Bold climbing requires technique with a wide margin for error, this can involve making moves using more strength than necessary, but remaining in better control.

Chris Moor leading *Satan's Slip* (E1), Lundy. Photo by Nick Smith.

The Mind

Trying

So far everything in this book has proceeded with one very big assumption: that you've decided to give a route a try. The one sure way of not doing a route, infinitely more effective than any of the usual mistakes we all make, is not to try it at all. That isn't of course, to say that you should just try everything regardless of how hard it is, but to improve it is essential to move outside our comfort zones, if only to learn where the improvements we need to make, lie.

Overcoming grade blocks

The most common reason for not trying a route is its grade. Grades were originally devised as a warning and they still serve well to steer us away from routes that we are not quite ready for. The problem with grades is that they are objective - a one-size-fits-all system that tries to guess how hard a given route will be for all of us.

The truth is that two routes at the same grade may feel very different. We all have our strengths and our weaknesses. Pick a route that plays to your strengths and you will probably be able to climb a couple of grades harder than if you found yourself on a route that preys on your weaknesses.

Because your subjective experience of a grade will vary significantly, mental blocks at particular grades are a nonsense. If you randomly picked ten routes of a particular grade, the chances are that some of them would feel a grade harder and some of them a grade easier, so if you have climbed ten routes at HVS - you've probably already experienced 'E1' even if you haven't climbed a route with that grade.

Often, just knowing the grade of the route we're trying is enough to affect our performance negatively, making us adopt a timid, defensive approach that is unlikely to succeed. Many personal bests are achieved when we accidentally get on the wrong route - thinking the grade is lower than it really is - resulting in a more confident, aggressive approach, which gets us to the top.

The obvious way to break into new grades is to second harder routes than you can lead - you will soon come to realise that you can do the moves and that there is protection. If you find yourself without someone who can lead you up harder routes, working routes on a top-rope, then headpointing them, is no different and has the same benefit of showing that grades are not barriers.

When it comes to start onsighting routes at a higher grade, it is good to have recommendations from friends who know our strengths and weaknesses and can suggest routes that accommodate them. Breaking into a grade nearly always involves ticking some 'soft touches' first - we all do it.

Finally, if you are fortunate to find a route with different grades in different guidebooks, you may wish to adopt the lower grade before you've done it and then settle for the higher grade when discussing it afterwards!

The Mind

Meilee Rafe and Paul Rowlands on *Valkyrie* (VS) The Roaches, Staffordshire, England. Photo by Nick Smith.

Saving it for the onsight?

This has to be the procrastinator's all time number one excuse. Saving routes until you know you will cruise them is never to experience them as the struggle they should be. Getting on a classic route that is well within your capabilities is often a bit of a disappointment. If you don't manage to onsight a classic, return a year (or so) later; you will want it even more and you will have a satisfying sense of just how much you have improved when you get it ticked.

Fear of failure

Whilst in trad climbing, fear of injury, or worse, has a natural cooling effect on our enthusiasm to 'have a go' on a route, it is quite rare for a route to be so poorly protected that failure will lead to anything more than disappointment. To climb well, you need to think of failure in a different way. Failure is the only way we learn what our weaknesses are - success teaches us that success feels good, failure teaches us how to get there. If you wish to progress in your climbing, you need to expect regular doses of failure and to learn from them. As you become a better climber, you will become more philosophical about failure and see that the success in trying your best outweighs the disappointment in the failure of that attempt. We stress that 'attempt' because you can never really fail on a route - only on an attempt. Think of a route as a student of music might think of a sheet of written music. If you play a wrong note, you can always return to the start and try again. The only true failure is when you stop trying.

The Mind

Divide and conquer

Still not convinced to get on that route? Looking up at an intimidating route can be enough to put you off, so try to look at it in a different, more positive way. Breaking a route down into sections is a great way of mentally undressing a climb. All but the starkest crack lines can be divided into sections, split up by breaks, rests, pieces of protection, whatever there is. As an example, the Snowdonia classic *Right Wall* on Dinas Cromlech is an E5 on many climber's tick list, but one that can be easily broken down into more manageable sections - some climbers have described it as three E3s one after the other - a far more inviting prospect for a keen E4 climber than one big E5.

When you're looking up at a route that you would like to try, but find it hard to commit to, consider the fact that you don't have to mentally commit to the whole climb. Break the route down into manageable sections and give yourself the option to retreat if you feel it's too much - perhaps not the most positive approach but infinitely better than staying on the ground and allowing the route to intimidate you. The higher you get on a route, the more reason you have to carry on, so any mental tricks that you can play on yourself to you to actually start a route are valuable tools.

> ### Anatomy of a route
> By breaking a route down into sections, it will often appear far more amenable. A long pitch will often have numerous rests where you can recover. The sections between the rests will always be easier, individually, than the route as a whole. A long E2, for example, could be viewed as three E1s climbed one after the other with reasonable rests in between. Simply by looking at a formidable route in a way that makes it appear more 'do-able' may be enough to give you the confidence to have a go - the first step in getting it done!

Climber on *Richochet* (E2) St. Govan's Head, Pembroke, Wales.

Using peer pressure

As social animals, our perception of what others think of us can be a very motivating force. If you've set yourself the goal of a particular route, and told your friends that you're going to give it a go, the thought of having to tell them that you chickened out may be enough to get you to rack up and go for it. Similarly, if you perform well with an audience, arrange it so you hit the crag with a big team. If not, sneak out mid-week - putting this sort of pressure on yourself may have the effect of turning you into a bag of nerves, unable to perform. How you use peer pressure is a very personal matter and only you will know whether it is likely to help, or hinder.

Reasons to be positive

If you find yourself lacking confidence on a route, or a section of a route, before trying it, take a moment to list as many reasons as possible that you have to be positive about succeeding. You will probably surprise yourself as to how many you can think of. Here are some examples:

+ You've climbed this grade before
+ You've been climbing well over recent weeks
+ The route favours your strengths
+ The route is well protected
+ Conditions are good
+ The technical grade is well within you, so lack of protection shouldn't matter
+ You've got new climbing shoes, gear etc.
+ You've got some good beta off the internet
+ Your mate did it last week and found it OK

Dealing with your doubts

Regardless of how many reasons you can think of as to why you should succeed on a climb, there are bound to be some doubts. After all, if you had no doubts whatsoever, it wouldn't be much of a challenge! While it's tempting to try to ignore them, bury them away and they will only resurface when things start to get tough - just when you need to be rid of them. A better strategy is to address your doubts one by one, and honestly deal with them by replying in a positive way. For example:

- *I've never climbed this grade before!*

+ You've climbed plenty of routes one grade below - and some felt quite easy.

- *It's a bit early in the season for this route!*

+ Getting this route would be a great start to the year.

- *This route's a crack and I'm no good at cracks!*

+ It's well protected and there is only one way to get better at them.

- *This route's really pumpy and I'm not fit!*

+ OK, I may have to take a rest, but I'll get a good work-out and can always come back to lead it clean later.

If you get a doubt that you really can't address, then maybe that's one you should heed!

- *This is a five pitch E3, I only climb VS and there's just two hour's light left...*

+ Better try something else!

The Mind

Human resources

The opinions of others can be an asset or a liability. A trusted friend climbing at your level or higher will be in a good position to recommend routes for you to try. A recommendation of a route, with the attached opinion that you should find it 'OK', is worth a year's training in terms of the amount of confidence it can give. A bad recommendation (a.k.a. 'a sandbag') is valuable only in that you know not to take advice from that individual again. Of course, if you happen to be sandbagged, and still pull it off, you get the last laugh.

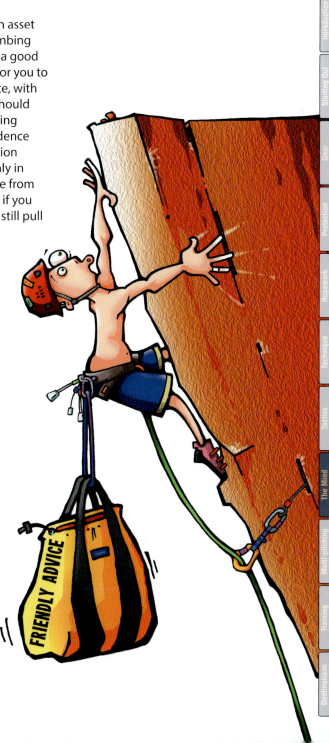

The Mind

Tales of woe

Climbers who have been thoroughly trounced by a route, especially men, frequently exhibit an evangelical zeal to warn everyone that the route is the domain of evil spirits and that their lack of success had very little to do with their climbing ability.

Such tales of woe are easy to take to heart - especially if a route is intimidating in the first place. Beware of reputations and keep an open mind about what to expect. Many reputations are the result of the Chinese whispers that breed and multiply in environments lubricated by pints of beer and the authors could fill a book with stories of unprotected routes that were anything but and so on and so forth - take no-one's word for it.

The Mind

225

Anne Arran on the first pitch of *Positron* (E5) on Main Wall, Gogarth, Wales. Photo by John Arran.

The Mind

Who's limits are your own?

When we start out climbing, the limits on what we attempt are necessarily set by those kind enough to take us climbing, however, the time will probably come when we need to spread our wings a bit and see what we're capable of. It is in these situations where the limits of those we climb closely with can become fixed to our own, and it takes a lot of willpower to overcome the natural reluctance we have to push ourselves beyond the boundaries of a more experienced partner.

If you find yourself in this situation then consider the fact that while experience is necessary to advance as a climber, it is not sufficient on its own. A climber with motivation, good physical condition and mental drive may be able to easily out-climb a partner with twenty years of experience and firmly set boundaries. Most 'mentor' partners will be delighted to be superseded by their 'students' and will happily hand over the lead to the new hotshot - it is the mark of a good teacher.

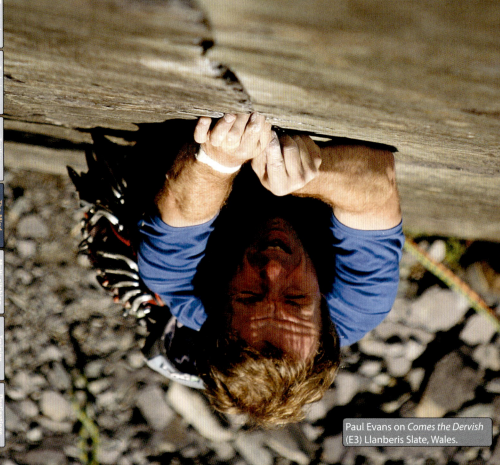

Paul Evans on *Comes the Dervish* (E3) Llanberis Slate, Wales.

The Mind

Swinging

In climbing partnerships, there is usually one partner more capable than the other - though probably not in every aspect. There are advantages and disadvantages in being the stronger or weaker partner. In our very first partnership, we are the weaker partner and have the benefit of being able to learn quickly from watching and learning skills from our more experienced partner.

A more experienced partner will give you confidence to attempt routes you otherwise might not and will set your expectations at a level higher than you can currently achieve. Nearly all top climbers become top climbers by climbing with other top climbers. If you are looking for the secret to stardom - this is it!

Being the more experienced partner is to be in a situation where you have less to learn from your partner, but as the 'leader' you will quickly learn to take a more responsible role, and your skills will rapidly sharpen in the absence of a partner who is always able to get you out of trouble and take over the lead if you flounder. Frequently being in the position of 'leader' is essential to realising your full potential as a climber.

Having a range of climbing partners, some more experienced, some less experienced is an important element in developing your ability as a climber. If you are in a situation where you have a regular climbing partner, and don't get to climb with other people much, make an effort to do so. Don't be afraid to team up with someone a lot better than yourself, but similarly don't overlook the benefits of taking an inexperienced climber out on the rock and taking the lead - just don't be surprised if they overtake you in the future!

Discussing options high on *Pinnacle Ridge Direct* (VDiff) East Face of Tryfan, North Wales. It is good for your climbing to have experience of being the most and least able partner in a team. Photo by Alan James.

Fear of succeeding

This is more common than many might imagine. There are a number of reasons why we may subconsciously throw a spanner in the works and snatch defeat from the jaws of victory. Here are some:

1) The route was your partner's idea and you've made it clear that you don't have a chance; you do, but don't want to prove your partner right.

2) You've got comfortable at a particular level and don't really want to move onto the next grade - if you move up a grade you may feel under pressure to climb at that level all the time.

3) You've had a long love/hate affair with a route and secretly fear that doing the route will leave you without a motivational force in your climbing.

4) Succeeding may well involve pushing yourself outside your comfort zone, where you are less able to stay in control and you may find yourself settling for comfortable failure rather than uncomfortable success.

Choosing to succeed

While we like to think that we always choose to succeed with what we are trying, when pushing our limits, success always comes at a price: feeling scared, being painfully pumped, bleeding from your fingers each time your push your tips into a thin crack, not having an epic story to tell in the pub and so on. Often, we will fail in our attempt not because we didn't have 'it' in us to succeed, but because we choose not to. This is often the case when we're pushing ourselves to our very limit, though sometimes we find other reasons for our failure rather than accepting that, at a subconscious level, our failure was a matter of choice.

Choosing to succeed can simply be a matter of accepting the price that has to be paid and asserting to yourself that this time around, you are choosing to succeed. Reliving past glories is a good way of convincing ourselves that the price is worth paying.

The mind and gear

Climbing protection has two roles to play - physically, it is there to stop our falls, but it also provides psychological support in spurring us on. An attempt is more likely to end because we aren't happy with the protection than because we physically can't do the next move. Often, it is psychologically advantageous to place more protection than is strictly needed in order to boost our mental morale, whether the physical cost of placing the extra protection is worth paying is a matter of judgement.

Anyone who has climbed with marginal protection will testify that what seems crazy from the comfort of flat earth, may make complete sense when you're runout on the lead. Placing protection that is barely able to support the weight of the quickdraw you've clipped to it clearly isn't a good idea from a 'fall arrest' perspective, but often, the mere act of having a rope leading upwards rather than downwards, and the visual impact of having something clipped is enough to get you through a bold section and out of trouble. Needless to say, 'psychological protection' is something that requires a calculated approach, though once in a while, it actually holds.

Cecile Rittweger on *Strapadictomy* (E5) Froggatt Edge, The Peak District, England.

Visualisation

Once we have done something, it is always easier to do it again than it was to do it the first time. Climbing a route you've done previously will usually feel a bit easier and if you've taken a safe fall from the crux of a route, it is easier to commit to it the next time around. It is just a shame that it is only after you needed that confidence that you get it. Visualisation is a means of cheating this paradox and saves a lot of time and repeated effort. When we visualise, the feelings can be so strong that part of the brain cannot tell the difference between the actual movement and the visualisation of that movement.

To visualise something, all you are doing is using your imagination to experience how it might feel, look, sound and even smell and taste. The more information you have about the physical space that you are visualising yourself in, the easier it is to believe your visualisation - it's hard to imagine yourself cruising through the crux of a route you've never even seen! Because of this, visualisation works best on routes that you have a good knowledge of, though that doesn't mean the technique cannot be used on routes you would like to onsight - but you would need to incorporate it into you route-reading to get the most from it.

How it's done

Like any other skill, visualisation is improved by practice. Start off by 'reliving' small parts of memorable routes where you have climbed well. Try to see what your eyes were seeing as you moved your eyes and head around searching for holds and protection. When you're happy with that, expand your sensory range to include the sound of your breathing, the click of karabiners snapping shut, the sound of the sea or the wind. Now include the tactile sensations: the roughness of the rock, the smoothness of the chalk, the tightness of your shoes, perhaps even a drop of perspiration as it winds its way over your cheek. Finally complete the picture with details such as the dry taste of your mouth and the odour of the air.

Viewpoints

The great thing about visualisation is you're completely in control. While in life we only get to view the world through our own eyes, when visualising, we can take any point of view we choose. It may be more helpful to view yourself from the viewpoint of a third person, allowing you to see more clearly the position you are in, something that may be difficult to judge when you are only seeing things through your own eyes.

Taking a moment to relax and visualise a climb before getting onto it can make all the difference.

The Mind

Visualising and headpointing

When you know a route intimately, you can boost your confidence by visualising yourself in great detail. If you've watched someone else on the same moves, you will have an even greater image of how you will look. When you are relaxed and undisturbed, take the opportunity to run through the moves from a variety of viewpoints. Make it as real as possible - if you are likely to be scared, then don't leave this out of your visualisation exercise. If you have repeatedly reached a point where you have backed-off, re-experience your anxiety in your visualisation, but feel yourself take a deep breath, push past it and watch what happens.

Visualisation and route reading

When you are reading the moves of a route, you can enhance the exercise by mentally projecting yourself onto the route. Visualising yourself on a route you have never attempted is always going to be the most challenging. Look at the holds and imagine how they will feel when you're hanging from them - where will your protection be? Visualising adds an emotional element to the task of extracting raw information about a climb. In addition to noting that there is a rest ledge at half height, imagine how good it will feel to reach that ledge and store up the expectation of a good feeling to keep you motivated on that tough first half.

If a route has an obvious runout, visualise yourself running it out. Pre-experience the focus you will have, see and feel the exposure, but at the same time give yourself credit for staying calm and focused on moving efficiently and securely. As the moves themselves will be uncertain, it may help to visualise yourself from some distance, where you can settle for an overall sense of upwards progress and calm, controlled, climbing.

Rob Greenwood on *Eroica* (E2), Pentire Head, Cornwall, England.

Visualising the negatives

So far, we've tried to see things in a positive light, by visualising how a climb will feel when all goes to plan, though of course in a believable context - there's no point visualising that you've got bionic strength or are completely fearless! There is an important role for visualisation in dealing with the negative aspects of a climb. For example, a climb with the potential for a big fall might not seem so repulsive if you can visualise yourself taking that fall, ripping that dodgy micro-wire, and swinging in space - maybe even laughing with your partner!

Neil Bentley mentally preparing for the best and the worst possible outcomes prior to making the first ascent of *Equilibrium* (E10) Burbage South, The Peak District, England.
Video still capture by Mark Turnbull.

Pre-programming responses

There is no sense in visualising a situation that glosses over climbing's inherent dangers. If a route you are visualising has a real hazard, then it is worth playing that scenario as a visualisation. So, for example, if you are visualising climbing a route where you will hit the ground if you fall, it would be a good idea to mentally prepare yourself to land as well as possible.

Similarly, if you are to attempt a route where a fall could leave you hitting a ledge, it would be worth running though in your mind the act of kicking yourself clear of the ledge in the event of a fall. Of course, you don't have to be the one falling to make good use of visualisation in this scenario, as the belayer, a pre-programmed response to give extra slack so that the falling climber is arrested clear of the ledge is also well worth taking the moment to make.

Dramatic visualisation

Visualising yourself from the perspective of a third person is a bit like watching yourself on a screen. Being able to do this automatically opens up a world of options for tinkering with what we 'see' and 'hear' depending on what changes in our behaviour we might be seeking. Want to get yourself motivated for a hard lead? Visualise yourself heroically cranking out the last moves of the route, disregarding the runout, before gracefully topping-out to a rapturous applause that doesn't quite drown out the 'Eye of the Tiger' soundtrack that's slowly been building … Okay not everyone's cup of tea, but you get the picture.

Alternatively, you may want to change behaviour that negatively affects your climbing by viewing it in a comic light. If you hate the fact that you get gripped when there's perfectly good protection at your feet, try visualising yourself in that situation but ham up your role to emphasise the ludicrousness of how it must appear to anyone watching. Add a Benny Hill soundtrack and 'canned' laughter to really make the point that if you saw anyone else behaving the way you do, you would think they were a bit crazy.

The Mind

Using video

Most climbers have an unflattering self-image. We naturally think of ourselves as looking a lot less smooth than in fact we are, most climbers who have watched video footage of themselves comment that they appeared far more relaxed and technically proficient than they felt at the time - an immediate confidence booster - so get that smart phone out!

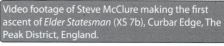

Video footage of Steve McClure making the first ascent of *Elder Statesman* (XS 7b), Curbar Edge, The Peak District, England.

The Mind

Positive encouragement

Being encouraged can be a real confidence booster and often makes the difference between success and failure when a route is approaching your limit. Developing a mutually encouraging relationship with your partners is usually a matter of giving encouragement in order to receive it. If your partner is being reticent, or is out of earshot, there's no harm in encouraging yourself with some insightful comments from the one you love.

When giving encouragement, it is important to remain positive in your wording as well as your intent. For example, if your partner was looking like they may give-up, 'don't give up!' and 'stick with it!' are both positive comments, but the first comment is worded negatively, while the second is worded positively. The positively worded encouragement will be more effective because it doesn't remind your partner of what they may be already thinking - telling them to 'stick with it' or 'go for it' is to suggest positive action, and is far more mentally 'digestible'.

You don't need to wait until things are looking desperate before making encouraging noises to your partner. Praise on a well executed move or a cunning rest, or a comment that the protection they just placed looked like a good one, all add up to a 'can do' atmosphere where quitting just seems out of place.

Having said that, don't over-do it. Partners who start encouraging from the first move make their shouts of encouragement on the crux less noticeable.

Lisa Rands soloing *Shine On* (E7) Stanage Edge, The Peak District, England. Having a good team to encourage you on is a big morale booster.

The Mind

Controlling your arousal level

The harder we are pushing ourselves, the higher our arousal level will become. Being highly aroused is our body's natural reaction to demanding situations - it increases the blood-flow to our muscles, speeds up our thought processes, and when we approach our limits, can induce a *fight or flight* response.

High levels of arousal do, however, have negative consequences. While our fight or flight response may be just what is needed to run away from a predator, or attack prey, it comes at the cost of our seeing with increasingly 'tunnelled' vision, and losing the fine motor skills that may be all that are keeping up on some marginal smears. This can lead to terrible technique and missing obvious holds simply because we are focusing too narrowly.

Clearly, there are benefits from being able to calm down while climbing. The best way is to take control of your breathing. Aroused breathing involves short quick breaths taken in through your mouth and employing the top of your lungs. Simply switching to taking long slow breaths through your nose and taking that air deep into the base of your lungs will start to relax you. Taking some time to relax and getting into a steady relaxed breathing rhythm before you set off on a climb is a great way to start as you mean to continue.

Doublespeak

Pressure can have negative effects when we're on a route. If you're taking some time to commit to the crux (with your freezing belayer weakly feigning patience) all you can do is wait until the right moment. Telling your partner you're definitely going to go for it this time can mount the pressure if you've said that five times already. Take the pressure off by telling your partner just that you're going to have one more look.

A regular partner will eventually learn your doublespeak and will be ready when you finally do go for it.

Climbers on *One Step in the Clouds* (VS) Tremadog, Wales. Moving above the belay can be a gripping moment - and an encouraging belayer can make all the difference.

Dave Pickford on *The Pulsebeat* (E5), Huntsman's Leap, Pembroke, Wales.

Focus

One of the real skills in climbing is being able to switch our mental focus. In climbing, everything has the potential to be critical: from the choices of holds, to the length of the extension we place on our protection, everything matters. When making a move, focus entirely on the move. There's no sense in thinking about that rusty old peg you just clipped, the best thing you can do is focus entirely on the movement, that way you are less likely to be *needing* that rusty old peg.

This is, of course, much easier said than done. A good way of helping yourself to switch your focus is to maintain a silent dialogue with yourself. It might go something like this:

"OK, I'm at the break, let's get a runner in"

[Switched focus from moves to protection]

"My size three cam fits well - now to check that it's well seated - looks good - now what sort of extension is needed?"

[Focus switched to ropework - and broadens to take in the whole route]

"There's a roof coming up so better use a long extender"

[Focus narrows in to selecting the quickdraw and clipping the cam]

"Now, what's coming up next?"

[Focus broadens to take in the next section of the climb]

"Looks like a tricky section to get to the base of the roof, but the holds are obvious - let's give it a go"

[Focus narrows onto the moves and the rock in the immediate facility]

"%&*! I'm wrong-handed - there's no way I can do the next move"

[Focus broadened to see the wider picture]

"Ah, there's a hold off to the side..."

[Focus narrows to make the moves]

As you can see, the focus changes both in its intensity and its subject. The skill is to exclude irrelevant items from your focus, while remaining able to broaden your focus under pressure when things aren't going as planned.

Tunnel vision

Being unable to broaden your focus is often referred to as *tunnel-vision*. This is particularly common on moves at our limit, where we naturally tend to focus on, not just what we are doing with our bodies, but on the minutiae of the holds we have our fingers on, to the expense of thinking about the rest of our bodies. Knowing you are climbing with tunnel vision is half the battle in developing the techniques to avoid it.

Next runner syndrome

This is when our passage up a route becomes entirely dominated by seeking out the next bit of gear. This often results in inefficient technique and placing unnecessary runners in a strenuous position because we didn't see the huge holds and obvious gear placements coming up. Climbing with only gear placement in mind feels like a chore and is rarely a satisfying experience.

Dave Coley leading off on the second pitch of *Il Risveglio di Kundalini* (VI) Val di Mello, Italy.

Multi-Pitching

If you ask experienced trad climbers to list their favourite routes, don't be surprised to hear a lot of multi-pitch routes quoted in the answers. Being higher above the ground can intensify the aspects people enjoy about climbing, and there is more of a sense that you are climbing as a team, with shared responsibility, especially if the route is very long, or if retreat would be complicated.

In practice, climbing a two- or three-pitch route requires only a few skills you won't already have as a leader of single-pitch climbs. This chapter will detail the things you definitely should be aware of before heading up a multi-pitch route, especially one you're expecting to find challenging.

Multi-pitching

A series of single pitch routes?

Sometimes when you break a multi-pitch route down, it is advantageous to think of it as just a series of single pitch routes, one after the other. If you can climb five or six HVS routes in a day then theoretically you should be able to climb a five-pitch route of HVS. There is a lot to be said for this as a good way of combating the psychological difficulties presented by multi-pitch routes, however it is worth exercising a little caution. A rest on the ground is better than a rest on a belay; you tend to rest longer and you are more relaxed. Also, five pitches up the exposure is significantly greater making the climbing more psychologically draining.

Before attempting a multi-pitch route here are a few other differences that you should consider.

Multi-directional belays

The most obvious difference you'll find when arranging a belay part-way up a crag is that you can't simply walk back from the edge as far as you need to find good belays. On most established routes you should be able to find reasonable options within a few metres of the stance. If in doubt place more gear, since five uninspiring pieces will make you feel a whole lot safer than two or three of them. A good trick is to climb up a little further and place a high runner, you'll probably be able to clip it as the first runner of the next pitch anyway.

The other main difference is that, whereas a ground belayer will always be pulled upwards and a top belayer always downwards, a mid-way belay should be safe for a pull in every direction. This is often easier to achieve if you're using cams, but particularly if your belay is made from wires or hexes you should be sure they won't all lift out when your leader falls unexpectedly and you're pulled violently upwards. If the route traverses from the belay you could end up being pulled sideways too. So make sure there's no unnecessary slack between you and the belay points or you could be dragged off balance and maybe have difficulty holding onto the rope.

Becky McGovern on pitch two of *Shadow Wall* (VS) Carreg Wastad, Llanberis Pass.
The belayer has three belay points, the sling over the spike will prevent him from being pulled sideways should his partner fall.
Photo by Alex Messenger.

Multi-pitching 241

Where to put the rope?

When on the belay, looking after the rope is an important factor in aiding smooth progression up a multi-pitch route. Often this will be easy if the belay has good-sized ledges of space where you can stash the rope as you take in, but sometimes you will need to consider other options to avoid creating a big tangled mess.

On smooth slabs there may be little for ropes to catch on beneath, so you may be happy to let the rope drop in loops many metres below. You can also use this approach on overhanging rock where the ropes dangle in free space however here you will find that the extra weight on the belay device makes efficient belaying awkward when your leader is climbing the next pitch.

As often as not, there will be sharp flakes, bushes or other things the rope could snag on below and around you, and if it's windy then long loops of dangling rope will end up in a horrible mess. In this case you should hang the rope in loops. If there's a good spike to hook them on you're in luck. Otherwise you can pass each loop across the belay (*see photo to the right*). Sometimes this causes problems in accessing the belay, especially if you aren't 'swinging leads' (*see page 242*) so in this case you can use a sling clipped to the belay, or a 'rope-hook' - a piece of kit specially designed for the purpose. If you decide to pass the rope through a sling, use a sling that's been 'doubled-up' rather than through the middle of a sling, that way you can release it if you get into any tangles.

When you're hanging the rope it's important not to make circular coils, which will tighten into a knot if pulled. Better

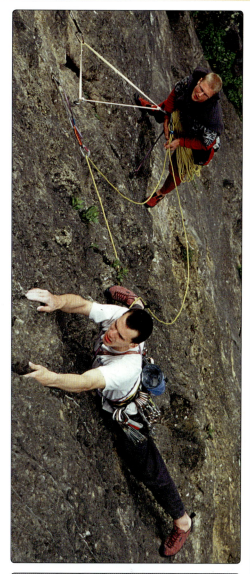

Dave Pickford keeps the rope organised as Chris Savage tackles the top pitch of *Psychopath Way* (E6) on Exploding Galaxy Wall, Avon Gorge.
Photo by Ian Parnell.

to pass loops alternately either side of whatever hook you're using. A useful tip is to make each loop marginally shorter than the previous one. That way when it comes to paying the rope out again you shouldn't have any loop tightening around another.

Tactical leading

The traditional approach, and in many cases the most efficient, is for a team of two to 'swing leads', i.e. to lead alternate pitches. There are several advantages. Firstly, the belayer stays in place so there is no need to spend time changing positions. Secondly, if you paid the ropes out carefully onto the ledge as your partner seconded the previous pitch, they should now be pulling from the top of the pile as your now-leading partner climbs on ahead. The third advantage is that the second may already have most of the gear needed to lead with, having taken it out of the previous pitch.

Linking pitches

If you're climbing well within your grade and placing relatively little gear, it can be more efficient for the same person to link a number of pitches in a row, missing out belays, and reducing the time needing to be spent exchanging gear.

Block leading

This is where one person leads a number of pitches in a row. For harder routes, a team can benefit from nobody having to climb two pitches without a breather in between. This approach is also common when one partner is a much more confident leader than the other.

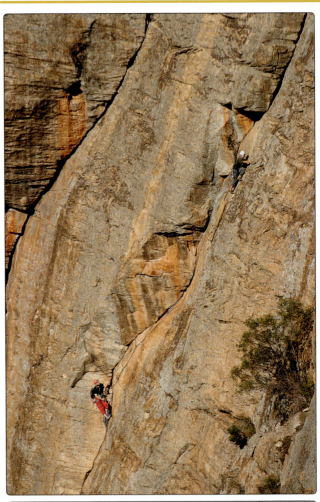

Climbers on the fourth pitch of *Skink* (18) Arapiles, Australia.

Planning

In reality the best approach will be different for every climb and for every team, so it's worth considering and discussing the options in advance. You may choose to combine swinging leads with block leading on the same route. Planning who leads what pitch is always worth taking time for - it may even give you a chance of avoiding leading the horrible off-width in return for letting your partner lead that nice-looking finger crack four pitches earlier!

Gary Latter and Jo George on *Mucklehouse Wall* (E5) Hoy, Orkney Isles, Scotland. Photo by Cubby Images.

Multi-pitching

Changeovers

If you do need to switch belayers on a stance you'll find it much quicker and easier if you've used slings rather than the climbing rope to equalise the belay. Many people carry a cordelette (a long loop of rope or tape - *see page 122*) specially for this purpose, as it may easily be knotted to exactly the lengths required. The changeover is then simply a matter of clipping into, and un-clipping from, a single equalised attachment point.

If you ran out of slings and needed to use the rope to equalise the belay, then you have three options:

1) Clip your partner's rope into each piece of the belay next to your own. The drawback is that with such a spider's web of ropes and knots it can be difficult removing your own ropes again once your partner has you on belay.

2) Replace your rope attachments with slings, now that your second has brought some up. This may sound like a good plan but in reality it will have few advantages over the first option and may mean you run out of slings again very soon.

3) Exchange ends of rope, which is particularly worth considering if you have had to climb any distance away from the belay to include additional anchors. Of course before untying you need to make absolutely sure you'll still be attached securely while you do so, which isn't always as easy as it sounds.

If you do switch belayers, and don't exchange rope ends, you'll find your ends are buried at the bottom of the pile. Maybe they'll pull OK anyway, but if they don't you could easily look down nervously from the crux to see your belayer wrestling with tangled spaghetti rather than paying attention. If in doubt it's worth spending a minute or two feeding the ropes through again to make sure.

Getting organised at the belay can take a lot longer than it should. Climbers on the stance of *Valkyrie* (HVS), Froggatt, The Peak District, England.
Photo by Duncan Skelton.

Multi-pitching

Passing gear

Inevitably you'll have to pass gear from one climber to another, and when you're tired from the last pitch or nervous about the next it can be very easy to drop some of your valuable, and possibly critical, gear. If passing directly, do it one piece at a time. If you end up passing more than one then state clearly how many you're passing so your partner knows to make sure they have them all. Better still don't pass gear directly at all, but instead clip it all into a loop of the belay. That way you'll each be able to work at your own speed and neither of you will be tempted to hold more things at once than you can reliably handle.

Bandoliers

Many climbers, particularly in the USA, like to keep their gear on a bandolier, which is a special padded shoulder-sling. This can make it very quick to hand over all unused gear, but at the expense of being somewhat more awkward to climb with.

For vertical climbs you may hardly notice the difference, but on slabs the gear will tend to swing forward and obscure your footholds, and on overhangs the gear will dangle behind you and be difficult to access.

Sean Isaac and Abby Watkins passing the gear on *Grand Wall* (5.11a) The Chief, Squamish, British Columbia, Canada. Photo by Simon Carter

Multi-pitching

Logistics

It goes without saying that on a long route you'll need to take everything you need with you. Depending on the length of the route this could mean a guidebook and a few snack bars; a water bottle, waterproofs, a head-torch and trainers for the descent; or even a porta-ledge, stove, dehydrated meals, sleeping bags and spare hardware.

Each route will be different, and before starting you'll have to balance the extra hassle of carrying things against the extra usefulness of having them with you. Only with experience will you know what's best, and even the most experienced big-wall climbers sometimes get it wrong.

Travelling light

If you're the kind of climber who clips many things to your harness 'just in case' you find a use for them, you may want to reconsider your strategy. With trainers, waterproofs and water to carry as well as your rack it's easy to encumber yourself enough to seriously affect your ability to climb, not to mention spoiling much of the enjoyment you're hoping to have. So trim your rack carefully.

Racking up for a route in Yosemite, California, USA. Taking only what you need is an important tactical decision that may determine whether you complete your route that day, or the following one.

Do you need a whole rack of microwires, or will a select few suffice?
Is there any point in taking both a belay device and a figure-of-eight descender?
Do you need a full-weight locking krab on every sling?

Multi-pitching

Moving fast

The big problem with taking too much gear is the extra time it takes to carry it. One virtual certainty is that if you take overnight gear you'll end up using it, as carrying it will slow you down so much you'll be left with little choice.

While staying safe is obviously high on the list of priorities, achieving this can be as much about moving quickly and efficiently as it is about belay systems and ropework. There are few climbing situations less pleasant or more dangerous than getting benighted on a long route with no easy options for retreat.

Avoiding benightment

The obvious way to avoid getting caught in the dark is to get up ridiculously early and walk-in before dawn - an 'Alpine Start'. If it's a long walk-in you could bivvy near the base of the route, especially if the descent will take you back that way. If the first pitches are relatively easy you could climb them before dawn with a head-torch.

If the first pitches are very hard you could climb them the day before, leaving a fixed rope in place to ascend in the morning. Fixing ropes is increasingly viewed as being a less than ideal style. While still very much a valid ascent, using fixed lines is a style that could be improved upon. However, if it's a choice between fixing a few pitches in advance, and either failing on a route, or having to haul heavy overnight gear, it can make a lot of sense to fix.

Being benighted on a route is never pleasant - Gaz Parry, Josh Bakker-Dyos, and John Hopkins at first light after being benighted on *Oceano Irrazionale*, (VII) Val di Mello, Italy.

Running it out

One mistake that British climbers in particular often make is to underestimate the time a route will take. We're used to pitches of 15-20m or often less, where unless you place gear every couple of metres there could be a very real chance of a ground fall. Doing this on a pitch of 50m or more will take a very long time, as will sorting that amount of gear again on each stance. Like it or not, if you're going to move efficiently on a big route you'll have to resist the temptation to put lots of gear in when it isn't very hard!

Further time can be saved by missing belays (stances) - long double ropes will make this much more possible.

Multi-pitching

Carry or haul?

Once you have decided what gear you are carrying on the route, you will need to choose how you are going to carry it all.

If it's a single-day route then any gear that you can't stuff in your pocket, or clip to your harness, probably isn't really essential. Plastic water bottles can be clipped on with a loop of accessory cord or finger-tape, and if the guidebook doesn't fit in your pocket you can use a small stuff-sac, or a pouch designed for the purpose. However, if the weather is changeable - particularly if you are somewhere like the Alps, where an innocent-looking shower can quickly become life-threatening without extra clothing - you may be better off taking a sack.

Carry

These days there are many sacks on the market, some of which are specifically designed for multi-pitch climbing with helmet storage flaps and water bladders built in, yet small enough to not restrict your movement. If you do a lot of multi-pitch climbing then investing in a sack like this is an excellent idea.

One question you should ask before setting off is: do we need to take two sacks? If it is just a few items like water bottle, descent shoes and some snacks then a single sack should be fine, and you can switch it between you on the belays. When carrying more gear you should consider splitting things equally between you and both climbing with it. For much of the route this may work well, but when the climbing gets near your limit this can start to look like a bad idea. In this case consider giving some, or all, of your load to the second to carry. This may seem unfair

Mark 'Zippy' Pretty keeping his balance despite carrying a pack along the top pitch of *Skeleton Ridge* (HVS) Isle of Wight's chalk classic.
Photo by Ian Parnell.

but if much of the climbing difficulty is psychological rather than physical, then they will effectively be on a top-rope while following relatively easy moves.

If your second isn't able to climb the pitch carrying all the kit they may decide not to climb the pitch at all, but to clean the gear out while ascending one of the lead ropes (while being belayed on the other) - *see page 152 for more on rope ascending.*

Chimneys and sacks
If you find yourself seconding with a sack, and have to climb a chimney, a good trick is to simply take your pack off, and attach it to your belay loop via a 120cm sling and let it hang below.

Multi-pitching

Haul

Hauling is hard work, takes up valuable time and is fraught with difficulties due to the potential for bags to get stuck and the need to free up a rope for the task. On single-day routes it should rarely, if ever, be necessary. That said, imagine a situation where neither leader nor second is happy climbing with a sack on and it makes sense to try to pull a bag up separately.

Assuming the bag itself is relatively light, say 15kg or less, the main issue is one of rope management. If the leader has been able to climb the pitch clipping only one rope you can haul on the other. If the pitch is less than half a rope length, the leader can drop a loop or a lead end to the second for them to attach the bag to. Alternatively, on a short pitch, the second can tie in to the middle of the rope and leave the bag perched on a ledge tied off to the rope end; then you can pull the bag up after the second has followed the pitch. When the leader is a little more than half a rope length away this last plan can still work, although you'll have to clip in and pull the bag up after you while you're still climbing the pitch.

The technique used to actually haul will depend on the weight of the bag. Loads up to about 5kg can be pulled up easily by hand. Beyond this you'll find it easier to clip the rope through a karabiner at head height, allowing you to pull down with one hand and up with the other. Much heavier again and you'll want to use a locking device (all rope ascenders work) allowing you to stop and rest from time to time during the haul.

Hauling a dedicated haul bag up the *Grand Wall*, (5.11a) Stawamus Chief, Squamish, BC, Canada. Photo by Simon Carter.

If you're expecting to be hauling frequently, or need to haul heavy bags, a wall-hauler device will make life much easier. These combine a low-friction pulley with a one-way locking mechanism, and are essential pieces of kit for multi-day big walls. For the heaviest loads, or if the bag needs to be 'encouraged' through trees or vegetation, you'll be able to apply much greater force if you pull the rope with a mechanical ascender or prusik, then you can use your full body-weight to help. An additional mechanical ascender, this time upside-down on the bag-side of the pulley, will increase your pulling power still further.

Left: A Petzl Traxion 'Wall Hauler' designed for hauling heavy weights up walls, a wall hauler integrates a pulley with a cam that allows the rope to move one way only.

Multi-pitching

Descending

A surprising number of climbing accidents happen on the way down. Maybe people stop concentrating so much once they feel the hard work is finished. Maybe they don't assess the danger highly enough, having completed what they see as the more risky business of climbing up. Or maybe it's just that by then people are most tired. Whatever the reasons, any fall when descending steep ground is likely to be severe, or fatal, so it's important not to let your guard down until you're safely back on the floor.

Very often it will be possible to walk down from a multi-pitch route and usually this will be your best option, but rarely can you lose 250m of altitude without either scrambling down some sections or walking considerably out of your way.

What is essential is that you know the descent options before you leave the ground. For straightforward walk-offs you'll want, as a minimum, a detailed description of the descent and the possible dangers. For more complex ones you'd be wise to make sure you have several hours of daylight left. If you can't guarantee that much, maybe it's worth walking up and down again to check it out before you try your route. An overlooked question you should ask others who have done the route before is not 'how was the climb?' but 'how was the descent?'!

If the light does start to fade, or if the path steepens worryingly, don't be slow in getting out a rope, especially if one of your party is a lot less confident on steep ground than the others.

Walking or scrambling down isn't always possible, and even when there is a walk-off it may be better to do a chain of abseils down the face you've just climbed. Rarely is this the case in the UK, as routes in mountain areas tend to have reasonable paths down, and those in other areas are usually short enough to descend in one double-rope abseil. But if you want to climb the Old Man of Hoy, or many of the higher rock routes in the Alps, abseiling will be the only sensible option.

Beginning the 50m free abseil back to the ground from pitch two of the *East Face Original Route* (HVS) on the Old Man of Hoy. Photo by Duncan Skelton.

Multi-pitching

Abseiling

It's easier to kill yourself abseiling than at any other time during a long climbing day. All it takes is one error: you don't put your abseil device on right; you put it on right but on the wrong rope; you don't realise how far you've gone and abseil straight off the end of the rope. There are many ways to get it wrong and almost every one of them will kill you. When added to that the fact that you are probably tired, it may have started raining and you could be shivering with cold, then you should begin to realise how important it is to double-check everything at every stage when abseiling.

Use an auto-locking abseil device, or a backup prusik (see page 148) and you won't fall if you get hit by loose rock, or lose control of the rope for some reason. It will also allow you to use both hands if you have to sort out tangles in the rope on the way down. If you don't have a locking system in place, you can free both hands by wrapping the rope a couple of times around your leg, but it's just as quick and invariably safer to use a prusik.

Tying an overhand knot near the bottom of the ropes will stop you abseiling off the end. You could tie knots separately in each rope but it's better to tie both ropes in one knot; not only is this quicker but it means all is not lost if you forget to untie the knot before pulling the rope.

One of your main concerns should be finding the next place to abseil from. Sometimes even fixed belay points are hard to spot - particularly if it's getting dark - and you won't want to go past as it can be hard and slow having to prusik back up again. If it isn't steep you can swing a few metres to either side to get a better look, and if you're descending the route you climbed you may be able to remember important details like traverse sections.

If you're abseiling down a diagonal pitch, you may have to place some gear from time to time and clip both of your abseil ropes in to guide your descent. The last person should be able to retrieve most if not all of these, but at the risk of taking a swing back each time they take a piece out. If the first person down keeps a firm hold of the ropes they can greatly reduce the swing. They can also help pull the last person across to the new belay.

Another big risk in multiple abseils is getting the rope stuck. If it's a long abseil the sheer weight of hanging rope will mean it isn't easy to pull, so minimising additional friction can be critical. Using a maillon (right) or a karabiner instead of threading nylon directly will help reduce the drag. If you use an overhand knot to join your ropes together the knot will have a tendency to roll around any edges it meets edge rather than butt up against them.

If you're not sure whether the rope will pull okay, get the first person down to try and pull it, while there's still time to make changes. Another good idea to speed up the descent is the first person down can begin threading the next belay while the second is abseiling - make sure you thread the rope you are going to pull though. The last person down can often help further by stopping on a ledge a short way down and pulling one rope through until the knot clears any edge near the belay. Note that this should only be considered if the rope is attached via a maillon or a krab, as pulling rope directly through a nylon belay can seriously reduce its strength.

Multi-pitching

Fixed belays

Luckily, where multiple-abseil descents are common, there will often be fixed belays at suitable points on the way down. Although usually reliable, you should check each one carefully for ageing and deterioration of any hardware (bolts, pegs, fixed wires, etc.) and especially software (slings or rope). If necessary, replace the slings with new pieces you brought up specially (you did bring some, didn't you?) Be particularly wary of abseil stations where there is no maillon or in-situ krab, as any fixed cord or webbing may have been melted and seriously weakened when previous people pulled their ropes.

Even if you're confident in the in-situ gear, it doesn't hurt to back it up while all but the last person goes down. This could mean putting an extra piece in somewhere, or just using an extra sling to back up any tat that's connecting different parts of the belay. If you're doing this it's very important that the fixed belay is still taking the strain and your additional gear is just a backup. Otherwise you still won't have tested the fixed gear properly when the last person has to go down.

If you're really concerned, and if you don't have any replacement tat to use, you can always abandon a sling or even cut a short length off the end of one of your ropes. Better that than getting scared stupid when you start to abseil, and far better than risking a belay failure.

If you find yourself abseiling from a belay so bad that you simply can't trust it, you can back it up for both parties by placing

Climbers descending from the *in situ* abseil point on the Lake District classic *North West Arete* (VS), Gimmer Crag. Photo by Ian Parnell.

gear on the way down and clipping your ropes in. When you get to the next belay, feed out enough slack for the next person to abseil, but keep them 'on belay', by keeping your abseil device on the rope. As your partner descends, they will need to remove the gear you've placed on the way down. If the worst thing happens and the belay rips, the gear between you will hopefully stop the fall in time.

Multi-pitching

Leaving gear

If you have run short of time, or if the weather has turned nasty, you could find yourself descending a route people usually walk down from. Most likely there won't be any fixed abseil belays and you'll have to fix your own. Then you have to balance the cost of the gear you're leaving behind against the increased safety of leaving it. Abseiling from just one bomber piece is always tempting, but unless you have exceptional ability to place and to judge the quality of your gear it can amount to rolling dice with your life. Two good pieces may be enough, as long as they are equalised, and as usual they can be backed up to a third to make doubly sure while the first person goes down.

Of course, wires are much cheaper to replace than cams, so if time is not critical it can be worth looking around for a while to find a couple of great wire placements reasonably close together. Another good idea is to keep a couple of old karabiners on your harness, perhaps use them to rack your wires on, so you won't have to leave your shiny new ones behind.

An old abseil station on the *Old Man of Hoy* in Scotland. A belay such as this can take some fathoming to work out that everything is clipped together and equalised - an easy assumption to make. Consider taking a knife to it and re-equalising if necessary. Photo by Duncan Skelton.

A low budget equalised abseil belay. Due to the low forces on the belay, it's acceptable to lark's foot the sling through the wires to save using karabiners - though of course it would be stronger to use karabiners throughout. The use of a maillon will allow the rope to pull much more easily.

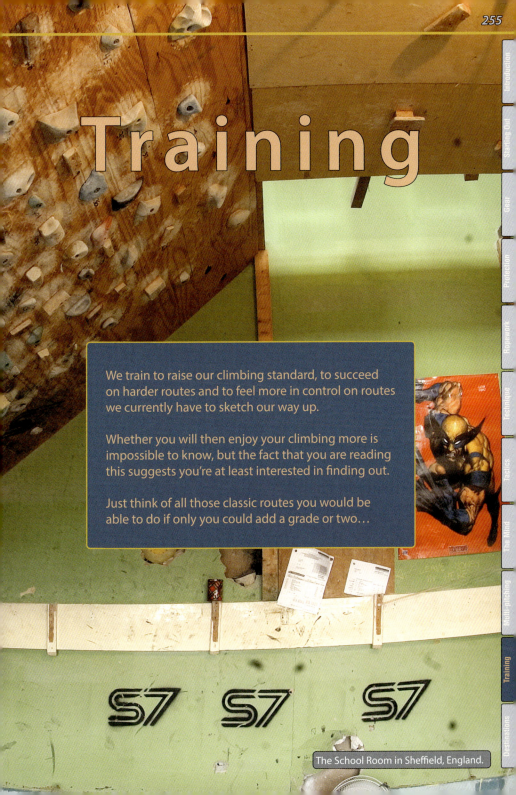

Training

We train to raise our climbing standard, to succeed on harder routes and to feel more in control on routes we currently have to sketch our way up.

Whether you will then enjoy your climbing more is impossible to know, but the fact that you are reading this suggests you're at least interested in finding out.

Just think of all those classic routes you would be able to do if only you could add a grade or two…

The School Room in Sheffield, England.

Training

Training for Trad

Most people can second or top-rope routes a good grade or two harder than they can lead. They're good enough physically and technically to climb harder, but not to cope with the extra skills and stresses involved in leading. It would make sense then, if you're a climber wanting to get up harder routes, to work on your leading skills so you'll be able to climb many of those routes you're already physically capable of. But mention training and people won't think of these aspects, they will instead conjure up images of climbing walls, pull-ups and campus boards.

The key to effective training is to target the parts of your climbing you want to improve and to take specific steps to achieve exactly that. Whether this means bouldering indoors, or leading lots of scary routes, if you're doing it specifically to help get better at some aspect of your climbing, then it's training.

Why not just climb?

Most of us aren't interested in sticking to a rigorous training programme, we just want to get better at climbing, so why not just go climbing? Isn't it true that 'the best training for climbing is climbing?'

Simply going climbing makes sense in that you'll be practising the full range of skills and strengths you need. It also makes sense in that the more training you do the more you'll enjoy it! However, getting out and climbing more routes isn't always possible and even when it is possible it won't always be the most effective way to improve. For example, most routes within your ability will have only a few moves, if any, that are near your strength limit. So if lack of strength is holding you back there are far more effective ways to increase your strength than simply climbing more routes.

Another reason why simply going climbing may not be the best way to improve is that we climbers are vain creatures, we tend to avoid things we're not good at, even if we know that by doing so we'll never get any better. We'd secretly like to be able to climb cracks well, or to keep calm when we find loose rock, but we'll never be able to do these things unless we first spend time doing things we aren't good at. For example, climbers who have difficulty coping with runouts often prefer well-protected routes, but continuing to climb only well-protected routes will be doing nothing to help them cope with runouts better in future.

Dave Macleod showing what hard training can prepare you for. *The Fugue* (E9), Glen Croe, Arrochar, Scotland. Photo by Dave Cuthbertson.

When to train?

You'll get the most benefit from training if you dedicate all of your climbing time and energy to it, but there is a balance to be drawn between improving your climbing and enjoying the fruits of your training gains. Also, your lifestyle inevitably will limit your available climbing time and energy. Even elite climbers rarely stick rigidly to training plans; they're human too! A good plan is to devote your weekday climbing to training and your weekends to achievement. Additionally, anything you're able to do to enjoy training more, or to gain more training benefit from your climbing, will be well worth doing.

Few people enjoy doing things they aren't good at, so if you've developed a weakness it's likely you won't enjoy the training needed to improve it. One approach is just to 'bite the bullet' and get on with it, but sometimes this can be intimidating and even counter-productive. You tell yourself you have to climb cracks next time out, you don't enjoy cracks because you can't climb them well, so you instinctively avoid going out! In this example you would be far better off deciding to climb, say, one crack climb per day when you go out. It won't improve your jamming skills as much as a whole day of it, but it will be far more effective than sitting at home avoiding the issue!

Planning your training

If you keep doing the same thing you will reach a plateau. Typically good training gains will be possible for three or four weeks by repeating the same type of exercise two or three times a week, increasing the intensity each session, after which time you should take a short rest and move on.

The stagnation will be psychological as well as physical and a change of training emphasis periodically can help keep you motivated. If you are able to devote plenty of time and energy to training, it is beneficial to have a clear plan, not just of what to train but also of how long to spend training it.

Planning such changes to your training focus is called 'periodisation'. It can help not only in getting the greatest benefits from your training, but also in maintaining your training enjoyment and motivation. Targeting a succession of weaknesses, each for a month or so, will also help focus your training. If you've identified many important weaknesses, you can't effectively address them all at once, so plan a six-month or one-year calendar and target each one individually for maximum benefit.

Physical and mental breaks

Just as it is important to know when to train, it is equally important to know when *not* to train. Make sure to give yourself a break from training, as it's beneficial both physically and psychologically to have a few weeks off at least once a year. Also, just as you should avoid pushing yourself physically when you're injured or ill, so you shouldn't push yourself mentally when you have other pressing things on your mind. Dangerous situations should be avoided when you aren't able to concentrate properly, but backing off routes can be psychologically harmful, so during a phase of mental training try to keep your life as free as possible from other stress. Lastly, there's nothing more motivating than getting up harder routes, so make sure you set aside some days for pushing your limits, even if this is just by trying a harder route at the wall.

Typical training plan

Month	Objective/Focus	Activity (sessions per week)
January	Build a good level of general climbing/training fitness. Also include stretching.	1 x general routes climbing 2 x low-intensity wall endurance training 2 x running/cycling/swimming
February	Build finger and core-body strength (after 5 days complete rest)	2 x targeted gym and systems board sessions 1 x general bouldering 1 x general routes climbing 1 x running/cycling/swimming
March	Build strength endurance (after 5 days complete rest)	2 x route lapping (different length routes) 1 x general routes climbing 1 x general bouldering 1 x running/cycling/swimming
April	Improve technique. Focus on route reading, resting/efficiency and gear placement/ropework	2 x specific technique practice 1 x general routes climbing 1 x general bouldering (strength-biased) 1 x running/cycling/swimming
May	Improve onsight mental performance by climbing runout routes 1-2 grades below your maximum	2 x specific weakness routes 1 x general bouldering (strength-biased) 1 x route lapping (30-50 moves) 1 x running/cycling/swimming
June	Hard target onsights	Climb as much as opportunity permits, but make sure you prepare for and attempt many routes at your ability limit, with adequate rest days.
July	Improve finger and upper body strength	2 x targeted gym and systems board sessions 1 x general bouldering 1 x general routes climbing 1 x running/cycling/swimming
August	Improve strength endurance (after 5 days complete rest)	Improve strength endurance (after 5 days complete rest)
September	Improve technique, focussing on maximising performance, precision footwork and timing	2 x specific technique practice 1 x general routes climbing 1 x general bouldering (strength-biased) 1 x running/cycling/swimming
October	Improve headpoint mental performance by climbing worked routes 1-2 grades below your maximum	1 x headpoint practice 1 x general bouldering (strength-biased) 1 x route lapping (30-50 moves) 1 x running/cycling/swimming
November	Hard target headpoints	Climb as much as opportunity permits, but make sure you prepare for, and attempt routes, at your ability limit with adequate rest days. Complement with light aerobic and general routes.
December	Rest	Have fun climbing wacky or obscure routes/problems, then give yourself a minimum of two weeks complete rest.

Training

Where to train

Weaknesses can be grouped into three categories: physical, technical and mental. The weakness you are working will largely dictate where you work it.

In general, physical attributes are most effectively trained indoors, or perhaps by specific use of certain bouldering or traversing venues outside. This way you can more easily concentrate your efforts on the right kind of holds, the right angled wall and the right duration.

Technical attributes such as movement skills, balance and jamming are usually best trained outdoors. Careful choice of venues and rock types will ensure the moves you do will resemble those on the routes you're training for.

Most mental attributes can only really be trained at the crag, although careful choice of venues and routes will be needed if apprehensions are to be reduced rather than reinforced.

Training at the crag

Because few of us are happy pushing our grade all day, it is tempting to spend much of the day on easier routes, clocking up 'mileage'. While this can be very enjoyable, it isn't an effective way to improve. Instead, try a climb you ordinarily wouldn't choose; something that will push you but without the ego gratification you normally would expect from trying so hard. Maybe a jamming crack, a thin bridging corner, or a fingery, bouldery route - whatever you aren't usually good at.

Alternatively, you may wish to spend time improving your technique by bouldering or top-roping something technical. The only sure way to get better is to practise and what better time to do so than when the alternative would be doing 'just another route'?

Jan Zbranek bouldering out *Old School* (V4) at Spittle Hill, Castle Hill, New Zealand - what better place to practise off-width climbing than on a hard off-width boulder problem?

Leah Crane competing indoors. Climbing competitions are great ways of getting a thorough workout - whether it's a fun local event or a World Cup!
Photo by Alex Messenger

Training

Physical training

There's probably more known about physical training for climbing than about any other aspect of climbing performance. Training theories for increasing performance in strength, endurance and flexibility have been adapted from other sports and there's plenty of climbing-specific knowledge now too. But while sport climbers and boulderers are usually keen to push their physical boundaries, trad climbers all too often hide behind the fact (excuse?) that there's more to it than just being able to pull hard. That may be true, but no amount of bravery or bottle will get you up a route unless you can pull the moves, and no amount of clever gear placement will get you up a sustained route you simple aren't fit enough for.

Almost all climbers would benefit from more rigorous or specific training, although to some, the idea of spending time on a campus board or pulling weights in a gym would be the antithesis of why they got into climbing in the first place!

The good news is that physical training isn't an all-or-nothing choice; simply by adapting your climbing behaviour at the crag you can get stronger or fitter and by careful use of climbing walls you can make even bigger gains.

Principles of physical training

Specificity - climbing requires very specific strengths and training must be focused on the muscles we use, rather than those we don't.

Overload - your body will grow to be comfortable with what you do with it, only by making it work harder will you cause it to **adapt** to the higher level.

Progression - Our bodies take time to adapt to increased demands. Training is most effective when we make small gains constantly over a long time.

Recovery - We need to rest to make the best of the training we've done, but not too long...

Reversibility - Use it or loose it! Training will make you stronger, but if you don't use that strength, you will weaken.

The *practicals* of physical training

Eat well - make sure you've plenty of energy by having a good meal several hours before your training session. You can't train well if you're running low, so if you're planning on training after work, make sure you have an extra-large lunch and maybe even a snack in the afternoon. When your training session is over, get some food in you as quickly as possible - it will aid your recovery.

Warm up - always make sure you are well warmed up before any hard training. You'll have less chance of injury and your training session will last longer and be more productive too. Expect to spend at least the first half hour warming up.

Hydrate - throughout the day you should ensure you are well hydrated. Keep an eye on the colour of your urine as an indicator - if it's dark, you need to hydrate now!

Warm down - at the end of your session, low intensity exercise - such as some easy routes, or a run/cycle ride home - will speed up your recovery.

Training

Working your weaknesses to achieve your goals

The best training for you will depend very much on your weaknesses, your goals and your body. If you're only interested in climbing a particular style of route, (for example, slabs) there will be little to gain from training something completely different (for example, thuggy overhangs). However trad climbing in general requires a huge variety of skills - covering all angles, techniques, rock types and degrees of protectability - and your weaknesses will certainly show up before long.

It is important to note that there is no one-size-fits-all training solution, only by understanding the general principles of physical training can you customise your training to best benefit your own climbing.

Identify your weaknesses

It's important to identify precisely what it is you need to train. If you fail on an attempt at a route it's tempting to assume you could have done that crux move if only you'd been stronger, but often lack of endurance or inability to recover is really to blame. Ask yourself if you could do the move after a rest on the gear: if you could, you don't lack strength, you just need to be able to use your existing strength for longer. Similarly if you lack core body strength you may not be able to transfer your weight through your feet well and you could mistakenly assume that your arms are just not strong enough.

Before you can train your weaknesses you first need to identify them, which requires brutal honesty. So perhaps enlist the help of a trusted climbing partner in filling in the table below. For example, if your goals are all on gritstone you may decide that footwork is very important (maybe a 9?) but that being able to cope with loose rock isn't (maybe a 1?). Note that the ability level is relative, so however well or poorly you climb overall, your weakest attribute should get no more than 2, and your strongest attribute should get at least 9. The higher the weakness factor for any attribute the more effort you should put into training it.

Attribute	A. How important it is for your climbing 1-10	B. Your current relative ability level 1-10	Weakness factor A x (10 - B)
Finger strength			
Upper body strength			
Endurance			
Recovery rate			
Technique			
Footwork			
Flexibility			
Placing gear			
Trusting gear			
Runouts			
Loose rock			

Training

Aspects of physical training

Physical training targets will fall into one of three groups:

1) General fitness - your ability to recover during easier climbing or while resting.

2) Strength - the ability to hold a position, or move from one position to another (doing it quickly is often referred to as 'power').

3) Strength endurance - maintaining your strength on a sustained route.

General fitness

An efficient cardiovascular system will help you train strength and strength-endurance more effectively, as you'll recover from each exercise and from each training session more quickly. Because of this, if you're thinking of embarking on a physical training programme to improve your climbing you should first make sure your general fitness is up to scratch.

A good way to improve your general fitness is alternating sessions of non-climbing aerobic activity (such as running, cycling or swimming) with sustained low-intensity climbing. The climbing should last for fifteen minutes or more without a break and should never be so hard you have to fight to stay on. Think of it as easy vertical jogging! It is possible to do this kind of training on routes at the climbing wall, climbing alternately up and down the same or nearby routes, but you'll need a very patient belayer! Climbing walls with auto-belay systems can be ideal and long traversing walls can be effective too. Otherwise you can link or repeat circuits on a bouldering wall, but be careful not to make the circuits too hard and be sure not to use any slabby rests!

After a month or so you should have a good base level of fitness and the benefits of continuing this kind of training will reduce; but as long as it doesn't leave you too tired to climb or to train specifically for climbing, a regular aerobic workout can help maintain your optimum weight and keep up your energy levels.

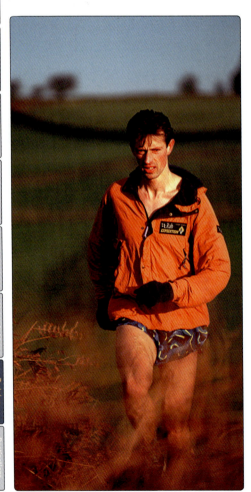

Al Powell running through the moors around Caley, Yorkshire, England. Photo by Ian Parnell

Strength

Quite simply, the stronger you are, the more chance you have of doing any given move. The shorter the route, the more likely it is that strength will be a critical requirement and no amount of general fitness or clever technique will compensate for fundamental weakness, particularly in your shoulders, arms or fingers.

Gaining strength can also help on longer routes. You can move more efficiently if you're not pulling your hardest and sometimes having the extra strength to pull through a hard move quickly can save a lot of time and energy.

To do hard moves you need to be fresh; a hard boulder problem will only be possible after a good rest, allowing you to use all of your strength. By the same reasoning, training strength is only really effective when you're well rested: to train for pulling hard you need to be fresh enough to actually pull hard! Trying powerful problems when you're pumped or powered-out may well be training something but it won't be training strength.

Specificity and isolation

The trick to making big strength gains is to make the exercises you do *specific* to the muscle groups and range of movement you want to improve. This is best achieved by isolating the muscles you need to strengthen and focusing your efforts on them. For example, it is better to train your fingers and your arms in *isolation*. In practice, this might mean doing finger-hangs on a fingerboard and then pull-ups on a bar.

Staying injury free

Pulling your hardest will incur the biggest risk of injury, so the importance of a thorough warm-up cannot be stressed enough. Start with general warming exercises such as running, then warm up the big climbing muscle groups first. Do plenty of non-pumpy moves on jugs, then gradually reduce the size of the holds and increase the diversity of the moves. Keep the moves fairly easy at first and gradually start pulling harder, resting frequently to make sure you don't get pumped. Crimping (pulling on very small finger holds), in particular, puts a great deal of strain on the joints and tendons of your fingers; so avoid using full crimps when you're training finger strength - better to use a combination of half-crimp and open hand positions.

Strength, of course, has it's limitations...

Training

Hypertrophy and recruitment

There are two elements to strength training. 'Hypertrophy' involves building muscle by increasing the number of your muscle fibres, this will increase your muscle mass, which may be fine for relatively small muscles like forearms, but if you apply this type of training to your quadriceps you can expect to gain some weight in muscle. 'Recruitment' is the ability to fire as many of your muscle fibres as possible. Perhaps surprisingly, much of our existing muscular potential is not available to us, at least not until we've trained our nervous system to co-ordinate more muscle fibre twitching at once.

Hypertrophy training

The way to build muscle fibre is to heavily load a muscle repeatedly between six and twelve times. The trick to making big strength gains is in making the exercises you do extremely specific to the muscle groups and range of movement you want to improve.

Muscle building in the gym

Gym equipment can be very good for arm, shoulder and torso exercises. With a little thought you can simulate pretty much any climbing movement and, because the load can easily be changed, you won't need to find a whole new problem when the first one gets too easy!

For example, to increase your mantelshelf (triceps) strength try doing dips on a set of parallel bars. Use either bungy-loop assistance or extra weights so that you can only do between eight and ten dips maximum. Do three sets of six on the minute, rest for ten minutes and repeat. You can use your resting time to work a different muscle group, such as finger strength.

Muscle building through bouldering

Most boulder problems are of a suitable length and bouldering can be excellent training for building strength. Problems should be between six and twelve moves long, very sustained, and on as similar holds as possible. Make sure you know the moves already, otherwise the load you subject your muscles to will decrease each time as you learn the optimal body positioning. Aim to repeat each problem three times, taking substantial rest in

Jamie Allen bouldering at The Foundry, Sheffield, England. Photo by Nick Smith

between.

Campus boards and system boards

Campus boards are common at many climbing walls and consist of a series of horizontal rungs on a high slightly-angled fixed board. They can be used for even greater gains in strength by enabling you to repeat exactly the same move each time. Plan on working each hand at least six times per set and if you complete your third set with strength to spare you should increase the difficulty next time by adding weight or using smaller or more distant rungs.

Recruitment training

Recruitment involves shocking muscle fibres into action by loading so extreme that you will only be strong enough for it during the short period immediately after your comprehensive warm-up. In practice, the exercises you do will be similar to hypertrophy but you should be pulling so hard you can only do two or perhaps three moves at a time.

Working a problem that's too hard for you can be effective, as long as you're not able to link more than a few moves at once. Take plenty of rest between attempts and stop trying the problem as soon as you aren't able to do moves you could do earlier.

Finger strength can be worked intensively by using a fingerboard at home. Find a hold on the board deep enough for only the first joint of your fingers. Using either one or both hands and if necessary adjusting the load by putting your foot in a variable number of bungy loops, find a combination you can hold for only 3-6 seconds. Keeping your shoulder and your elbow slightly bent will help prevent injury. Repeat your maximum-duration hang eight times, resting for around thirty seconds each time. In subsequent sessions you may find you're stronger and can hang for more than six seconds, so raise the difficulty level by reducing the amount of bungy assistance. Eventually you may even be able to move onto doing this with just one hand but take care to avoid injury and start off using a bungy for assistance.

Zlu Haller on *The Joker* (V9) Spittle Hill, Castle Hill, New Zealand. Recruitment training through very short boulder problems at your very limit is a great way to learn to use more of the muscle that you've already got.

Strength endurance

The key to being physically able to climb most trad routes is having good strength endurance. Looking for holds, trying different sequences and placing gear all take their toll on our muscles. Success will often depend critically on your forearms' ability to keep working at quite a high level. Training strength endurance will keep the pump at bay for longer.

The way to do this is to get pumped - frequently and severely! Like taking foul-tasting medicine, you know it's going to be unpleasant but you also know it's the best way to get better, so just swallow it!

The more often your arms are forced to cope with sustained activity, the more effective they will become at clearing the lactic acid your muscles inevitably produce. If you're lucky you'll learn to like the feeling of being not-quite-pumped and you'll enjoy trying to push it ever further.

Working strength endurance indoors

When most people visit climbing walls they're largely working on strength endurance, but if you have a haphazard approach to which routes you try and when, the benefits won't be nearly as great as they could be.

Using routes

After a thorough warm-up you should be aiming to climb the same length of route - ideally the same route - up to five times in a session, with 10-15 minute rests between. The route you choose should be sustained and very close to your maximum grade, which is harder than you can onsight, so choose something you know already and feel you can get only just get up in one go. Many walls are 10-12m high, meaning routes typically involve only 20 moves or so, which is about the minimum length for strength endurance training. Longer routes can be simulated by climbing up, down and up again.

Thea Williams leading at The Foundry wall, Sheffield, England. Photo by Nick Smiith.

Circuit training

A good alternative to climbing routes is to do circuits on a bouldering wall, as you have full control over the grade, the length and the type of moves involved, although you'll probably have to spend a whole session 'working' a circuit before you'll be able to train on it effectively. An advantage of boulder circuits is that you won't be limited by the height of the wall, so it's easier to create circuits of exactly the right length, and you can train alone.

Try to vary the length of the routes or circuits in different sessions. One plan is to spend one session doing 20-30 move routes/circuits and another session - a couple of days later once you've recovered - doing longer ones of 40-50 moves. If you're doing longer routes you'll need more rest between them, between two and three times the time it takes to climb the route. If the route, or circuit, is slightly too easy or slightly too hard you can adjust the resting time so that you can only just get up it each time.

Keep it specific

One mistake people often make is to train on overhanging walls of 12m or so, then go out and climb 30m vertical routes. Certainly there will be a training benefit, but the closer you can make the training mirror the climbing, the more effective it will be. Also, if you're top-roping indoors on familiar routes you will be moving continuously, which is a poor simulation of onsighting routes outside, where you often have to stop to think and to place gear. Leading routes indoors is better, as you have to stop and clip, but you can further emulate this by forcing yourself to lock certain holds (maybe every third hold) one-handed for five or ten seconds.

Another trick is to climb with five spare quickdraws on your harness and to transfer all of them from one gear loop to another between each clip. If you're using circuits on a bouldering wall, you can slow yourself down in exactly the same way - if there are some bolt-hangers, hang quickdraws off them and clip them as you go around - just tie a short length of rope to your waist and clip away.

Lastly, if you fall mid-route, or mid-circuit, and have the ability to carry on (such as if your foot slipped), then get straight back on and continue - the route you're on is a means to an end and getting a clean ascent is of no importance.

Strength endurance training at home just requires a bit of imagination and plenty of dedication. John in Pristina, Kosovo, trying to stay in shape without access to a wall or a crag.

Technical training

You can improve your climbing technique just by climbing a lot, but like other aspects of training, the more you focus on a specific weakness the more effective your training will be. This is where it pays to be self-critical, or at least to have friends who are happy to criticise your technique for you!

Most technical aspects of climbing are best learned and trained when you're near the ground. If you're not confident in your ability to place wires, cams or any other pieces of gear well, try placing fifty of them within reach of the ground at various points along the foot of a crag. Hang on each one to test it and you'll soon find which work well and which don't. An added bonus is that you'll learn how to get stuck ones out again as well!

Movement skills are also best trained near ground level, or at least with the safety of a top-rope or good protection. First identify specifically what you need to get better at, then find places where you can practise these specifics in safety. Bouldering is often best for this, although if there aren't appropriate moves near the ground you may have to use a rope. For instance, if you have trouble keeping in balance when you're climbing aretes, go to a bouldering area where there are lots of aretes to practise on. Similarly, if you find it hard to avoid cutting loose (swinging foot-less) when climbing roofs, find a section of crag that's very undercut near its base, so you can experiment safely and without getting pumped.

Learning techniques and being able to apply them is clearly important, even essential, but often the most effective technical advantages are subtle. Whether to use your heel or your toe on a particular hold? To change feet or step through? To pull up and then lock, or use momentum and dyno? Mastering these subtleties will not only get you up boulder problems you otherwise may find impossible, they will also help fend off the pump on a long pitch and make insecure moves above gear feel more solid.

Penny Allchin bouldering at The Edge Wall, Sheffield, England. Photo by Nick Smiith.

Thinking carefully about every aspect of your body and its balance is the key to good technique. If you're surprised when a hard-looking move feels easy, ask yourself why that is? What was the 'trick' that made it all feel less steep, or that made such small holds feel good enough? Watch some of the better climbers at the crag or at the wall to see how they do the same moves as you. Often you can learn from watching good female climbers, as they will rarely pull through hard moves on strength alone unless there's little alternative.

Bouldering in groups will help you learn from each other, but remember there are usually several ways to do the same move. What works well for someone else will not always work well for you, so keep an open mind and always be on the lookout for subtle adjustments that could turn out to be critical. A good idea is to start making up your own problems; trying to set a problem that you can do but your friends can't will get you thinking carefully about the differences in your climbing styles, strengths and techniques.

If you do use bouldering as a means to improving your trad climbing technique, remember that the level of insecurity you find acceptable when you're at bouldering height may be very different from when you're facing a lead-fall. Once you've done a problem try it again but this time try to keep in perfect balance throughout. This may just mean pulling harder, but often it won't be possible unless you optimise precisely how you grip each handhold and carefully refine your footwork - precisely the things you want to become second nature while leading. Keep working it until you're sure you've found how to do it with minimum effort and maximum security!

David Schinzel bouldering at Spittle Hill, Castle Hill, New Zealand.

Psychological training

As climbers we choose which crags to visit, which routes to try, what gear to carry and where to place it. We 'read' sequences from below and gauge the quality of holds, rests and protection in advance. We 'trust' each gear placement differently, depending on our experience, our fears and our scepticism about whether any tiny piece of alloy could hold our entire falling weight! All this presents us with a great many opportunities for negative thinking and it may only take one small irrational fear for us to fail on our attempt.

Of course our fear is important; it keeps us from killing ourselves on dangerous routes we aren't good enough to climb. But very often our fears are unfounded, or at least exaggerated. As we saw in The Mind chapter (*page 206*) the mind is frequently the weakest-link, so anything we can do to train it is bound to have an immediate benefit to our climbing ability.

Is your mind your weakest link?

The best way of assessing your mental strength is to climb for a while with someone much better than you. He or she should soon be able to judge whether you're backing off routes because there's a real chance of hurting yourself or whether your fears are largely unfounded.

At the same time you'll also be able to learn from their judgement, their reasoning and their advice. But there are plenty of ways you can help yourself, even without changing your usual climbing partner.

Mind training

The first step, as ever, is to work out what you need to get better at. If it's a particular type of route that you're avoiding, try lowering your grade expectations on routes of that type until you get more confident. It won't please your ego in the short term but ultimately it may do wonders for your all-round competence.

Trusting your gear

If you don't trust the gear you're placing you can put in plenty at ground level and test it, but no matter how much you know the gear is good, the idea of falling off can still be terrifying. This is hardly surprising: we spend much of our climbing time desperately trying not to fall, so we're unlikely to be over the moon when it happens!

But people fall onto good gear all of the time, and even though it's not something to make a habit of, it clearly isn't the end of the world.

Fall practice

Falling isn't an everyday part of our climbing; it's something we have to learn, just like any other technique. Trusting your belayer doesn't come easily either. Of course they are watching, they are holding the rope and they know not to let go when it comes tight; but knowing all of this is no substitute for really experiencing it.

Climbing walls are perfect for practising falling, as they offer a reasonably safe environment in which to practise. You can do the same on a crag, but back up your top runner with two, three or even more bomb-proof pieces - as many as you need to remove from your mind even the slightest worry about gear failure.

First make sure your belayer is fully aware of what you're about to do. Climb a steep well-protected route and clip a bolt or a collection of utterly perfect pieces six metres or so above the ground. Make sure there aren't any ledges or large protruding holds directly beneath you. Enlist a third person to 'back up' your belayer by loosely holding the 'dead' end of the rope a couple of metres from where it leaves the belay device (alternatively have your belayer tie a simple overhand knot at that point in the rope), then:-

1) With your waist just above the highest clipped runner, have your belayer take the rope tight and lock it off, then drop onto the tight rope.

2) Do the same again, but this time have your belayer lock the rope off without first taking it tight. You will fall a metre or so further due to the slack in the system.

3) The same again but this time let go without your belayer having yet locked off the rope. You may go down slightly further again as the belay is locked off, but it shouldn't be far.

4) Repeat steps 1-3 from a point one metre higher, but falling onto the same gear.

Practising falling can help you build essential faith in the rope and belay system. The more irrational fears you can remove, the better you will be able to concentrate on the rational ones!

Trusting yourself

A common rational fear is when a climb doesn't have bomb-proof gear, where trust in your own ability is needed to compensate for lack of trust in the gear. To many people this is really what trad climbing is all about. It's not about making climbs safe by using technology - you could do that with a top-rope or by sport climbing. It's about making climbs safe by learning judgement.

We're all used to crossing roads in busy traffic. We judge the size of the gap, the speed of the cars, the width of the road, the chance of tripping and all manner of other factors. If we get it badly wrong we'll get hurt, but this rarely happens. With practice, children get better at crossing roads in heavy traffic. The gaps don't get bigger, the cars don't go slower, but we learn to judge situations better and we learn to trust our own judgement.

Trad climbing is just like crossing a road. One important way of getting up harder climbs is by improving your judgement, and you can only do that by practising. The moment you climb above gear your brain will be constantly assessing possible outcomes, and constantly learning. By placing gear just one metre further apart than you normally would, you will be training yourself to cope with runouts. If you get scared when runners are by your feet, do slightly easier routes and don't put gear in until the last good piece is beneath your feet.

Only through practice will you learn to feel in control when you're above your gear and if you practise often on routes where there's plenty of gear options you'll be far happier climbing routes where there isn't. If you get into the habit of doing this regularly, you'll add spice to every lead except your hardest grades, and training may never have felt so good!

Matt Goode on *Lost Arrow Spire* (5.10d/A0) Yosemite, California, USA.   Photo by Alex Messenger

Destinations

The best way to improve your trad climbing is to get out on the crag and do it. You should aim to experience different rock types, try long sustained routes, try short sharp routes, climb on steep stuff, climb on slabs, climb in the mountains and climb on sea cliffs. The more you experience, not only the better you will become at dealing with unforeseen circumstances, but also the more rewarding your climbing will be.

For many people trips to far away destinations are what climbing is all about. The following section should give you a few pointers to possible locations around the world. The list is far from exhaustive but covers the most important areas.

Destinations

Britain

Britain has long been recognised as the home of trad climbing. From early explorations in the late 19th Century to the present day, the leading British climbers have all been measured by their ability to climb harder and harder trad routes. There have been forays into aid climbing, and sport climbing, indeed there are many fine sport climbing venues in Britain, but most climbers would agree that the trad experience is what makes climbing in Britain so special.

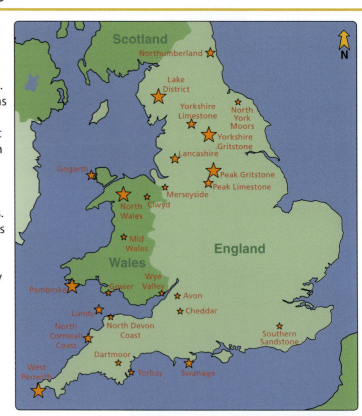

Southern England

Rockfax guides print and app - Dorset (2012), West Country Climbs (2010), Southern Sandstone Climbs (2017)

Alison's Rib (Diff), Bosigran, West Penwith, Cornwall, England. Photo by Mark Glaister

Much of the best trad climbing in southern England is on the fine sea cliffs of the Devon and Cornwall coasts which provide some of the most dramatic and atmospheric routes anywhere. Of particular note is West Penwith where the whole coastline is littered with cliffs of granite. There are more big limetone sea cliffs at Swanage and superb granite on the Island of Lundy. For inland destinations the granite tors of Dartmoor offer similar climbing to the famous gritstone crags in the North, plus the sandstone in Kent has always been a popular destination although top-roping is the norm here. The limestone gorges of Avon and Cheddar are

Destinations

Northern England
Rockfax guides print and app - Eastern Grit (2015), Western Grit (2008), Peak Limestone (2012), Northern Limestone (2015), Northern England (2008)

The most famous and popular British climbing is found in the Peak District where the gritstone edges offer single pitch trad climbing at its best. The World's most popular crag - Stanage - is home to nearly 1200 routes with many more on the near-by edges along the eastern Peak District and to the west in Staffordshire. The limestone of the Peak District is also a worthy destination offering both a mix of trad climbing and sport climbing. Further north the gritstone of Yorkshire has many fine crags which offer equally good trad climbing. Once again the limestone of Yorkshire has a mix of sport and trad. The Lake District is a rival to North Wales as the best mountain trad climbing venue with many fine long routes on great mountain crags. In addition to these major venues are many other diverse locations like the beautiful sandstone of Northumberland and the dramatic quarries of Lancashire.

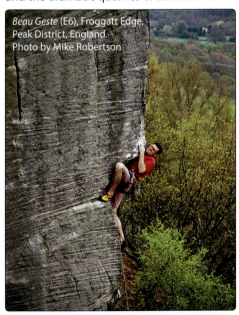
Beau Geste (E6), Froggatt Edge, Peak District, England. Photo by Mike Robertson

Capital Punishment (E4), Idwal, North Wales. Photo by Sherri Davy

Wales
Rockfax guides print and app - North Wales Climbs (2013), Pembroke (2009), Clwyd Limestone (2015)

The rugged landscape of Wales has much to offer. In particular the mountain crags of Snowdonia are amongst the oldest and best-loved trad climbing areas in the world with superb crags like Clogwyn Du'r Arddu, Dinas Cromlech and Idwal Slabs to name three. Surrounding the mountains are many more equally fine crags offering excellent trad climbing on a variety of diverse rock types. Famous crags include the accessible routes at Tremadog, the unique slate climbing near Llanberis, and the huge sea cliffs at Gogarth. Almost as revered as the North Wales mountains are the sea cliffs of Pembrokeshire - miles of limestone cliffs offering thousands of trad routes.

Destinations

Scotland

For such a small country, Scotland offers a wealth of traditional climbing, much of it steeped in a rich history. It is renowned for its impressive mountain cragging, sea cliffs, sea stacks and lowland crags in some of the most beautiful locations in the UK. The rock types vary depending on area but most abundant is schist, gabbro, granite, sandstone and gneiss. If you make the effort to travel to some of the more remote areas you will be often be rewarded with a huge crag (or mountain) to yourself. The best time of the year is usually May and June – generally warm, sunny and pre midges, and September and October can also be very good.

For the mountain areas Cir Mhor on Arran offers impeccable granite slab climbing. In Glencoe Buachaille Etive Mor's Rannoch Wall gives steep, exposed climbing in an incredible situation, Aonach Dubh has great historic classics and the Etive Slabs are a must! On Ben Nevis climbs have an almost alpine "big-feel" in summer with classic ridges and historic routes at all grades. The Isle of Skye has Sron na Ciche, the most immaculate gabbro in the UK and Carmore Crag offers a remote experience but is worth every step of the long walk-in. Up in the Cairngorms Shelterstone Crag has some great long and hard routes on immaculate granite. Another granite crag is Hells Lum which has routes at more modest grades. Finally there is Creag an Dubh Loch, one of the finest granite cliffs in the country for the VS plus climber.

For low-level cragging there is Glen Nevis, Creag Dubh and Diabaig which are all quality locations. The sea cliff areas of Reiff and Sheigra give great atmospheric climbing in a superb settings. The Pass of Ballater is a sunny venue with good granite.

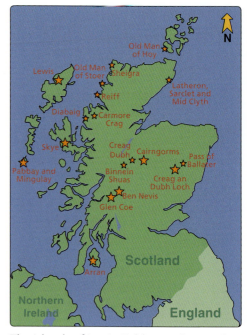

The islands of Lewis, Pabbay and Mingulay in the Outer Hebrides offer some of the best sea cliff climbing in Britain in truly stunning locations. Sea stacks worth seeking out include The Old Man of Hoy – a truly memorable excursion!, and the Old Man of Stoer.

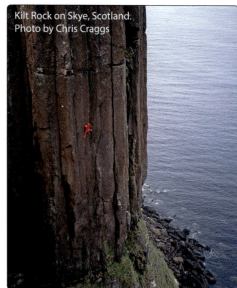

Kilt Rock on Skye, Scotland. Photo by Chris Craggs

Destinations

Ireland

The best crag in Ireland is Fair Head: a big steep crag of dolerite columns with imposing lines, many of which are two and three pitches in length. Also in Northern Ireland are the Mourne Mountains: a number of crags scattered across a compact and wild mountain range made of rough granite, the best are the Binnian Tors and Lower Cove. Be prepared for the long walk-ins, which contribute to the remote wild atmosphere. Near Dublin the smooth granite of Dalkey Quarry offers trad climbing in a suburban location. The touristy valley of Glendalough has become the mecca for Irish bouldering recently, but also hosts some fine long routes of all standards on impeccable mountain granite. Luggala, in the Wicklow Mountains, is an imposing and steep granite crag with some surprisingly amenable long routes which weave their way through the crag's complex layout.

Over in County Clare is Ailladie (*Aill an Daill* - The Burren), a sheer limestone crag which faces west across the open Atlantic. In the winter it is a wild and weather beaten place but in the summer it can be a glorious suntrap.

Spain

Rockfax guide print and app - Costa Blanca (2013)

As in many parts of Europe the majority of the accessible cliffs in Spain have been bolted up to provide the convenient sport climbing that has become so popular. Despite this there are extensive 'terrain d'aventure' venues; these are cliffs that have been left with minimal fixed gear (often just the belays) and are scattered all over this big country. On top of this, the majority of the bigger cliffs are simply too large to be fully bolted and on these a trad climbing experience comes into its own. Settled weather and a long season means that Spain is a year round destination and is especially suitable as a winter venue when northern Europe is cold and grey.

Even the popular sport climbing destinations have some trad lines - usually the big gnarly cracks - as well as whole areas to go at. For example even the Costa Blanca, one of the best known sport climbing venues in Europe, has such fine challenges as the Peñon d'Ifach, the Puig Campana and Ponoch.

Alpine Areas

Rockfax guides print and app - Chamonix (2016), The Dolomites (2014)

The European Alps is a five hundred mile arc of mountains which are best known for big snowy North Faces and multi-day climbs involving huts, glacier crossings and pre-dawn starts. Despite this there is a wealth of great trad climbing on offer which doesn't require a full-on alpine style - although the routes are usually bigger than you might be used to and one eye must be kept on the weather to avoid afternoon thunderstorm epics. Often the belays are fixed which makes retreating in the event of difficulties straightforward. Around Chamonix Mont Blanc are some fine granite crack-lines and walls which have mostly been left as trad challenges. At the other end of the Alps the steep limestone classics of the Dolomites have have much to offer those wanting to test themselves on some of the most impressive cliff faces around.

In between these two major areas are many great cliffs, from the granite slabs of Eldorado and Handegg in central Switzerland, to the varied limestone faces of the Arco and Lecco regions of northern Italy, and on to the major crags of the Kaisergebirge and Ratikon in Austria. Most of these areas also have plenty of accessible sport climbing crags as well for those who are happy to mix their climbing styles.

Krystal (V+), Swiss Granite. Photo by Chris Craggs

Destinations

Norway
Rockfax guides print and app - Lofoten Climbs (2017)

Norway has long been the dark horse of European trad climbing with masses of great rock and a long tradition of self-sufficiency in the mountains. Stories of horrendous weather and man-eating mosquitoes have kept the crowds away - but slowly the truth is asserting itself and increasing numbers of climbers are making the trip to the land of the north-men. Stretching over 1000 miles from end to end, from the southern tip all the way up to the Arctic Circle and beyond, there are fine cliffs of high quality volcanic rock - many of which await their first route. Sea cliffs, valley crags and mountain settings, all tastes are fully catered for. Long-standing areas such as Romsdal, Innerdalen and Lofoten are available along with more recently developed venues; Rogaland, and Nissedal in the south and Fugløya and Kvaløya in the far north for example.

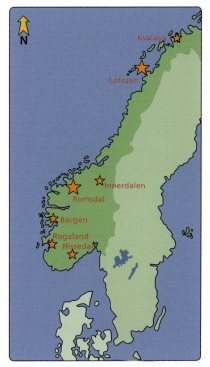

Mot Sola (6-), Nissedal, Norway. Photo by Chris Craggs

Rest of Europe

Germany and Czech

The Elbesandstein area in eastern Germany and over into the Czech Republic offers bolted climbing with a trad feel about it. Much of the protection is hand-placed in the shape of knotted slings although big iron ring bolts tend to be placed near the hardest sections. Leave your metal trad rack at home though.

Malta

There is also a lot of trad development on the islands of Malta and Gozo mostly by ex-pat Brits. In total there are around a thousand routes both on inland crags and dotted around the coast.

USA

Yosemite Valley is the 'big apple' of American climbing. The Valley is rich in history, rich in atmosphere, rich in big walls, soaring crack lines, blank slabs, small cliffs, medium-size cliffs and boulders. Neighbouring Tuolumne Meadows is at a higher elevation and offers accessible summer cragging on beautiful granite domes.

In the Southern Sierra, the lemon-lichen encrusted granite Needles are a crack paradise.

Further south is Joshua Tree, a complex area of quartz-monzonite high desert domes. Its quality and proximity to Los Angeles means that it is has been well developed.

Las Vegas and the Red Rock Canyons of southern Nevada are a vast area of sandstone canyons featuring single and multi-pitch routes of all grades.

Utah is blessed with an incomprehensible amount of rock; Moab is the place to base yourself for the cam-gobbling cracks of Indian Creek and the equally famous desert towers. Near Salt Lake City are the Cottonwood Canyons. Three hours up the road in Utah, City of Rock gives great climbing in a high desert setting.

In Colorado Eldorado Canyon, the Flatirons and Boulder Canyon are located next to 'climbing town USA' - Boulder.

In Wyoming is Devil's Tower. The easiest route up this monolith is the Durance Route a 5.7 with many harder routes.

The East Coast has Cathedral and Whitehorse Ledges in New Hampshire; granite multi-pitch right next to the climbers' town of North Conway. New York State has the Gunks which may hold the candle as the most popular cliff in the USA and rightly so; the rock is perfect quarzite and the trad climbing exceptional.

Canada

Canada is renound for its world-class ice and alpine climbing especially around the Banff and Lake Louise areas. The Bugaboos and the Cirque of the Unclimbables are two of the best high-quality alpine areas in the world. For exceptional roadside cragging (above Hwy 99) the number one destination in Canada is north of Vancouver in British Columbia; a place called Squamish. One-pitch cragging, multi-pitching, hard free, hard aid and bouldering, Squamish has it all, and on the most perfect of granite. Good conditions can be found spring through to early winter. Further east, near Penticton, is Skaha, another major accessible cragging

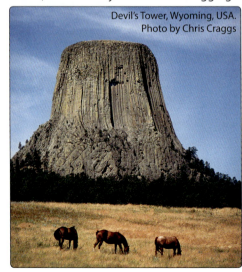

Devil's Tower, Wyoming, USA. Photo by Chris Craggs

Australia

Australian trad climbing is well established and thriving at the world renowned Mt. Arapiles. 'The Arapiles' has hundreds of outstanding single and multi-pitch climbs of all difficulties and is a good place to hook-up with other climbers at its sociable crag-side campsite. Within an hour's drive of Mt. Arapiles is the Grampians National Park. The climbing here is dotted about on some magnificent cliffs that have a first-rate mix of both single and multi-pitch climbs and classics throughout the grades. Close to Sydney are the Blue Mountains which is home to a vast number of sandstone crags. For the visitor the best places to head for are the small towns of Blackheath and Katoomba, from which the best crags can be reached by car. If the weather is really hot then the best choice is to head for the granite of Mt. Buffalo mid-way between Mt. Arapiles and The Blue Mountains.

Mt. Buffalo is a beautiful area with both single and multi-pitch climbs but this time mostly in the mid to upper grades. For those after something a little bit different the desert crags of Moonarie in South Australia will give a feel of the outback, whilst the sea cliffs and mountain basalt in and around Tasmania will reward the more adventurous who crave a bit of solitude.

New Zealand

New Zealand's trad climbing is limited at present, but is easily combined with the multitude of other activities on offer in this outdoor wonderland, including some surprisingly good sport climbing. Undoubtedly its best crag is Whanganui Bay on the shores of the North Island's Lake Taupo. However it lies on a Maori Reservation and access is complicated and often restricted; a bit of research prior to a visit is advised to avoid disappointment. More convenient for the visitor is the urban but excellent Mt. Eden Quarry in Auckland that provides many basalt testpieces. Most of the other good trad lines are located in predominantly sport climbing locations although for those looking for rock climbs within a mountain setting, the Southern Alps of the South Island offer a lifetime of exploration.

Eternity Road (22) Whanganui Bay, New Zealand. Photo by Mark Glaister

Destinations

South Africa

South Africa is a fantastically varied and exotic country with world class climbing of every kind. For the best concentration of trad crags fly in to Cape Town and visit the likes of Table Mountain, Wolfberg and Tafelberg – memorable climbs of all grades, on immaculate rock. If roadside convenience is your thing then don't bother, South Africans are well used to three hour walk-ins, but the rewards are excellent. Further afield there is more adventure trad-ing than you can wish for. Try the Drakensberg for big walls, the highest waterfall in the world, with rumours of banditry and troops of baboons on the snow line for company.

Middle East

Wadi Rum in Jordan is the best and most accessible of the Middle Eastern countries with extensive and well-developed climbing on huge sandstone walls which offer single and multi-pitch trad climbing across the grade range. Beyond that there's the granite in the Sinai, which is well regarded and the metamorphosed limestone of the Hajar mountains in Oman. A lot of trad routes have been climbed by ex-pat Brits in the mountains along the UAE/Oman border.

Destination web sites

The following websites are well established and present good information on climbing in their home countries. Some of them have online shops (or links to online shops) where you can buy area guidebooks. Also try Google of course.

Mainly UK
rockfax.com - *see box opposite*
ukclimbing.com

Rest of Europe
planetmountain.com - Italy
camp2camp.org - France
escuelasdeescalada.com - Spain
climbing.de - Germany
lezeck.cz - Czech Republic

North America sites
rockandice.com - USA
climbing.com - USA
supertopo.com - USA
gripped.com - Canada

Rest of the World sites
climbing.co.za - South Africa
climb.co.nz - New Zealand
thecrag.com - Australia

Drakensberg Mountains, South Africa.
Photo by Matt Heason

Acknowledgments

Rockfax 'PLUS' Series

Two other books in the Rockfax 'PLUS' series.

SportCLIMBING+
Covering all aspects of sport climbing. It follows a similar approach to this book, focusing on the positive things people can do to improve their own performance

WinterCLIMBING+
A similar approach is taken for winter climbing covering everything you need to get out in winter conditions safely.

Rockfax Trad Guides - Print and App

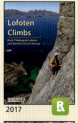   
2017 — 2016 — 2015 — 2015

2015 — 2014 — 2013 — 2013

2012 — 2012 — 2010 — 2009

Rockfax produce guidebooks to trad climbing and sport climbing areas across Europe. These are all also available in the Rockfax App which gives interactive coverage and is fully integrated with the UKClimbing web site Logbook system.
More info - rockfax.com

Android version in 2017

Thanks are due to all of the following who have assisted in the publication of this book:

Additional photographers

Duncan Skelton, Alex Messenger, Nick Smith, Ian Parnell, Dave Cuthbertson, Chris Craggs and Simon Carter.

Photographic subjects

Alex Hughes, Alex Mason, Alex Barrows, Steve Ramsden, Paul Evans, Meilee Rafe, Katherine Schirrmacher, Luke Roberts, Pat McBride, Rob Greenwood, Chris Moor, Cecile Rittweger, Lucy Creamer, Max Adamson, Mike Grant, Anne Arran and Miles Gibson.

Illustrations

Ray Eckermann

Companies

Wild Country, DMM, Petzl, Five Ten, Mammut, Black Diamond and the BMC.

Other contributions

Dan Middleton, Mick Ryan, Chris Craggs, Mike James, Jo George, Matt Heason, Toby Foord-Kelcey, Alan Stark and Dominic Green.

Index

A abandoned gear 72, 93
abseiling 144–151, 251
  auto-blocs. 148
  belays 126, 144
  dramas 150
  fixed anchors 252
  hazards 147
  joining ropes 147
  leaving gear 253
  missiles 148
  multi-pitch 251
  passing a knot. 151
  rope doesn't reach the ground . . 150
  with a pack 150
abseil inspection. 215
abseil rope knot 147, 251
access 15
acid and gear 56
acknowledgments 285
adjective grade. 26
Adrian Berry 6
Aliens 44
Alpine coil 104
anchor . . . . see belays
annual goals 212
arete technique 177
arm-barring 186
arousal level 235
arresting a fall 22, 128
ascending ropes 152–153
ATC Guide 152
auto-blocs. 148
auto-locking abseil device 251
auto-locking belay device 33
B back-and-footing. 188
back-clipping 116
backpack. 54
balance. 163–164, 169
bandoliers 245
behaviour 15
belay device 22, 33
belaying 108–114
  basics 108
  direct 127
  double ropes 114
  escaping the system 112
  lowering. 111
  magic/guide plate 111
  paying out. 110
  sliding method 111
  taking in 109
  through the top piece 127
  tying off a belay device 112
belays 118–126
  belays and screwgates 118
  changeovers. 244
  close belay points 120
  direction. 118
  distant belay points 121
  equalising 118, 123
  fixed. 126
  ground anchors 119
  multi-directional. 240
  no belay? 126
  passing gear 245

  protecting a traverse 124
  sitting or standing. 127
  using slings 122
  using your ropes as a sling . . . 121
  where to belay. 124
  where to put the rope 241
benightment 247
beta 192
biners . . . . see karabiner
block leading. 242
board lasted 30
bold routes. 216
bolts 90
bomb-proof wire. 62
boot squeeking 198
bottom roping 154
bouldering 13, 189, 266, 271
bouldering mats 94
bowline 99
breaking a route down 220
buddy system 22
building a rack 52
building belays. . . . . see belays
butterfly coil 104
C calls 24
Camalots. 44
camming devices 44, 76–86
  camming angle 79
  camming range 44, 76
  flexible-stemmed 81
  micro-cams 83
  off-set 80
  orientation. 80
  removing 84
  reverse strength. 83
  rigid-stemmed 81
  testing your placement 84
  walking 77, 83
campus boards 266
cams. . . . . see camming devices
caring for your gear 56–57
carrying gear. 248
chalk-bags 21, 32
changeovers 244
chicken-winging 186
chimneys 188
chockstones 187
choosing the right placement . . . 62
circuit training 269
climbing calls 24
climbing fast 247
climbing outside 14–15
climbing shoes 30–31
  cleaning 198
clipping hangerless-bolts 69
clipping protection 116–117
clothing 198
clove hitch 103
coiling a rope 104
cold weather 195
communication 24
conditions 195
cordelette 122
cord slings 92
corner technique 176

cracks 179–188, 199
croll 153
crux move 26
D day goals. 212
descending. 144, 250
Destinations **275–285**
  Alpine Areas. 280
  Australia and New Zealand . . . 283
  Britain 276–278
  Ireland. 279
  Middle East 284
  Norway 283
  Rest of Europe 283
  South Africa. 284
  Spain 279
  USA and Canada 282
  Web sites 284
dirt and gear 56
double bowline. 99
double fisherman's knot 101
double ropes 38, 113–115, 134
doublespeak 235
double stopper. 98
doubts 222
down-climbing 158, 192
drag 132
dramatic visualisation 232
drop knees 170
dynamic belaying 140–143
dynamic ropes 38
Dyneema. 46, 92, 101
E edging 168
Egyptians . . . . see drop knee
encouragement 234
equalising belays. 118, 145
escaping the system 112
esoteric wire placements 69
ethics 15
evaluating runners 68
extender . . . . see quickdraws
extending protection 136–138
F failure to success 204
fall factor. 130–131
fall forces 128
falling off. 214–215
  ropework 156–157
fall practice 272
fear of failure. 219
fear of falling. 214
fear of succeeding 228
figure of eight 98
figure of eight on a bight. 100
finger jams 180
finger locks 180
fist jams 183
fixed belays 126
fixed rope abseil belays 144
flagging 170
flash 192
focus. 237
foot jams 182
footwork 162–164, 180
free climbing 192
French prusik 102
friction hitch . . . . . . see Italian hitch

Index

Friends 44, 79
frogging 169
Gastons 187
Gear 29–57
  backpack 54
  bandoliers 245
  belay device 33
  building a rack 52
  camming devices 44
  chalk-bags 32
  climbing shoes 30
  cordelette 122
  harness 32
  haul bag 249
  helmets 34
  hexes 42
  karabiners 37
  nut key 33
  prusik loop 34
  quickdraws 46
  rope ascenders 50
  rope-bags 54
  rope-bucket 54
  rope protector 144
  ropes 38
  shunts 50
  skyhook 205
  slingdraws 48
  slings 46
  tri-cams 42
  wires 40
gear and falling 215
gear and the mind 228
gear loop 32
general fitness 264
girth hitch . . . . see lark's foot
Glycaemic Index 198
goals 208–213, 263
grade blocks 218
grades 26–27, 218
groove technique 176
ground belays 119, 142
ground-up 204
guidebooks 15
gym training 266
half ropes 38
handholds 172
hand jams 182
hand-stacking 186
harness 20, 32
hauling 249
headpoint 192
headpointing 204–205, 231
head-torch 51
helmets 34
hexes 42, 74
HMS karabiner 37
hot weather 195
how cams work 78
how the system works 22–23
hypertrophy 266
impact force 38
indoor climbing 11, 12, 268
injury 265
in situ protection 60, 89

interlinking wires 67
Italian hitch 103, 111
J jamming technique 180–183
jamming wires 68
jams and cams 183
John Arran 6
joining ropes 147
jumaring . . . . . . see ascending ropes
K karabiners 37
  badly loaded 107
knots 98–102
  abseil rope knot 147, 251
  bowline 99
  clove hitch 103
  double bowline 99
  double fisherman's knot . . . 101
  double stopper 98
  figure of eight 98
  figure of eight on a bight . . . 100
  French prusik 102
  Italian hitch 103
  lark's foot 102
  overhand knot 100
  prusik 102
  reef knot 101
  strengths 106
  tape knot 101
krabs . . . . see karabiner
L lark's foot 102
laybacking 175
leading 19, 22
  on multi-pitch routes 242
leading gear 40
leading rack 52
leaving gear 145
leg jams 187
lifetime goals 211
linking pitches 242
locked-off 22
logistics for multi-pitch 246
lowering 111
lowering off 126, 203
M Magic Plates 51, 111
maillon 251
manteling 173
marking gear 57
micro-cams 83
Micro Stoppers 68
microwires 40
Mind 207–237
  fear of falling 214–217
  fears 228
  focus 237
  goal setting 208–213
  trying 218
  visualisation 230–233
mind training 272
Mini Rocks 68
Mini Traxion 51, 155
missiles 148
multi-directional belays 240
Multi-Pitching 239–253
  carry or haul? 248
  changeovers 244
  descending 250–253

  differences 240
  logistics 246
  tactical leading 242
multi-pitch rack 52, 246
Münter hitch . . . . . . see Italian hitch
N natural thread 87
next runner syndrome 237
non-verbal calls 24
notched karabiner 37
notchless karabiner 37
nut key 33
nuts . . . . see wires
nylon on nylon 106
O off-fingers 181
off-fists 183
off-set cams 80
off-set wires 40, 64
off-widths 186–187
  clothes 187
  footwork 187
onsight 192, 219
opposing wires 70
optimising a rack 201
oval karabiner 37
over-cammed 77, 84
overhand knot 100
overhang technique 178
P padding 166
palm taping 185
partners 226, 234, 235
passing a knot 151
passing gear 245
peer pressure 222
pegs 89
Petzl Shunt . . . . see Shunt
physical training 262–269
planning your training 258
positive encouragement . . . 234
preparation 196–201
pre-placed gear 193
pre-programming responses . . 232
Protection 59–95
  bolts 90
  bouldering mats 94
  camming devices 76
  esoteric wire placements . . . 69
  evaluating your placement . . 68
  hexes 74
  how cams work 78
  in situ protection 89
  opposing wires 70
  pegs 89
  removing wires 72
  tat 92
  Tricams 75
  using slings 87
  wire placement tricks 66
  wires 62–65
prusik 34, 102
prusiking 152
psychological training . . 272–273
pulley effect 128
pulleys 51
putting on a harness 20
Q quickdraws 46, 136

Index

R rack 52, 200–201
racking up 200
rappel . . . . see abseil
recruitment 267
redirectional base runner . . . 138–139
reef knot 101
removing cams 84
removing wires 72
resting 202, 258
retainers 47
re-threaded figure of eight 98
retreating 158
retrievable rope belays 145
retrievable sling belay 146
Reverso 152
rigid-stemmed cams 81
ring locks 181
Rockfax publications 285
rockovers 174
rocks 40
rock shoes . . . . . see climbing shoes
rope ascenders 50
rope-bags 54
rope-bucket 54
rope-cutters 51
rope drag 132
Ropeman MK2 50
rope protector 144
ropes 38, 132, 241
Ropework 97–159
 abseiling / rapelling 144
 ascending ropes 152
 belaying 108
 building belays 118
 clipping protection 116
 coiling a rope 104
 dynamic belaying 140
 extending protection 136
 fall factor 130
 falling off 156
 hazards 106
 keeping ropes straight 132
 knots 98
 redirection 138
 self-belaying 155
 top-roping 154
 understanding forces 128
 using double ropes 113
route goals 212
route reading 199, 231
RP microwires 40
rucksacks . . . . see backpack
running belay 22
S salt and gear 57
sandbag 223
sawn-off peg 205
Screamers 46
screw-gates 37, 118
sea-cliffs and gear 57
seconding 17, 22
seconding rack 52
selecting the right wire 64
self-belaying 155
setting the wire 65
shaking out 171

Shunt 50, 148, 152, 155
side-on climbing 170
side-pulls 172
simultaneous abseiling 149
single rope abseil with two ropes . 147
single rope ascenders 50
single ropes 38
skyhook 205
slab climbing technique . . . 166–168
sliders 40
slingdraws 48, 136
slings 46, 87
slip lasted 30
slopers 172
smearing 167
snap-link karabiner 37
solid-gate karabiner 37
soloing 193
Spectra . . . . see Dyneema
sport climbing 16, 214
spotting 159
stacking wires 66
stainless steel pegs 89
stamina . . . . see endurance
Starting Out 9–27
 access and behaviour 15
 chalk-bags 21
 climbing outside 14
 communication 24
 ethics and styles 15
 getting into trad climbing 10
 grades 26
 how it all works 22
 indoor leading 12
 indoor top-roping 11
 leading trad 19
 moving from indoors 11
 moving from outdoor bouldering . 13
 putting on a harness 20
 seconding 17
 sport climbing 16
static ropes 38
stopper 40
straight-arming 171
straight ropes 132–134
strength 265
strength endurance 268–269
stuck wires 72, 93
style 192–194
sunlight and gear 57
superlight rocks 40
swaged wires 40
swapping 170
swinging partners 227
system board . . . . . see campus board
T tactical racking 201
Tactics 191–205
 conditions 195
 headpointing 204
 preparation 196–201
 styles 192
 when climbing 202
taking in while paying out 115
tape gloves 185
tape knot 101

tape slings 92
taping for cracks 185
tat 92
TCU 44, 76
teacup jam 183
technical grade 26
technical training 270–271
Technique 161–189
 climbing different rock features . 176
 cracks 179
 feet 162
 handholds 172
 jams and locks 180
 off-widths 186
 slabs 166
 special techniques 173
 taping 185
 walls 169
the mind . . . . see Mind
thread-back buckle 20
three-way pull 107
Tibloc 50
top-roping 154
trad climbing 7
Training 255–273
 for Trad 256
 physical training 262–269
 psychological training 272
 technical training 270
training at the crag 260
training goals 263
training plan 259
Traxion Wall Hauler 249
Tricams 42, 75
trip goals 212
trusting your gear 272
trying a route 218–225
tunnel vision 237
twin ropes 38
two handled ascenders 153
tying off a belay device 112
tying-off pegs 89
U undercuts 172
understanding forces 128
unzipping runners 138
using of micro-threads 69
V video use 233
visualisation 230–233
W walking cams 77, 83
wall climbing technique 169–171
warming up 197, 262
where to train 260
wire-gate karabiner 37
wire placement tricks 66
wires 40, 62–72
Y yo-yo 192
Z Z clipping 117
ziplock buckle 20, 32